THE
PLYMOUTH TO YEALMPTON RAILWAY
(The South Hams Light Railway)

by
Anthony R. Kingdom

DOMINE · DIRIGE · NOS   VIRTUTE · ET · INDUSTRIA

ARK PUBLICATIONS (RAILWAYS)

First published in 1998 by ARK PUBLICATIONS (RAILWAYS), an imprint of
FOREST PUBLISHING, Woodstock, Liverton, Newton Abbot, Devon TQ12 6JJ

British Library Cataloguing in Publication Data
A catalogue record for this book is available from the British Library
ISBN 1-873029-07-1

0-6-0PT No. 5412 waits at Yealmpton Station on July 31st 1946 before
making the return journey to Plymouth (Friary).

S. C. Nash

ARK PUBLICATIONS (RAILWAYS)
Editorial, layout and design by:
Mike Lang

Typeset by:
Carnaby Typesetting, Torquay, Devon TQ1 1EG

Printed and bound in Great Britain by:
The Latimer Trend Group, Plymouth, Devon PL6 7PL

Cover photographs:

Front — (Top) A photograph taken at Friary Station on August 30th 1945, with
0-6-0PT No. 3705 on a Yealmpton branch train and with a
Turnchapel branch train partially hidden behind it.

H. C. Casserley

(Lower) An official GWR Company's photograph of Yealmpton Station
taken just after the opening of the line in 1898.

British Railways Board

Back – 0-6-0PT No. 5412 and auto coaches Nos. 71 & 74 at Steer Point
Station in 1947.

D. A. Thompson

CONTENTS

ACKNOWLEDGEMENTS

The author wishes to extend his grateful thanks to all those, past and present, for their generous assistance given in a wide variety of ways during the preparation of both this book and its predecessor, *The Yealmpton Branch,* which was published in 1974 and upon which this new edition is based.

Blue Circle Industries plc; British Gas, South West; British Rail Records Office, Kew; British Railways Board; Camas UK Ltd; Central Library, Plymouth (Local Studies Department); City of Plymouth, Directorate of Development; City of Plymouth, Highways Planning Department; *Evening Herald;* Kitley Estates, Yealmpton; Newton & Noss Local History Group; Plym Valley Railway; *Plymouth Extra*; Plymouth Railway Circle; Signalling Record Society; *South Devon Times;* Wembury Local History Society; *Western Independent; Western Morning News;* Wild Swan Publications; Yealm Hotel, Newton Ferrers.

W. C. Beard; F. Bennett; S. J. Broad; R. Cawse; J. Crocker; Mrs N. C. Croft; F. J. Cross; M. T. Daniels; A. Davies; Miss E. Dennis; W. Dennis; G. St C. Ellis; C. Fennamore; R. H. C. Fice; C. Foster; P. H. Gatley; B. C. Gunton; E. M. Hall; Mrs D. Joll; I. R. Lanyon; F. W. J. Lawrance, O.B.E.; P. Lucas; R. G. Perryman; H. Pitts; P. J. Powell; G. Pryer; C. Richardson; Mrs I. Rickard; Mrs E. Rundell; R. C. Sambourne; M. Stone; B. Y. Williams; R. Wilson; R. Zaple.

Special thanks are due to the following:-

Larry Crosier for the intricate descriptions of the line's signalling and its equipment; Bryan Gibson for his detailed information on railway and omnibus time tables; Paul Karau for permission to reproduce photographs of G. N. Southerden from Wild Swan Publications; Alan Kittridge for the detailed information on ferry boats and their services; Eric Shepherd for the use of his personal notes and observations on the branch.

(Photographs are acknowledged individually in most instances)

FOREWORD

Many members of my family have been railway enthusiasts and there is a long history of family interest and involvement with railways – and especially with the Great Western. I was therefore delighted when I was asked to write the foreword to this short history. The Yealmpton branch was formally opened by my grandmother in 1898 and as a small boy, many years later, I well remember watching trains crossing Laira Bridge.

I have however two regrets, firstly that I should be helping to write its epitaph and secondly that I never travelled on this line. Having followed the line on the map it must have been a very picturesque route – and what a pleasant and relaxing way to commute to work in Plymouth!

On a more serious note, branch lines, such as this, which probed and penetrated the depths of the country, have considerable implications for the historian. They played a key role in opening up and developing rural areas in the era before motor transport. Like so many other institutions however we took them for granted – and it was only after they were closed that their importance was appreciated.

It is fortunate that Mr. Kingdom has been able to complete this short history whilst the line can still be traced and whilst records and memories are still available to him. It will be a valuable adjunct to local histories and will, I am sure, be enjoyed by all who read it.

Morley
5th May 1974

The luncheon ticket issued for the opening of the line on January 15th 1898.
Courtesy of Miss E. Dennis

PREFACE

The Yealmpton branch ran for over six miles in an easterly direction from Plymouth, crossed the River Plym and then ran parallel with the River Yealm estuary for much of its latter part.

In many ways it must surely have been unique in the annals of railway branch line history. It was opened as a passenger line no less than twice and was relegated to a goods line an equal number of times.

The terminus, Yealmpton, was in fact a 'through' station. Its track ran on many yards past it to end abruptly in dense woodlands. The original terminus, Modbury, was never reached.

Yealmpton was even to have been a junction, for at one time it was planned to lay a spur leaving the branch at Puslinch, making for the village of Newton Ferrers. Alas only the opening ceremony was performed, a little excavation and the first sod cut towards this grandiose scheme.

Running rights were give by the former LSWR for Yealmpton trains to use their track, in order to reach the branch and to enable them to cross the River Plym. In later years the branch was also to operate from the then Southern Railway station at Friary.

Its passenger carrying life amounted to some thirty-eight years in all, whilst its total life exceeded that by only a further twenty-four, making a grand total of sixty-two short years. Being opened as late as 1898, it was much younger than most of its contemporaries in Devon and Cornwall, and consequently suffered from the competition of the motor car much earlier in its life.

Despite the very short passenger life of the line, however, it was remembered by many generations with nostalgic affection. It brought back memories of Sunday School outings, busy market days, summer river trips and simple journeys to and from school and work, and also memories of the wartime years, fuel crises, of renewed peace, of nationalisation and of the renewed worship of the motor car. It was the car that won and sadly the branch itself became a memory.

Prior to the line's 1930 closure to passenger traffic, all trains to and from Yealmpton terminated at Plymouth (Millbay), so it is from here that the full journey must be described.

Anthony R. Kingdom
1974

5

INTRODUCTION

It was during the 1960s that I first commenced research on the railway line that held such prolific memories of my wartime youth. Its beauty and continuously varying scenery fascinates me as much today as it did then. It was the epitome of a GWR country branchline, set, as they often were, in the aquatic and sylvan environment of the beautiful English countryside, for which there is no equal anywhere in the world.

Now, in 1998, I find myself returning to my roots, figuratively speaking, not by just updating my first efforts as an author, which culminated in 1974 with the publication of *The Yealmpton Branch* by the former Oxford Publishing Company, but by completely re-writing it! Most of what was contained within the Introduction of my first book on the line is still applicable and cannot be improved upon. It is, therefore, considered prudent that it should re-appear, at least in part, on the previous page as a Preface.

The main difference in my approach to this new history, apart from the inclusion of the copious amounts of new information and photographs that I have amassed, is to describe the geography of the line in 1930, the year of closure. In addition, I have been able to include a totally new chapter devoted to post-closure developments as well as appendices to cater for extraneous information, such as ferries and bus services, and other miscellaneous data.

Finally it is with great pride and much pleasure that the 'Holbeton, Yealmpton and Brixton Society' saw fit to include my name upon their commemorative plaque that is affixed to the wall by the former entrance to Yealmpton Station.

Anthony R. Kingdom
Thalassa
Newton Ferrers
Devon
March 1998

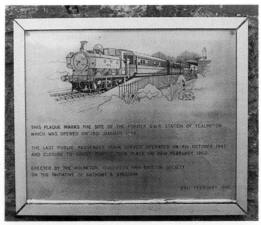

The commemorative plaque mentioned above.
It was erected on February 29th 1980 – exactly
20 years after the last train left the branch.

THE ROUTES DESCRIBED

(a) Plymouth (Millbay) to Yealmpton, *circa* 1930.

Millbay Station during 1930, the last year of operation of the Yealmpton passenger service, was a constant hive of activity. This, however, was nothing new as it was the main terminus of the GWR at Plymouth and, as such, dealt not only with the Ocean Liner and Ocean Mail traffic from its adjacent docks, but also with the main line and branch line traffic (both passenger and goods) to and from the entire GWR system.

The layout was spacious, and the main building was an elongated one constructed in an extended 'Y' plan of dressed limestone lined with red sandstone in a contrasting style. It was bordered on one side by Adelaide Road, and by Bath Street on the other: the latter was the boundary of the extensive goods depot situated on the far side of the main line into the docks which, in turn, ran to the west of the station site on a dropping gradient.

At the front of the building were several pairs of heavy wrought iron gates. These were utilised to control the various entrances to (and exits from) the platform area, and each sported a GWR gilt-painted monogram cast in the same metal. Adjacent to them, on the outside, was the station forecourt. This, in turn, led onto Millbay Road and was overlooked by The Duke of Cornwall Hotel, the latter, situated on the opposite side of the road, having been built in 1866 to cater for the then comparatively new railway traffic to the town. Through this same road, incidentally, ran a single line of the Plymouth

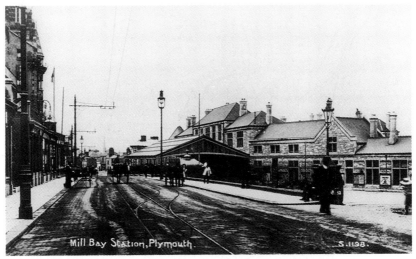

Plymouth (Millbay) Station in all its former glory. Originally the terminus of the South Devon Railway, it had been reconstructed and enlarged by the GWR during the late 1890s.

Author's collection

7

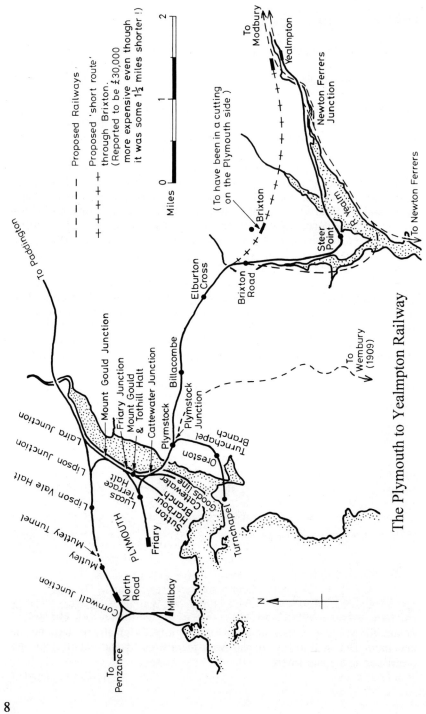

Proposed Railways

Proposed 'short route' through Brixton. (Reported to be £30,000 more expensive even though it was some 1½ miles shorter !)

(To have been in a cutting on the Plymouth side)

Miles 0 1 2

To Tavistock

To Modbury

Yealmpton

Newton Ferrers Junction

R. Yealm

Brixton

Steer Point

To Newton Ferrers

Brixton Road

Elburton Cross

To Wembury (1909)

Billacombe

Mount Gould Junction

Friary Junction

Mount Gould & Tothill Halt

Cattewater Junction

Plymstock

Plymstock Junction

Oreston

Turnchapel Branch

Laira Junction

Lipson Junction

Lipson Vale Halt

Mutley Tunnel

Cornwall Junction

Lucas Terrace Halt

PLYMOUTH

Sutton Harbour Branch

Cattewater Goods line

Friary

Turnchapel

North Road

Millbay

To Penzance

N

The Plymouth to Yealmpton Railway

8

The less impressive interior of Millbay Station, c1912.

L & GRP

Corporation Tramway: a passing loop for trams proceeding to and from West Hoe, as well as the city centre, was situated just to the north of the station forecourt.

Although the station forecourt led principally onto Millbay Road, mention must be made of the fact that it was also connected, by means of a private thoroughfare, to Adelaide Road, and thence to Union Street. Interestingly enough, this road had to be closed one day per annum in order to comply with the minimum legal requirement for the substantiation of its private status.

Internally, the station had four platforms. Nos 1 & 4 were used for local and stopping traffic, whilst Nos 2 & 3, their tracks equipped with a double crossover, were used for the 'up' and 'down' main lines for originating and terminating traffic. Consequently, the Yealmpton-bound train would normally depart from platform 4, thereafter steadily climbing towards its first stop – Plymouth, North Road.

Immediately upon leaving the station boundary, and the 'up' main line secured, the train crossed over Union Street by means of the giant, multi-track steel bridge known locally as 'Union Street Arch'. This typical Victorian structure carried some ten tracks, with pointwork catering for a further six. It had replaced the original South Devon Railway bridge, dating from 1848/49, on the reconstruction and enlargement of Millbay during the late 1890s, and not only served as a bridge, but, with its long abutment at the southern end, provided considerable accommodation for the stabling of horses employed in connection with the GWR road delivery fleet for freight and parcel traffic. Arches within the adjacent embankment were deep and extensive, and those surplus to the GWR's requirements were rented out to small businesses.

9

The locally known 'Union Street Arch' viewed from its eastern side, c1948.

British Railways Board

The views from the train as it crossed the bridge were panoramic. The city centre, ensconced around the mother church, St Andrew's, lay to the east; Union Street, Stonehouse and, further in the distance, Devonport lay to the west. In addition, to the north, lay a landscape of housing developments, such as those at Stoke, Milehouse, and Peverell, although they could not actually be seen from the train at this point.

Immediately beyond the bridge, Millbay signal box was passed to the east of the line. Constructed in 1914, this 115-lever box consisted of five wooden sections mounted upon a brick base, the rear of which stood high above the built-up area between Devonshire Lane and Summerland Street, which ran parallel to Union Street to the south.

From here, the line proceeded to cross King Street by means of another bridge, this time constructed of dressed limestone and carrying only six tracks and a crossover, before continuing further northwards past the extensive carriage sheds and cleaning plant that lay on either side of the main running lines. These buildings, in fact, had been constructed upon the site of the former South Devon Railway's engine sheds below Harwell Street, and were overlooked by All Saints Church. Moreover, the GWR had a motive power depot here, a situation that was to exist until 1931, when the new MPD (originally opened at Laira in 1901) was enlarged.

As the last outposts of Millbay were passed, so came the approach to Cornwall Junction. Here, the signal box was situated to the west of the line and at what, ever since the construction of a through main line from North Road Station into Cornwall, was effectively the southern apex of a triangle. Apart from having overcome a complicated reversing entry into Millbay, this additional line had meant that trains setting out from, or terminating at,

Millbay could enter, or depart, in two directions: eastwards under Patna Place or, as before, westwards over Stonehouse Pool viaduct, adjacent to Victoria Park. In the event, the Yealmpton-bound train took the easterly course and therefore proceeded to pass under Patna Place bridge, which carried North Road over the line at m.p. 245¼. It was also near this point, within the triangle and to the west of the line, that there was situated a large turntable that had been constructed in 1912, together with three access roads and a siding.

A study of the turntable constructed in 1912 and situated to the west of North Road Station, clearly showing the three access roads and the siding. The lines running from the centre to the right of the photograph are those to and from Millbay, and North Road West signal box can be seen in the middle distance.

W. E. Stevens

Still proceeding eastwards, the train eventually reached the far end of Cornwall Junction at the rear of houses in Albert (later Bayswater) Road. It then negotiated another bridge, that carried the two main lines over Pennycomequick Hill (near the junction of Saltash Road with Alma and Stuart Roads), immediately prior to passing North Road West signal box on the northern side of the line. This box, also constructed of timber on a brick base, contained 59 levers and, as its name implied, guarded traffic to and from the western end of the station.

At this time Plymouth, North Road was a moderately sized station consisting of four main platforms and three/four loading bays, and on arriving there one could compare what was an austere 'joint GWR/LSWR affair', built originally in 1877, with the grandiose design of the terminus, Millbay. Nevertheless, passengers awaiting the Yealmpton train from here did have a grand view to the north, namely the wide expanse of the fields of

11

Central Park, together with the maroon and cream trams and buses ascending and descending Alma Road as they served the north of the city and their adjoining depots at Milehouse. In addition, to the east, could be seen the main lines passing under the bridge carrying Sutherland Road on its way to join Apsley Road, Maple Grove and Beechwood Avenue. In Apsley Road, adjacent to the line, stood an imposing building constructed entirely of red brick with a red tiled roof; this was the Royal Eye Infirmary.

North Road Station, looking westwards towards Millbay, c1921.

L & GRP

Leaving North Road Station, the train passed North Road East signal box which was constructed in like manner to its sister box to the west. But then, after a distance of only 27 chains, the train ground to a halt again – at Mutley Station. Constructed in a deep cutting, it was overlooked by Apsley and Station Roads to the north, and by Napier and Gordon Terraces to the south, and had been built to serve the Mutley Plain area before the joint GWR/LSWR station at North Road was conceived. At one time, therefore, it had also been the last stop before Millbay, where all trains had previously terminated.

A small, main line station, Mutley had its booking office and waiting rooms on the 'up' platform, housed in a slender (but neat) building with a capacious canopy, its edge adorned with cast iron 'lions heads'. Connecting the 'up' and 'down' platforms was a typical GWR footbridge which enabled passengers to enter, or exit, via Napier Terrace, or to await 'down' trains in the small waiting room at its base on that side. Despite its close proximity to North Road, it was a busy station serving the shopping and densely populated areas around it. Mutley Plain could be seen from its platforms to the east, striding sedately over the impressive structure of Mutley Tunnel. The grey limestone face of the tunnel, with its prominent arch and keystone, framed the darkness and gloom of its interior. This contrasted strongly with the bright red, white and yellow of the 'home' and 'distant' signals on their short white post to the left of the tunnel mouth. This, and the former scene, was dominated by the twin square towers of Mutley Baptist Church, standing high above it to the south-east.

A view of Mutley Station showing the southern end of the tunnel, c1921. Above the tunnel lies Mutley Plain, while adjacent to it can be seen Mutley Baptist Church.

L & GRP

Lipson Vale Halt, looking towards the rear of Mutley Plain and with the spire of the former Mutley Methodist Church just visible in the distance, c1922. To the left of the 'Pagoda' shelter can be seen part of the Beechwood's pie factory.

L & GRP

13

Leaving Mutley Station, the main line passed quickly through the deepening cutting before entering the slightly curving, 183 yards long, tunnel itself. At its eastern end, below Moor View Terrace, and parallel to Lisson Grove to the north and Alexandra Road to the south, Mannamead signal box was reached, closely followed by Lipson Vale Halt. This halt, with its wooden platforms and corrugated 'Pagoda' shelter, was overshadowed by the eminence of St Augustine's Church and the height of Beechwood's factory chimney, both on the southern side, and was sandwiched between Ashford Road and Alexandra Road. Access to it was provided by means of a gate in Ashford Lane and also by steps adjoining the over-bridge at the eastern end of its platforms.

Once past Lipson Vale Halt, the train emerged out on to an embankment and provided its passengers with a sudden view of the wide expanse of green fields stretching into the distance towards the village of Egg Buckland. Southwards, however, lay the densely populated Lipson Vale residential area, the neat rows of terraced houses creating a stark contrast. Meanwhile, it was not long before Lipson Junction (some 1¼ miles from Mutley Station) was being negotiated, so terminating the Yealmpton branch train's run over the main line.

The train now headed in a southerly direction and went past the rear of Lipson Junction signal box, on the western side of the 'famous' Laira triangle. This triangle had been created when its third side was constructed in 1890 so as to permit access to the then newly constructed LSWR station at Plymouth Friary. In order that the Yealmpton trains could reach the LSWR branch line from Plymouth Friary to Plymstock, further lines had been laid between the GWR lines at Mount Gould Junction to join up with those of the LSWR at Cattewater Junction. (In addition, Mount Gould Junction catered for entry to Laira Yard to the east, for main line access to LSWR Friary, and the GWR Sutton Harbour branch to the west. Complicating the trackwork still further, the 4' 6" gauge track of the Plymouth & Dartmoor Railway/Lee Moor Tramway crossed the Yealmpton branch west of Mount Gould Junction on its way to Sutton Harbour.)

Returning to the journey, at the southernmost tip of the Laira triangle the line, still double at this point, entered a deep cutting as it approached Mount Gould Junction. At this point it ran parallel to The Embankment, a large straight roadway running along the western bank of the wide estuary of the River Plym, whose waters were often stained milky white by discharge from the Lee Moor Clayworks high up on Dartmoor.

At Mount Gould Junction the branch proper commenced and, immediately after passing under Lanhydrock Road bridge, the site of the former Mount Gould & Tothill Halt was reached. It was a small halt with no buildings, and its entrance was by a swing gate within the railings adjacent to the bridge: at the time of our journey the latter was all that remained. Progressing southwards, the line then crossed The Embankment at an oblique angle by means of one of two steel girder bridges, the second, a short distance to the west, belonging to the SR and providing independent access to Cattewater

Junction, and thence to Plymstock and Turnchapel from Plymouth Friary, via Lucas Terrace Halt.

Above: An extremely rare photograph dating back to the early 1900s depicting the short-lived Mount Gould & Tothill Halt. Taken from a distance, where Mirador Place and Heathfield Road are now situated, it clearly shows the bridge carrying Lanhydrock Road over the line before joining The Embankment.

Author's collection

Below: The 'kissing gate' entry to the former Mount Gould & Tothill Halt as existing up until the bridge renewal during the 1980s.

A.R.K.

An unusual, but historically important, view of the double track of the Yealmpton branch leading towards Cattewater Junction from Mount Gould Junction in the early 1900s. On the centre line of the scene, from left to right, are Cattewater Junction signal box, the GWR and LSWR bridges over Embankment Road, and the LSWR bridge over the GWR Sutton Harbour branch and the 4' 6" gauge track of the Plymouth & Dartmoor Railway/Lee Moor Tramway. The LSWR bridges carried the Turnchapel/Cattewater branches.

J. B. N. Ashford

A view, from the road bridge, looking northwards towards Cattewater Junction signal box in the 1950s, showing the goods line dropping away to Cattewater Wharfs and the rising gradient of the Yealmpton/Turnchapel line before it reaches the bridge over the River Plym.

W. E. Stevens

At Cattewater Junction the hitherto double track of the Yealmpton branch reverted to single track as it joined up with the SR, over whose lines the GWR had running rights to Plymstock. However, just beyond this junction, where the complexity of trackwork involving two companies was controlled by Cattewater Junction signal box (situated to the west), the SR branch line itself diverged into two single lines. One, a goods only line, dropped away on the west bank of the river to Cattewater Wharfs; the other, on which, of course, also ran the Yealmpton-bound train, continued to hug the river on a rising gradient until finally crossing to its eastern bank by means of a four-section, lattice-type, steel girder bridge. Supported upon tubular steel legs sunk into the river bed, this bridge ran almost parallel to the locally famous 'Iron Road Bridge' which had been opened by the Duchess of Clarence on July 14th 1827 after being constructed of cast iron during 1824/25 and engineered by James Rendle.

The LSWR bridge over the River Plym, as viewed from east to west, c1964. Near the centre of the photograph, Cattewater Junction signal box can be seen in the distance, soon after its closure.

A.R.K.

Once over the river, the line soon crossed a smaller over-bridge above the road (named 'The Ride') into Chelson Meadow from the A379. From here, in an easterly direction, it then ran parallel to Billacombe Road upon an embankment, with quarries to the north and Mill Pond to the south, until reaching Plymstock Junction and Station – the point at which, to the south of Pomphlett Quarry, the SR Turnchapel branch diverged southwards from the GWR Yealmpton branch. (It is interesting to note that at the time of our journey, and just to the south of the station, there stood the old 'Abbots Mill' from which much goods traffic was generated. It was, in fact, the old Pomphlett Tide Water Grist Mill, built in 1392 and operated continuously until 1923 by water-wheel, and then by electricity. Owned by the Dukes of Bedford until 1864, and subsequently by the Mitchell family, it had later been

A view of the line looking eastwards towards Billacombe, showing the steel bridge that carried it over 'The Ride' into Chelson Meadow, c1964.

A.R.K.

Plymstock Station, looking eastwards as a train arrives from Yealmpton in the early 1900s. The line veering away to the right of the photograph is that of the Turnchapel branch.

L & GRP

auctioned in 1922 and passed into the possession of the Plymouth Co-operative Society.)

Although, as already stated, the branch to Yealmpton started at Mount Gould Junction, to many people the 'true' starting point was here at Plymstock Station, at a distance of 6 miles 44 chains from the terminus. Whatever, upon leaving the station (described in part (b) of this chapter), Plymstock's 'down starting', the rear of the 'up home' and the 'up fixed distant' signals were passed in quick succession as the line initially took an easterly direction, still on an embankment, to run parallel to Billacombe Road and above Billacombe Brook. (This brook ran firstly into the tidal Mill Pond, through the old mill, and thence on to Pomphlett Creek.) However, passing below Pomphlett Farm, at m.p. $^1/_4$, the line took a more southerly curve and then continued past m.p. $^1/_2$. Beyond this, it entered a cutting before reaching the 'down fixed distant' signal for Billacombe Station, followed, after m.p. $^3/_4$, by an even longer cutting at the rear of Billacombe Villas. From here, after passing under Colesdown Hill road bridge, it then entered the confines of Billacombe Station itself.

A photograph of Billacombe Station taken from Colesdown Hill road bridge on March 19th 1955, showing the dusty stone-crushing equipment of Moore's Quarry immediately to the north.

E. R. Shepherd

Situated on a site later to be dominated by the lineside, dusty stone-crushing equipment of Moore's Quarry to the north, Billacombe Station was the first of the three principle stations along the 'true' branch and featured a small, but elegant building of dressed limestone edged with Staffordshire blue bricks. Its blue/grey slate roof gave way to a neat canopy of steel ironwork supported from the main stonework by three large girders securely embedded therein. This framework, in turn, held a glass-panelled covering and supported a wooden skirt formed by vertical planking, holed out and cut into pointed ends for a decorative effect. Accommodation consisted of a 'Booking Office & Waiting Room', 'Ladies Waiting Room' and 'Gentlemen's Toilet'. The platform was fairly long, and the main entrance to Elburton Road was situated at its western end, secured by two large steel gates.

In addition to the main station building, there were two matching buildings, one being the goods shed, with its own small platform. Alongside an accompanying siding, and adjacent to it, was the goods office. This was a smaller building used by staff dealing with the invoices for the incoming and outgoing merchandise of the station.

The road access to Moore's Quarry ran under the line between the station and the goods depot. The crossover from the passing loop to the goods siding started on this quarry road access bridge and ran in a south-westerly direction from it, branching into two further goods sidings in the process. Just to the east of the platform was situated m.p. 1.

Leaving behind this busy little country branch line station, the line next advanced towards m.p. 1^1/4, near which was a footpath level-crossing, and on through a steep-sided cutting below Moorcroft Quarry before crossing over Stag Lane and traversing an embankment to reach m.p. 1^1/2. From here, there followed another deep cutting carrying the line under Haye Road bridge and on past m.p. 1^3/4, to the north of Standarhay Nurseries and The Minses. It then approached the next stopping point from a north-westerly direction: Elburton Cross, 1 mile and 77 chains along the branch, was but a small passenger halt catering for the village after which it was named.

This halt, built as an afterthought to the planned branch, consisted of a long, stone-edged platform equipped with a rather austere wooden building. It was constructed of lateral planking with a flat sloping roof and served as a 'Waiting Room'. On the eastern side of this building stood a cast-iron gent's urinal, the sole toilet facilities available here!

Access to the halt was provided by a 'kissing-gate' in Sherford Road, situated on the southern side of the bridge which carried this same road over the line. The main exit, on the other hand, was by way of a gate in Station Road, which was a cul-de-sac leading off from The Minses. Over this exit stood a large 'Way Out' sign, constructed in a like manner to the over-sized 'Elburton' nameboard and clearly outlined by a rising bank, on top of which were the telegraph poles carrying the signal wires.

Departing from Elburton Cross, the train immediately passed m.p. 2, went under the high brick arch of the aforementioned Sherford Road bridge and on through a deepening cutting. Beyond the cutting there was a series of embankments which had to be crossed before m.p. $2^1/4$ and m.p. $2^1/2$ were each passed in turn. By then it had plunged into yet another deep cutting as the line veered in a southerly direction past the 'down fixed distant' and the rear of the 'up advanced starting' signals of the next stop – Brixton Road Station.

A train arriving at Elburton Cross on its way to Yealmpton prior to the 1930 closure to passengers.

Lens of Sutton

Brixton Road Station, photographed in 1921 looking towards Elburton and sporting a 'LSWR-type' striped canopy!

L & GRP

Here, the line passed under a steel over-bridge (supported on heavy brick abutments) that carried the A379 Plymouth to Kingsbridge Road on its journey eastwards, and then doubled into a passing loop upon entering the station.

On arrival, the station building was found to be virtually identical to that at Billacombe, and there were also two matching buildings. One, a goods shed, was situated just behind it at an angle of 45 degrees, while the other, a goods office, lay parallel to (and behind) the main station platform. In addition, at the southern end of the platform, there had been a signal box, but at the time of our journey this had long since been removed.

To the south of the station a double goods siding left the branch in a north-easterly direction (the opposite direction of our journey), while at the other end was the only entrance. This was provided by means of large double gates at the foot of the hill from Brixton village, which was built astride the A379. It was also about half a mile away – the reason why the station carried the suffix 'Road'.

Shortly beyond Brixton Road Station came the start of some of the most picturesque scenery imaginable as the train recommenced its journey southwards by the quiet waters of Cofflete Creek. In doing so, it passed the hamlets of Torr and Wapplewell, which were in clear view from the carriage

A study of the picturesque section of the line running through Brixton Torr, beyond Brixton Road Station.

C. Fennamore

windows as the train negotiated a high embankment at that point. Breaking into the sylvan scene briefly, were two over-bridges crossing the by-roads in from the A379 at 2 miles $61\frac{1}{4}$ chains and 2 miles $71\frac{1}{4}$ chains respectively. One ran in from Chittleburn Cross past what, in later years, was to become Otter Nurseries, en route to Wapplewell and Spriddlestone: the other ran in from the A379 via Combe and Holbay Cottages before joining up with the first.

As the train headed south over a series of small embankments, passing the rear of Brixton 'up fixed distant' signal and m.p. 3, another bridge, over a small back road in from Brixton itself, was crossed at 3 miles 10 chains. From here, the next cutting reached was to the north-east of Weston Park Wood at m.p. 3¹/₂, and from there the line veered on a steady curve, through a series of deep cuttings skirting the high ground to the south-west of South Farm at m.p. 3³/₄. At the end of the cutting m.p. 4 was passed and, with it, another steel girder over-bridge carrying the small road in to Steer Point. This road bridge served a brickworks, an oyster fishery, and Steer Point Cottage, part of the Kitley Estate.

As the train emerged from under the bridge, so it entered Steer Point Station. Although only a halt (not officially so), with no buildings of

A steam railcar arrives at Steer Point Station from Yealmpton. This very familiar scene is believed to be dated 1928, the year that the GWR sought economies to maintain passenger services.

Lens of Sutton

architectural note, Steer Point was perhaps the busiest stop along the line. Here passengers could catch the ferry to Newton Ferrers and Noss Mayo, further down the River Yealm. In addition to plentiful passenger traffic, a large amount of freight was handled, the greater part of this being various types of bricks (including 'GWR' bricks) from the adjacent brickworks.* The

* This may seem an incongruous setting for such an industry, but the 'South Hams Brickworks' had come about because of the presence of large clay deposits, of the highest quality, in the immediate vicinity. Originally, before the arrival of the railway, the factory (which was coal-fired) had sent most of its bricks away by river and sea, but since the turn of the century it had been served by rail and its own private siding. Situated to the east of the station, and almost completely screened by trees, its position was pinpointed by its tall chimney.

brick traffic was supplemented by the more usual coal, animal feeding-stuffs, farm produce, and oysters from the nearby fishery.

The construction of the station was the usual platform of earth infill edged with large paving stones, and the well to line level was brick-lined, this replacing the original wooden planking and truss construction of 1898. Along the entire rear of the platform were iron railings, which also formed the boundary to the road into the goods yard. The station building itself was austere in design, namely a corrugated iron construction ribbed with wood. The usual facilities were provided in the form of a 'Waiting Room/Ticket Office' with a 'Ladies Toilet'. The 'Gentlemen' sign appeared at the distant end, and lighting was by oil lamp throughout.

On leaving Steer Point, the line continued still in the gentle curve which had commenced before entering the station, only now in a north-easterly direction through a deepening cutting, passing m.p. $4^1/4$, and out onto an embankment; this had been built with spoil from the cutting as the line protruded outwards into the waters of Mudbank Lake. The latter, in fact, was a small creek off the River Yealm, adjacent to Broad Ooze, that extended northwards into Fish Pond – a freshwater lake resulting from the damming of the stream feeding into it. Known as Silverbridge Brook, this, in turn, originated at Beechwood (near Sparkwell) on the southern slopes of Dartmoor and flowed down to the east of Brixton village and thence through the eastern part of the Kitley Estate.

From the embankment, reinforced with rows of large boulders to protect it against tidal erosion, the line was then carried over Mudbank Lake by means of a bridge to its eastern bank, where a second embankment, similarly reinforced, had been built with spoil excavated from the deep cutting through the rocky terrain at nearby Warren Point. This bridge, incidentally, known as

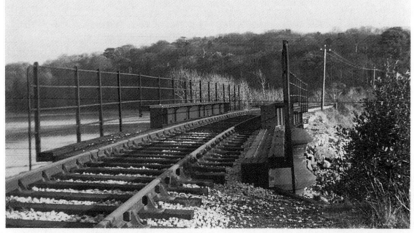

Cylinder (or Barrow) Bridge which carried the line over Mudbank Lake.

C. Fennamore

24

Cylinder Bridge or, sometimes, as Barrow Bridge, derived its name from its mode of construction, namely four large cylinders sunk into the bed of the creek: the centres of these had been filled with hardcore and topped with large limestone slabs to support the main span of the bridge over the water and the ends of the two spans connecting it to the two embankments.

Continuing what had now become the final part of our journey, one needed to pause in order to contemplate the vast array of breath-taking beauty and variety of wildlife on view. The River Yealm is no less than three-eighths of a mile wide at this point, wider than anywhere else along its entire length, or, indeed, its mouth. Views across to its south-eastern bank (towards West Wood) were furnished with copious amounts of dense woodlands of both conifers and deciduous trees. Down river, to the south, further woodlands, namely Crawl Wood, almost completely obscure the first habitations of Newton Ferrers, with its twin village, Noss Mayo. These pretty fishing villages overlook Noss Creek to the east of its confluence with the River Yealm. They were, unfortunately, out of sight from the train, but could be visited, by ferry, from Steer Point Station.

To the east lay Puslinch House and its accompanying estate. Nearer to the line was situated 'The Saltings', an assembly point for migrating birds. Often, in this haven for bird life, large flocks of Canada geese fly in on the rising tide to join the mute swans, various gulls and numerous waders, including curlews and oystercatchers. If one is particularly fortunate the neon blue dash of a kingfisher may also be seen. High trees provide the habitat for herons and buzzards, which continually circle for fish and rodents respectively, whilst along the river bank otters play.

The cutting immediately beyond the eastern embankment, on the middle of which stood m.p. 4½, took the line through the southern tip of Warren Wood. Here, there was also an accommodation bridge over the line, which had been built by the GWR in order to maintain a right of way from the beautiful Kitley Estate (home of the Bastard family) to Warren Point and a nearby landing stage. The bridge itself was a rather ornate affair, being made of steel with lattice sides and with its main girders holding 4"-thick timbers slotted into their 'I' sections.

After passing under this bridge, the line continued in an easterly direction and ran along an embankment on the northern bank of the river, which also formed part of the boundary of the estate. The entire length of the river bank along this section to Kitley Quay was marked with cast iron boundary posts sunk into the river bed. It was also reinforced with stonework in order to protect the line from tidal erosion. At a point approximately midway between m.p. 4¾, at the eastern end of Warren Wood, and m.p. 5, just prior to Kitley Quay, was Kitley Quay Cottage with its attendant boathouse. Constructed as part of the estate, and standing out into the River Yealm upon its own quay, this cottage could hardly have been situated in a more tranquil setting. Much the same applied to Kitley Quay itself, although this had not always been the case for it had been built to facilitate the unloading of coal barges and used as such in earlier days until the river silted up. Access to it from the estate,

Kitley Quay Cottage, part of the Kitley Estate, viewed from its eastern side at around the turn of the century. In the background can be seen the South Hams Brickworks.

Courtesy of Mrs. J. Chudley

incidentally, was by means of passing under a small-span steel bridge with brick abutments.

Continuing the journey through this most beautiful of scenery, now to the south of Fish House Plantation yet still close to the water's edge on an embankment, the hitherto gentle down gradient gradually changed to a gentle up gradient as m.p. $5^1/4$ was approached. Passing m.p. $5^1/2$, the train then had to cross a series of minor embankments as the line veered away from the river to pass under a bridge at 5 miles 53 chains. This, in fact, was Yealmpton Road bridge – a misnomer, for in reality it carries the minor road in from the A379 to Newton Ferrers. Spanning a cutting more than 40 feet deep, the bridge itself is built of brick.

Emerging from this deep cutting, the line immediately joined another embankment which was, arguably, the longest along the route, for it ran the entire length of the meadowland to the south of Western Torrs. Another underpass, for cattle and farm traffic, was crossed at m.p. $5^3/4$ as the train engaged a dropping gradient. Then, at the end of the embankment, came the largest engineering structure to be encountered, namely the bridge that carried the line over the River Yealm. This, in fact, was the only crossing of the actual river on our journey and, here again, was an area of outstanding beauty, a small weir, some 60 feet below the top of the bridge, adding to the overall charm. As for the bridge, it consisted of two spans. One extended over the river, while the other (smaller) passed over an adjoining road leading into The Clam from Puslinch, although to all intents and purposes it was a rough cart track. The supports were a large brick pier standing in the river and two abutments on either side, also of brick.

Above: Approaching an accommodation level-crossing near Puslinch is 0–6–0PT No. 738 with a train for Yealmpton on April 26th 1930.

B. Y. Williams

Below: Another view of the level-crossing, taken some 20 years later and showing also the bridge carrying the road from the A379 to Newton and Noss. This bridge still carries heavy local traffic to and from these villages, via Puslinch, every day.

C. Fennamore

Above: The view from the top of the road bridge shown in the previous photograph, looking down some 40 feet into the cutting as 0–6–0PT No. 1252 approaches with a train from Yealmpton on, or around, July 8th 1924.

H. C. Casserley

Below: Another photograph of 0–6–0PT No. 1252 probably taken on the same day, only now captured a little further along the line at m.p. $5^3/4$ and heading for Yealmpton, adjacent to Yealmpton 'Meadows' and the upper, non-tidal reaches of the River Yealm.

H. C. Casserley

The largest engineering feature on the Yealmpton line was the bridge carrying it some 60 feet above the River Yealm, depicted here during the 1950s. *Above:* The top of the bridge viewed from the trackbed, with the 'down fixed distant' signal and Waltacre in the background. *Below:* The southern side of the bridge, showing the span over the road leading into The Clam from Puslinch and the other striding the river.

C. Fennamore

Once the train had crossed the bridge, m.p. 6 and the 'down fixed distant' signal for Yealmpton were passed, with the latter being situated some 728 yards from Yealmpton signal box; a considerable distance in signalling terms. Nevertheless, it was at this point that the final run into Yealmpton Station effectively began ...

During this latter stage of the journey the train had, first of all, to traverse a small level-crossing equipped with hand-operated, farm-type gates, which connected Waltacre to The Clam, to the east of Western Torrs. It then had to skirt the old quarries below Rounds Nest and pass over a low steel bridge at 6 miles 9¼ chains that provided access to an accommodation road formerly serving the old quarries, but now serving the houses in Waltacre, from Boldventure. Finally, after passing behind the houses at Boldventure and

The final cutting at the rear of Boldventure, c1950. It was here that the rock-shifting explosion occurred in 1947 (see text in phase 5 of the next chapter).

C. Fennamore

negotiating another level-crossing (similar to the former, but close to m.p. 6¼ and giving right of way between Boldventure and Torr – Dixon Terrace), the train had to run out onto its last embankment. This gave the line the correct height for the station layout, crossing, in the process, Torr Road bridge – yet another single-span steel bridge with blue Staffordshire brick abutments. Just prior to, and just beyond, it were the rear of the 'up advanced starting', the 'up starting' and 'down home' signals for Yealmpton, while under it passed the B3186 (Newton Ferrers/Noss Mayo) road connecting with the A379, alongside which stands the village.

Yealmpton was the terminus of our journey, even though it had been built and designed as a 'through station'. This was because originally the line was to have been extended to Modbury, some 4 miles to the east, but sadly this never came to pass. In the event, the track layout consisted of a passing loop

30

A general view of Yealmpton Station, looking eastwards and taken at around the time of World War I.

Lens of Sutton

some 17½ chains long, which ran well past the platform and ended approximately 70 yards from the stop blocks. Interestingly enough, the platform itself differed from those at the other two stations (Billacombe and Brixton Road), which had vertical brick faces to track level: here it consisted of stone slabs as edging and dressed limestone forming the vertical face down to track level.

The main building was situated to the right (south) of the track as the train entered and was a limestone-faced structure identical to those already seen at the other two stations. Immediately alongside it, to the east, stood a signal box built of lateral wooden planking on a brick base, and beyond that, at the far end of the platform, was a water crane – the only watering point for engines working the 'true' branch. This derived its supplies from a large, square water tank standing on four girder legs on the river side of the station site and which, in turn, was filled with water from the river by means of an oil-driven pumping engine contained within an adjacent corrugated iron pumping house.

Behind the main building, to the west, was a large brick-built goods shed, with its 'through road', and three further goods sidings, complete with a hand-operated crane. In addition, immediately behind it were the cattle pens with their 'through road' to the cattle truck washing-troughs of blue Staffordshire brick. These five sidings then converged into one, which itself joined the running line and its loop by means of a 'double slip' facing the stop blocks. Adjacent to the 'double slip' was situated m.p. 6½, and a little further on was the final bridge; this was an accommodation over-bridge

31

connecting the village (via the river bank) to Higher Torr and Black Torrs in conjunction with a footpath.

Passengers alighting from the train found the way out of the station involved walking around the main building and turning right down the access road that also served the goods depot and coal sidings. At the lower end of this road they then had to walk through two large iron gates constructed of old boiler tubes in traditional GWR style, before joining the B3186 (crossed some minutes earlier whilst aboard the train) at the foot of Torr Hill.

(b) Plymouth (Friary) to Cattewater Junction (for Yealmpton), *circa* 1941.

The second terminus (1941 to 1947), Friary Station, depicted here during the busy 1920s. The Yealmpton-bound trains during the 1940s would leave from the far bay, adjacent to the signal gantry.

Lens of Sutton

The wartime re-opening to passenger traffic during 1941 (eleven years after closure in 1930) closely followed the closure of Millbay as a passenger station. These two incidents had a common factor, namely the Plymouth Blitz (March/April 1941), for the Yealmpton branchline was re-opened primarily to assist the nocturnal evacuation of the civilian population from Plymouth to escape further bombing, while the railway complex at Millbay had suffered heavy damage. In fact, the giant goods depot at Millbay had been totally destroyed by fire, and emergency action by the GWR had decreed that the passenger station adjacent to it should cease as such and operate as a goods handling depot until the cessation of hostilities. As a result, and so as to avoid congestion at North Road, it was decided that the resumed service should operate out of the Southern Railway's terminus at Plymouth Friary.

A building of grand proportions, complete with its own stationmaster's house, Friary Station had been constructed of dressed limestone and opened by the LSWR as its main Plymouth terminus on 1 July 1891; this had followed the opening, on 2 June 1890, of the Lydford to Devonport (Kings Road) line. It was situated at the end of Beaumont Road, adjacent to the crossroads by St Jude's Church, and a full description of its somewhat complex layout appears in one of my other books entitled *The Plymouth to Turnchapel Railway (and The Cattewater Goods Line)* – ARK Publications (Railways), 1996. Suffice to say the passenger platforms were situated on the northern side of the site, and it was from a small bay platform (No 4 road) that the Yealmpton-bound train departed during the six years of passenger operation until the second, and final, closure in 1947.

From Friary, the train headed eastwards and quickly joined the main 'up' line near the spot where Friary 'B' signal box was passed to the south of Knighton Road, which ran along a high embankment. Then, as the main 'up' and 'down' lines picked up the goods lines emerging from the station below Desborough Road, Friary 'A' signal box was passed. Here, the embankment fell away to leave passengers a clear view over St Jude's and Mount Gould as the main lines veered away to Friary Junction. Just beyond this point, however, the train left the 'up' main line, still in an easterly direction, crossed the 'down' main line and climbed onto a high embankment carrying the single track of a branch line. This was actually the Turnchapel branch/Cattewater goods line, and, after passing alongside the SR Motive

Two photographs of Lucas Terrace Halt taken by the author in 1964. *Above:* The view eastwards showing the Turnchapel/Yealmpton line on an embankment adjacent to the SR main lines to and from Friary, and with the River Plym and the Lanhydrock Road bridge in the background. *Overleaf:* The view westwards towards Friary Station.

Power Depot, with its long straight shed and turntable, the train gradually eased to rest for its first stopping point along it – Lucas Terrace Halt.

Opened in 1905, this halt consisted of a precast concrete structure, serving as a small shelter/ticket office, and a long single platform, its entire length being of stone and earth infill with concrete slab edging to a loose chippings surface. It was situated on the southern side of a low over-bridge which carried the branch and main lines, each having their own arch, over Lucas Terrace, and the only passenger access to it was by means of a winding, stepped walkway from the road below.

After departing from Lucas Terrace Halt, the train headed southwards and proceeded to cross the GWR Sutton Harbour branch and the Plymouth & Dartmoor Railway/Lee Moor Tramway over a steel girder bridge with lattice sides, this whilst negotiating a severe curve.

It then proceeded in much the same direction until reaching a similar bridge (situated just to the west of a more substantial GWR girder bridge

34

Lucas Terrace Halt in its heyday with a SR class '02' and ex-LSWR 'gate-type' coaches bound for Turnchapel on May 22nd 1935.

H. C. Casserley

A well-known photograph of Plymstock Station taken during the early 1900s. It shows the Yealmpton platform with its enamel nameboard of LSWR design, which was painted blue and white, and also the canopy built by the LSWR for the GWR.

Lens of Sutton

35

Two more views of Plymstock Station, taken by the author and showing the ('temporary') concrete station buildings constructed by the SR to replace those destroyed by wartime enemy action. *Above:* Looking westwards towards Plymouth and showing the wooden signal box. *Below:* Looking eastwards towards Yealmpton. (N.B. These photographs were taken c1963, before the site was demolished and prior to the provision of new South Western Gas Board sidings and transfer plant in 1966.)

which had been built especially for the section of the Yealmpton branch from Mount Gould Junction) that carried the line over The Embankment. From there, it was only a short distance before the train arrived at Cattewater Junction and continued to Plymstock Station (and beyond) along the same route as that used for the original passenger service up until 1930.

Plymstock Station (which has not previously been described here) had been built by the LSWR and, in its original form, consisted of an ornate corrugated building with an additional 'lean to' housing the gentlemen's toilet. Attached to it was also a vertical planked platform shelter with glazed ends and a wooden canopy decorated in wrought ironwork. Facing the GWR line, which passed its northern aspect, this contrasted starkly with the LSWR side for the Turnchapel branch, as here there was no covering at all! The platform, meanwhile, was a slightly curved affair backed with a wooden fence, and this led off to the station's only exit into Billacombe Road.

Unfortunately, the air raids of 1941 were responsible for the partial destruction of the station and resulted in the SR building 'temporary' structures on the site, using the same platforms. These consisted, primarily, of an ugly precast waiting room and a very small ladies and gents toilet built of wood under an asbestos roof (similar to the replacement signal box), and were to remain in situ until eventually being demolished during the early 1960s.

Compared to 1930 and earlier, the appearance of Plymstock Station was by no means the only difference that the wartime traveller on the Yealmpton branch would have noticed. Certainly one of the more obvious would have been the occupation of the three stations along its route by railway staff and their families, and each of them being 'sealed off' by means of a concrete post and wire fence: the doorways opening out onto the platform at each station, incidentally, were linked in the form of a corridor by a purpose-built wooden structure.

Tickets were made available on board each train, but at Yealmpton a 'Pagoda'-type corrugated ticket office was provided adjacent to the exit. In addition, a small concrete block building was erected at the far eastern end of the platform to serve as a ladies and gents toilet. In the meantime, the brick base of the former signal box had sprouted wooded sides with wire netting windows and been covered by a corrugated asbestos roof – it had become a chicken house!

It was these sights, together with lines of washing and also occupants staring out of the station windows at those staring in at them from the trains, that the wartime travellers would recall on their journeys to and from Yealmpton, a situation that existed even into the immediate post-war years, until October 1947.

37

(a) Plymouth (Millbay) to Yealmpton.

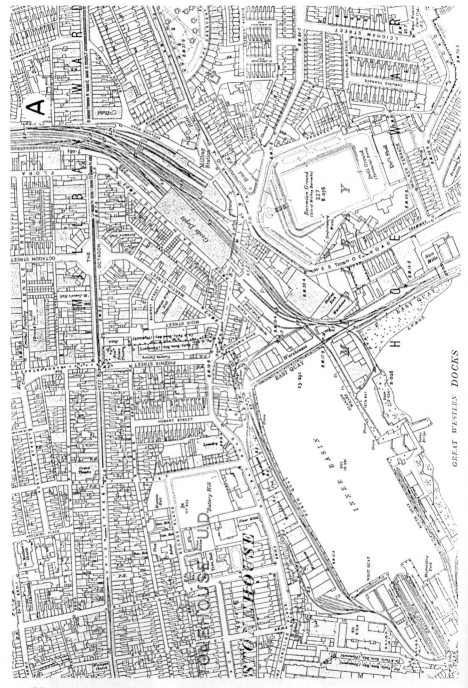

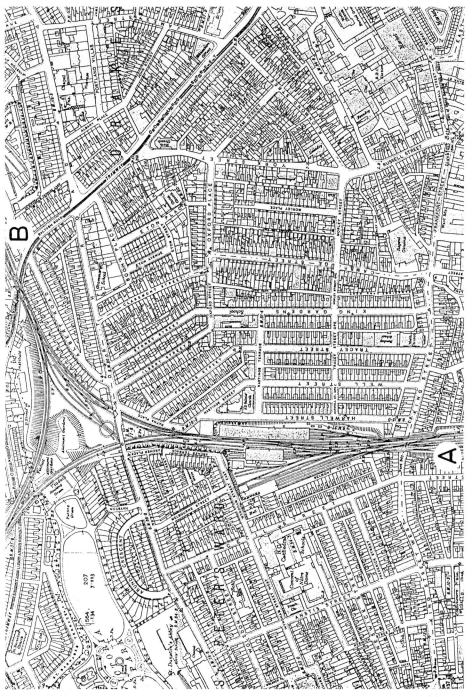

39

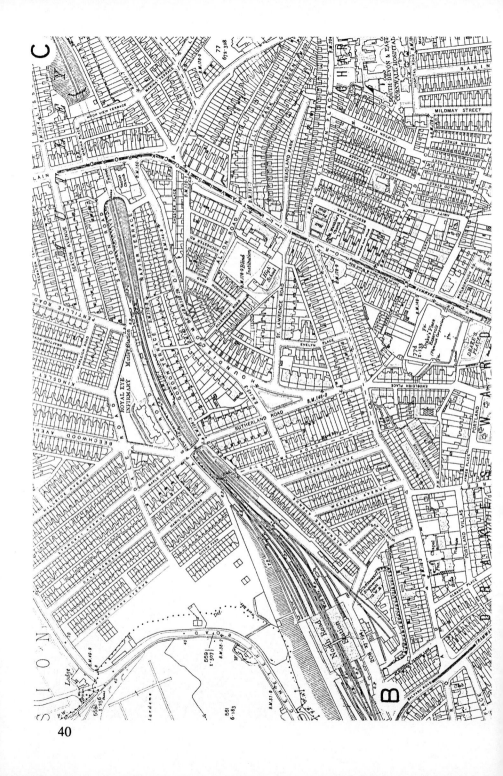

41

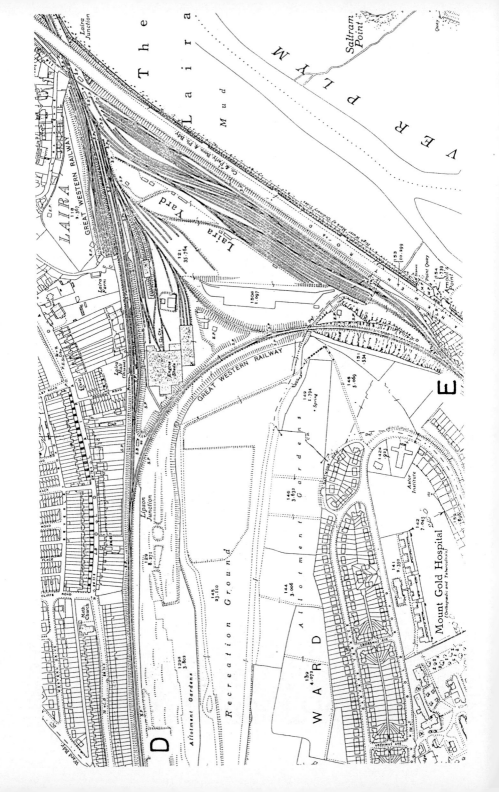

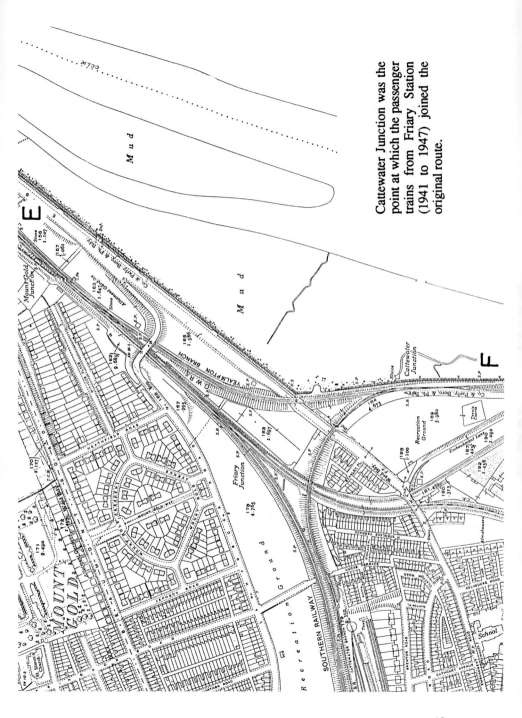

Cattewater Junction was the point at which the passenger trains from Friary Station (1941 to 1947) joined the original route.

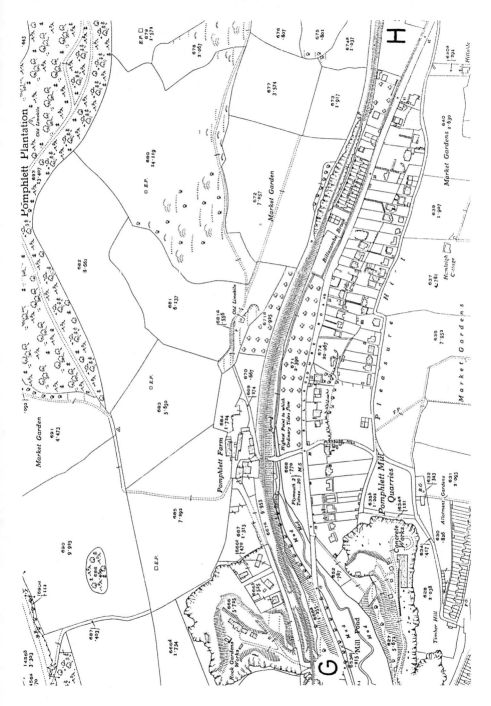

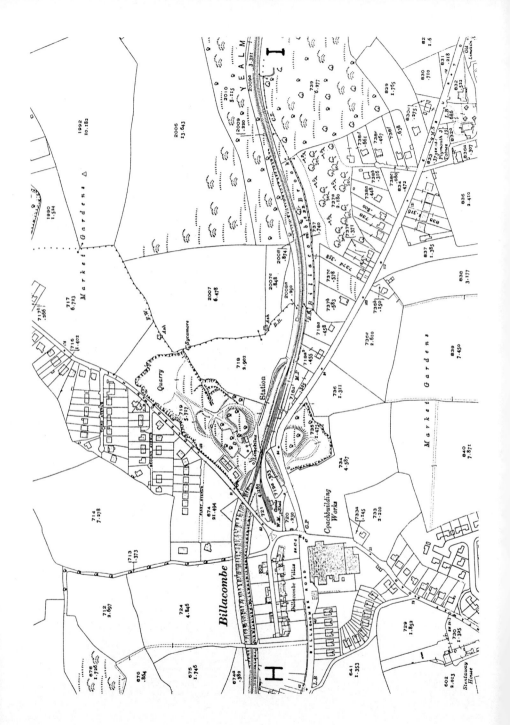

46

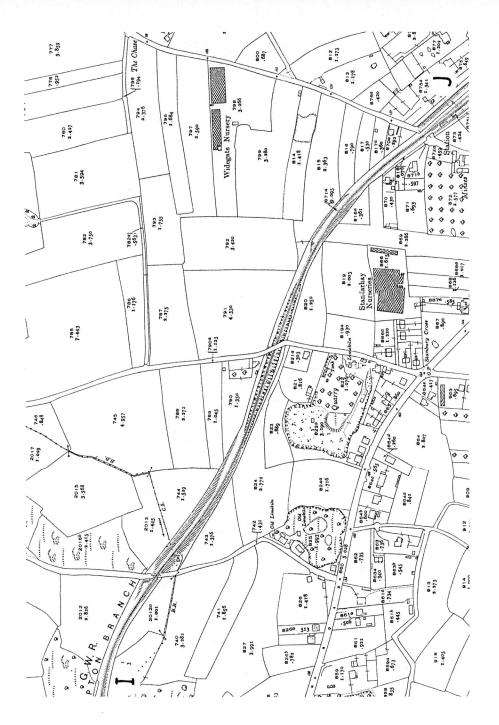

47

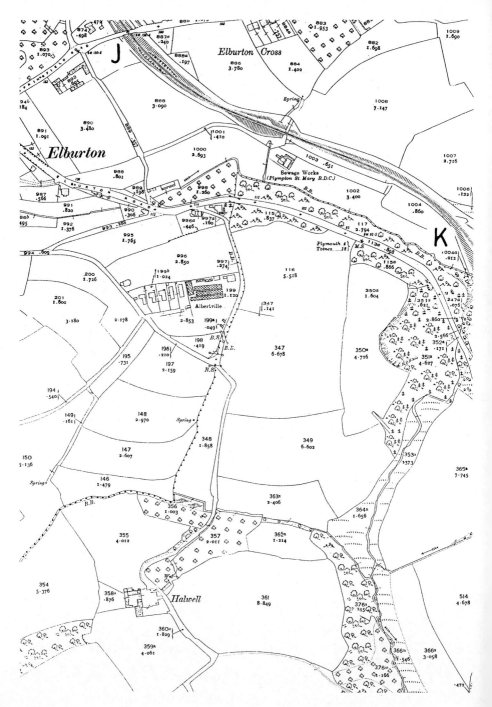

48

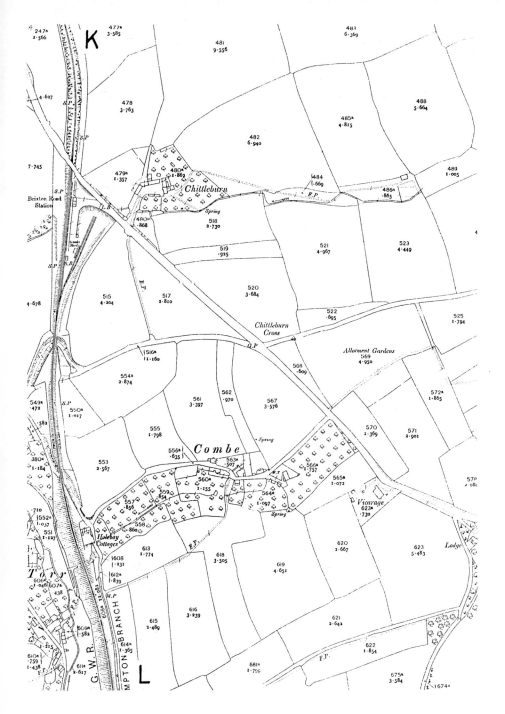

49

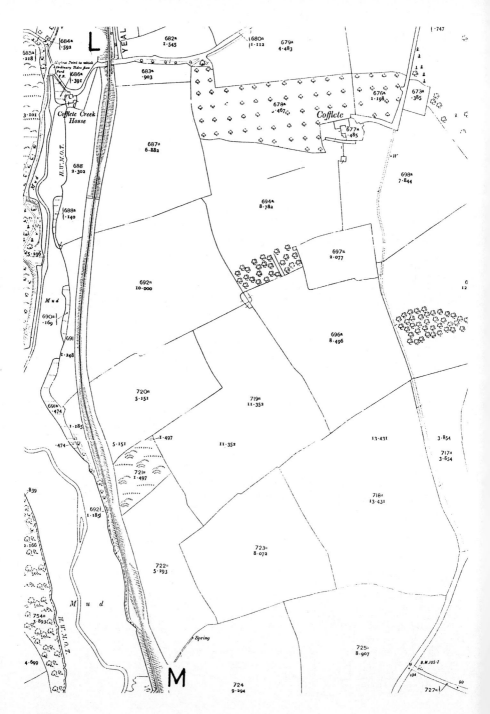

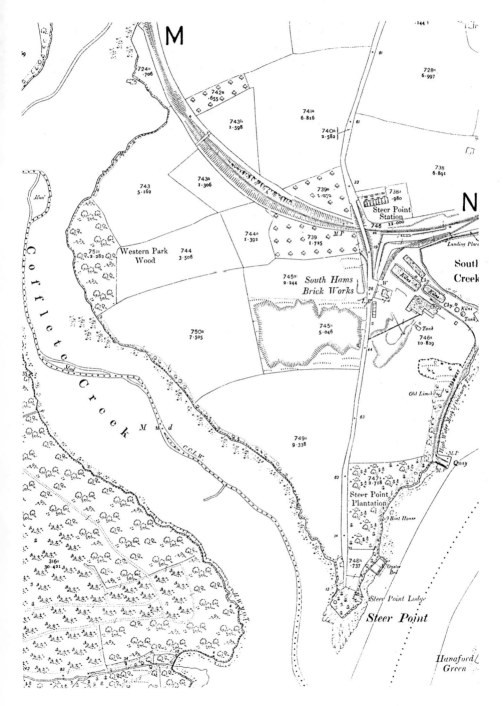

724ª
·706

742ª
·655

743ª
1·598

741ª
6·816

740ª
2·582

·144 ¹

728ª
6·997

738
6·891

743
5·162

743ª
1·306

739ª
3·070

738ª
·980

Steer Point
Station

746 13·000

Landing Place

32

81

61

Mud

75ª
2·282

Western Park
Wood

744
3·506

744ª
1·392

739
1·725

M.P

South
Creek

745ª
2·244

South Hams
Brick Works

Kiln A

Chy

Kilns

Chy ᴮ

Kilns

Tank

Mud

750ª
7·505

745ª
5·046

Tank

746ª
10·829

Old Lime Kiln

Coffete Creek

Mud

C.C.L.W.

749ª
9·338

63

High Water Mark Ordinary Tides

M.P

Quay

62

747ª
2·718

Steer Point
Plantation

Boat House

316ª
30·431

M.H.W.M.

14

13

748ª
·737

Oyster
Bed

Steer Point Lodge

Steer Point

142

83

Hanaford
Green

51

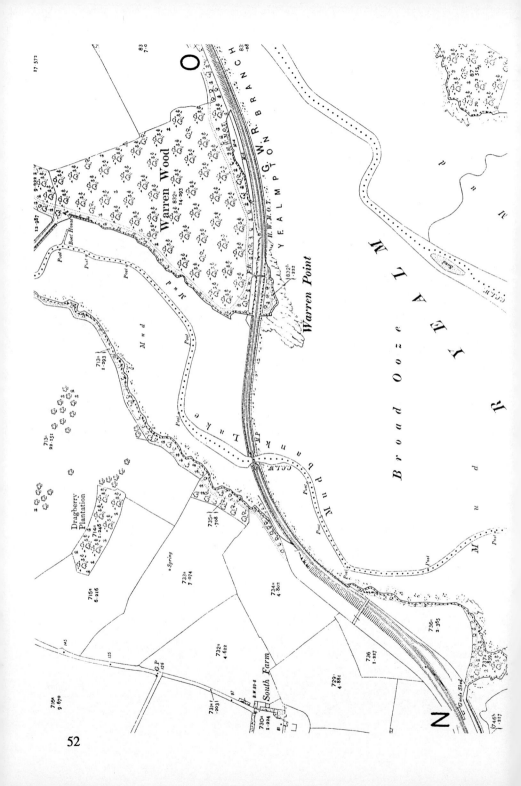

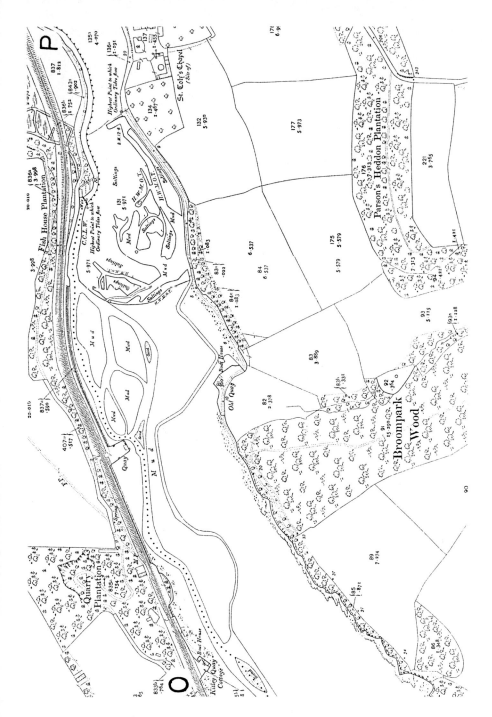

53

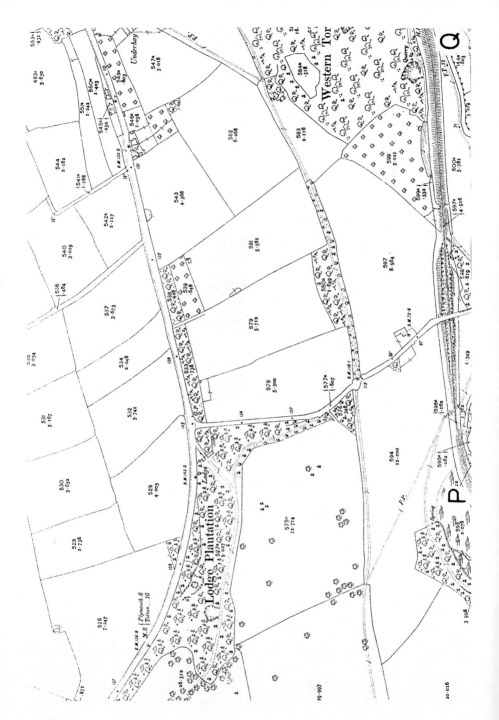

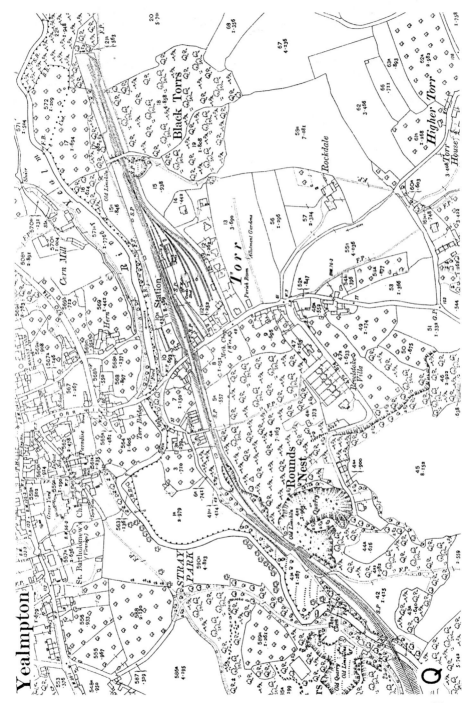

(b) Plymouth (Friary) to Cattewater Junction.

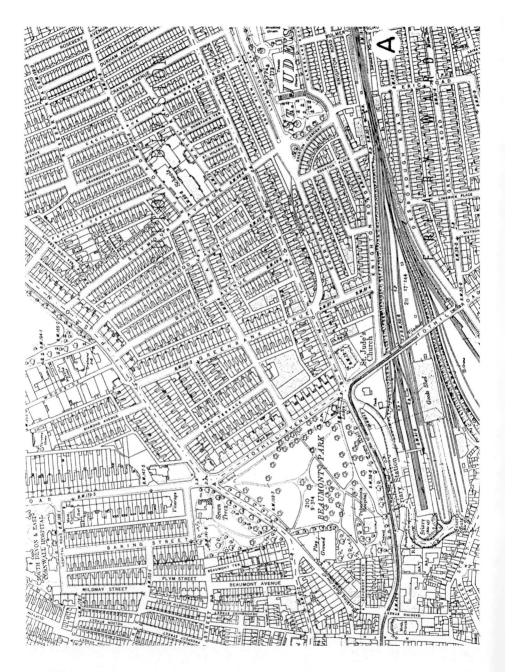

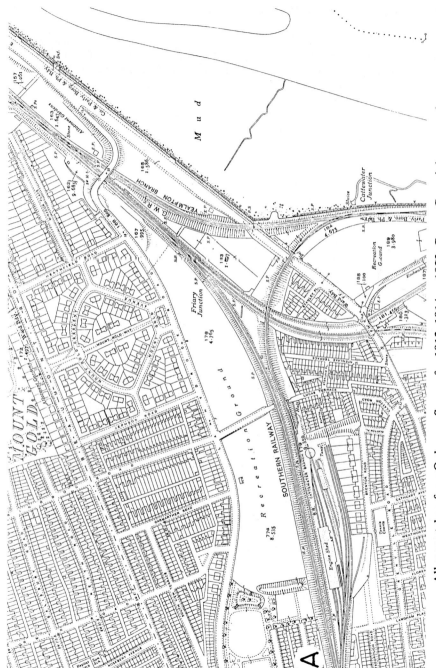

THE YEALMPTON BRANCH – HISTORY

The history of the line will be dealt with in six phases, but its chequered career will not be recounted in every detail for two reasons. Firstly, its very early demise clouded the accuracy of remaining records and, secondly, the 'heavy reading' produced by an over-detailed succession of historical facts and dates are of interest to only the most avid historian. Therefore suffice it to record only the more dominant and interesting facts that gave the line its many lives before its final demise.

Prelude – The proposed Plymouth to Modbury Railway

Plymouth & Dartmoor Railway Co., 1883.
(Galbraith & Church, Engineers)

The route of the railway proposed in 1883, from Plymouth to Modbury, included running along the *western* side of Cofflete Creek (passing over Foxes' Cove in the process), crossing the river just to the south of Steer Point and then running along the *eastern* side of the Yealm estuary, keeping to the east of Hanaford Green. Continuing through Puslinch, it was then to have crossed the

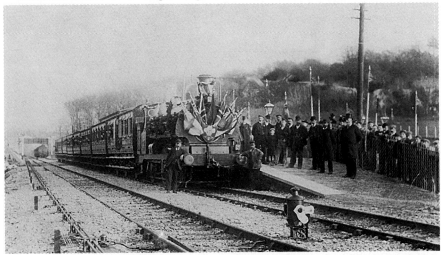

Conjecture and speculation still surround this photograph over 20 years after its publication in the forerunner to this book, *The Yealmpton Branch*. Originally purporting to depict the opening of the Yealmpton Railway, the photograph has since given rise to a number of alternative suggestions. The best explanation, however, is that it depicts a train returning to Plymouth (Millbay) from Yealmpton on the first day of public operation – Monday, January 17th 1898. If so, it would probably have been the 2.30pm ex-Yealmpton train as photographs of trains earlier that day would have been impaired by poor, winter light. (The GWR Company's official photograph of the opening of the line by Lady Morley appears on page 66)

Courtesy of Mrs D. Joll

river again just to the north of Torr, before proceeding towards Modbury. (Later the Devon and South Hams Light Railway Company was to propose building an extension from Yealmpton to Totnes, via Modbury, Aveton Gifford, Kingsbridge (with a branch to Salcombe), Slapton and Dartmouth, but this, too, fell by the wayside.)
In 1887, however, another plan was deposited showing the line that was subsequently constructed:-

Phase I – The preamble and conception by the Plymouth & Dartmoor Railway Co.

Plymouth & Dartmoor Railway Co., 1887.
(Galbraith & Church Engineers – signed J. C. Inglis)

Plymouth & Dartmoor Railway Co. – Meeting 9th December 1887.

Minute 81: Seal of the Co. to be affixed to petition for bill authorising an extension of the Co's line to Modbury, on the solicitors reporting that the solicitor, engineers and others had agreed not to look to the P & D R Co. for any costs in respect of the capital to be issued by the intended bill.

G.W.R. Traffic Committee – Meeting 14th August 1895.

Minute 18: In reference of minute No. 19 of the meeting of the board held on the 21st March last, the General Manager submitted a plan of the proposed railway from Plymstock to Yealmpton. He stated that it is proposed to erect four stations on the line viz: at Billacombe, Brixton, Steer Point and Yealmpton respectively, as shown on the plan submitted, and that the cost of the works is estimated as follows:

Engineering, including land	£87,187
Locking and signalling	£1,095
Telegraphs	£750
	£89,032

The estimate for telegraphs includes a sum of £174 in respect of work between Cattewater Junction and Plymstock which it is considered should be done by the P. & D. Co. and it is proposed to ask that Co. to defray this expense.
The committee approved the plans and estimates and agreed to recommend the Board to authorise the works to be proceeded with.

G.W.R. Engineering Committee – Meeting 16th October 1895.

Minute 26: Recommendations as to the mode of carrying out authorised works were submitted and approved as follows:

Construction of Railway between Plymstock and Yealmpton £87,178.

By Contract
Earthwork, laying ballast and permanent way, fencing, brickwork, masonry and ironwork etc.   Estimated £64,500

By Company
Supply of permanent way materials, ballast etc. Estimated £22,678

G.W.R. Traffic Committee – Meeting 20th November 1895.

Minute 25: The following expenditure was approved after consideration of each case and examination of the plans and estimates and it was agreed to recommend the Board to sanction the same:
Elburton Cross on the South Hams Extension.
Construction of platform with shelter and urinal thereon £215

G.W.R. Engineering Committee – Meeting 18th March 1896.

Minute 27: Recommendations as to the mode of carrying out authorised works were submitted and approved as follows:
Elburton Cross, Yealmpton Line
Provision of a stopping place £215
By Mr. John Aird at the schedule attached to his contract for the Yealmpton Line. Estimate £215

Plymouth & Dartmoor Co – Meeting 17th June 1896.

Letter was read dated 27th March 1896 from G.W.R. relating to the construction by them of this company's line between Plymstock and Yealmpton proposing that the traffic would be more efficiently worked between the junction with Plymouth & Dartmoor railway and Plymstock if the electric train staff system were introduced and stating the cost would be £174.

G.W.R. Engineering Committee – Meeting 11th November 1896.

Minute 31: Read report upon the progress of the works of the Yealmpton line. An expenditure of £1,500 was approved in carrying out various accommodation works for the Duke of Bedford, Mr. Bastard and Mr. Collins – Splatt respectively which have been agreed to since the contract was made with Mr. Aird for the construction of the line. The works will be carried out by Mr. Aird upon the schedule of prices attached to his contract.

Great Western Railway Company
General Manager's Office,
Paddington.
20th October, 1897

Sir,
I beg to state for the information of the Board of Trade that the works in connection with the construction of the new railway from Plymstock to Yealmpton, authorised by the Plymouth and Dartmoor Railway Act, 1888, the powers contained in which were transferred to this Company by the G.W.R. Act (No.2) 1894, are approaching completion; and I hope shortly to be in a

position to send you plans and particulars of the works in question.

I am Sir,
Your Obedient Servant,
For J. L. Wilkinson.

Great Western Railway Company
General Manager's Office,
Paddington.
26th November, 1897

Sir,
With reference to your letter of 21st instant (R12116) I beg to inform you that the new line of railway between Plymstock and Yealmpton has been completed and may be inspected at any time convenient to the Inspecting Officer. The usual detail plans and statements are sent herewith.

I would mention that Col Yorke RE proposes to take other inspections in Cornwall during the latter end of next week and it has occurred to me that probably he might be able to make it convenient to take the inspection of the new Yealmpton line while in the West.

I am Sir,
Your Obedient Servant,
For J. L. Wilkinson.

RAILWAY DEPARTMENT,
BOARD OF TRADE,
8, Richmond Terrace
Whitehall, London, S.W.
Dec 7, 1897.
Sir,
I have the honour to report for the information of the Board of Trade, that in compliance with the instructions contained in your minute of the 27th Nov, I have inspected the new line from Plymstock to Yealmpton on the Great Western Railway.

The line, which is single throughout (with sidings at some of the intermediate stations) commences at the junction at Plymstock with the L & SW Rly and terminates at Yealmpton, the total length being 6 miles 38^1/$_2$ chains.

Land has been purchased for an additional line of rails, and the width at formation level is 107 feet. The gauge is 4' 8^1/$_2$" and the width between the running line and the sidings is 6' 6".

The steepest gradient has an inclination of 1 in 60, and the sharpest curve a radius of 15 chains.

The permanent way is laid with rails weighing 76 lbs per yard and cast iron chairs weighing 36 lbs each.

The sleepers which are creosoted are of the usual dimensions, and the line is well ballasted with broken limestone.

There are numerous cuttings, the most important of which have depths of 40 ft while the principal embankment has a height of 45 ft.

The fencing consists of wooden posts and eight wires with straining points at suitable intervals.

There are 16 bridges under and 11 over the line.

Two of the under bridges and three of the over bridges are constructed with arches resting on masonry abutments, faced with brick. The remaining bridges have steel girders or steel troughing.

There are no public road level crossings, no viaducts and no tunnels and there are only eight small culverts.

The works all appear to be substantially constructed and to be perfectly stable. The girders have sufficient theoretical strength and those under the line gave inordinate deflections under test.

There are five stations on the new line, viz Billacombe, Elburton, Brixton, Steer Point and Yealmpton.

These all have platforms 300 ft long except Elburton, where the platform is 223 ft long.

At Billacombe, Brixton, Steer Point and Yealmpton the usual accommodation is provided, including booking offices, waiting rooms and conveniences for both sexes, but at Elburton there is merely a waiting room and urinal, with no booking office or ladies room. It is not intended at present to man Elburton station and the issue of tickets to and from this place, and all platform work will have to be attended to by the guard of the train calling there. As there will be no one to light the station lamps, it will be necessary under these circumstances to prohibit the use of this station after dark.

The line is to be worked on the electric staff system, as to which the usual undertaking is to be provided by the company, and the section will extend from Plymstock to Yealmpton, so that no signals are required or provided except at these two places. All intermediate siding connections being locked by the key on the train staff.

Plymstock signal box, which is on the L & SW Rly will be separately reported on.

Yealmpton signal box contains 23 levers of which 18 are in use, and 5 are spare, and the only requirement noted, is that levers nos 19 & 23 should interlock.

There are the following ground frames to work the various siding connections, all of which are locked, as already stated by the key on the staff; viz –

Billacombe – 1 ground frame containing 5 levers, all of which, are in use.

Brixton – 2 ground frames, the west frame contains 2 levers, and the east frame 4 levers, all in use.

Steer Point – 2 ground frames, the west frame contains 3 levers in use and 4 spare levers, while the east frame has 2 levers, both in use.

This line is in excellent order, the only point requiring alteration being that short lengths of railing are required over the tops of the wing walls at several of the under bridges.

Subject to these railings being fixed, with the alterations in the locking at Yealmpton (which I have already referred to) being made, within a month, I can, as the arrangements are in all other respects satisfactory, recommend that the Board of Trade sanction the opening of this new line for passenger traffic.

I have the honour to be,

Sir etc, etc,

Col H. A. Yorke R.E.

R. *13888.*

Copying

8 Dec. 189*7.*

Sir,

    I am, &c., to transmit to you the enclosed Copy of Colonel Yorke's *Report of his inspection of* the new line from Plymstock to Yealmpton,

on the Great Western *Railway, and to inform you that, subject to compliance with the requirements of the Report, they sanction* the *use* of the Line in question for passenger traffic.

    I am, at the same time, to request that you will acquaint this Department when the requirements referred to have been complied with.

I am, &c.,

Signed
Francis J. S. Hopwood.

The Genl. Manager *of the* Great Western *Railway* ~~Company.~~

63

Board of Trade,
8, Richmond Terrace,
Whitehall, London SW 1
December 15th, 1897

Sir,

I have the honour to report for the information of the Board of Trade that while inspecting the Plymstock and Yealmpton Branch I also inspected the Cattewater and Plymstock Junctions of the London & South Western Railway.

The former junction is the point where the Laira Loop line on the Great Western Railway joins the London & South Western line from Friary Station, Plymouth to Plymstock and Turnchapel; and the latter is the place where the Plymstock and Yealmpton line diverges from the Turnchapel line.

Cattewater Jcn signal box contains 29 levers in use and 8 spare and the interlocking is correct.

Plymstock signal box contains 21 levers all in use, 4 of them being "push and pull" levers. The interlocking here is also correct. At this place the two lines are joined by what is known as a "Single Junction". According to Board of Trade Requirement No. 10 the junctions between two single lines should as a rule be formed as "double junctions". But as the traffic at Plymstock is for the present not likely to be heavy, the single junction arrangement need not, I submit, be objected to, especially as there are loop sidings into which goods trains can be shunted so as to permit passenger trains to pass them.

If however it should become necessary hereafter for passenger trains to and from Yealmpton to cross each other here, a proper passing loop with up and down platforms will have to be constructed, and when this is done a double junction between the two branch lines should be substituted.

I have the honour
etc, etc, etc,
Sgd H. A. Yorke.

G.W.R. Board Meeting – 6th January 1898.

Minute 22: The common seal of the company was authorised to be affixed to the following document:
Undertaking to the Board of Trade to work the single line between Plymstock and Yealmpton upon the electric staff system.

Minute 23: The Chairman mentioned that the line from Plymstock to Yealmpton would be ready for opening by the 15th instant, and that the Countess of Morley had consented to perform the ceremony upon that date.
It was agreed to run a special train for the Directors and Officers from Plymouth to Yealmpton on the date named in connection with the ceremony.

Great Western Railway Company
General Manager's Office,
Paddington.
11th January, 1898

Sir,

Adverting to your letter (R13,888) of the 8th ult enclosing copy of Col Yorke's report of the new line from Plymstock to Yealmpton, I beg to enclose herewith an undertaking, signed and sealed on behalf of the Company, as to the mode of working the traffic over the said new line.
Will you kindly acknowledge receipt.

I am Sir,
Your Obedient Servant,
For J. L. Wilkinson.

The GREAT WESTERN RAILWAY COMPANY as owners of the single line of Railway between Plymstock and Yealmpton hereby undertake to work the said single line of Railway upon the Electric Staff System.
Dated this Sixth day of January, One thousand eight hundred and ninety eight.

(Sgd) Emlyn
Chairman
(Sgd) F. K. Mills
Secretary

Great Western Railway Company
General Manager's Office,
Paddington.
18th January, 1898

Sir,

Adverting to your letter of the 8th ult, relative to the inspection by Col. Yorke of the new line from Plymstock to Yealmpton, I beg to say that the requirements mentioned in the report viz:- the interlocking of the levers at Yealmpton and the provision of short lengths of railing over the tops of the wing walls of the underbridges has now been carried out.
Will you kindly note.

I am Sir,
Your Obedient Servant,
For J. L. Wilkinson.

The slowness of the shutter of a very early camera catches the tape dropping as the first train enters Yealmpton Station on Saturday, January 15th 1898. The locomotive, a 4–4–0 'Duke' class, was appropriately named *Lady Morley* for the day.
A GWR Company official photograph, courtesy of British Railways Board

Phase 2 – 1898 to 1930: The opening and early life

The best account of the actual opening of the line is recorded in the *Railway Magazine* of February 1898, page 186, *viz:-*

> The Countess of Morley on Saturday, January 15th opened for traffic a new line of railway, constructed by the G.W.R. from Plymstock to Yealmpton, a distance of six and a half miles, the total distance from Plymouth (Millbay) being nine and a half miles.
>
> The new line passes through a beautiful part of Devonshire, and the district opened up will probably become a favourite tourist resort.
>
> A double loop line has also been constructed at Laira to give direct access between the G.W.R. main line and the Plymstock and Yealmpton branch. The line between Plymstock is single throughout, the running gradient being 1 in 60, and the sharpest curve having a radius of 15 chains.
>
> On the new line there are five stations, *viz,* Billacombe, Elburton Cross, Brixton Road, Steer Point and Yealmpton, all, with the exception of Elburton, having ample goods in addition to passenger accommodation. There are some thirty bridges, of which the two largest are over the rivers Kitley and Yealm. There are no tunnels or viaducts, but several deep cuttings were necessary, some of them through hard rock.
>
> A special train of first class saloon carriages left Millbay at noon on Saturday for Yealmpton. Quite appropriately the train was drawn by an engine named *Lady Morley* and was gaily decorated with evergreens and flowers and a trophy of flags in front.
>
> The G.W.R. provides a service of four up and four down trains daily (Sundays excepted) between Plymouth (Millbay) and Yealmpton.
>
> A luncheon followed the opening ceremony and was served in the company's goods' shed which was gaily decorated with flags, bunting and flowers and transformed into a festive looking dining room. (See list following.)

ARRANGEMENTS FOR THE OPENING
OF THE SOUTH HAMS RAILWAY

Receipts in donations with tickets sold.   £86. 10. 0d
Decorations given by W. Bastard of Lyneham, for erection outside
Manor Office and at the bottom of Bowden Hill.
Decorations for the other end of the village were given by Mr. Snawdon.

Dr. to the Snawdon Bros, 41 Bedford Street & 9/10 East Street,
Plymouth. Manufactory – Yealm Bridge, Yealmpton.
Fitting up railway committee luncheon room at Yealmpton Station   £9. 0. 0d

Dr. To James H. Keys, Commercial & General Printer (Publisher of
The Plymouth Comet), 7 Whimple Street, Plymouth.
150 Ivory, gilt bevelled cards – luncheon tickets.   7. 6d   (37¹/₂p)
100 Posters – Anniversary Opening.   8. 6d   (42¹/₂p)
150 4-page menu cards – ivory, gilt bevelled cards, printed
blue bronze, and 1 card specially printed in silver bronze.   £1. 17. 0d   (£1.85p)

Parlayes.	1. 4d	(8p)
Cards for dining places.	1. 0d	(5p)
TOTAL	£2. 15. 4d	(£2.76½p)

Luncheon Account – H. Matthews, Confectioner, 11/12 Bedford Street, Plymouth.

To luncheons for band/navvies/railway officials etc. – 48 @ 2/6d (12½p)	£6. 00. 0d
To luncheons for 83 guests @ 5/6d (27½p)	22. 16. 6d
To luncheons for tickets sold at Yealmpton – 35 @ 5/6d (27½p)	9. 12. 6d
Wines etc. (as detailed below)	23. 18. 0d
TOTAL	£62. 07. 0d

List of wines etc:-

39 Bottles	–	Large	Champagne at 10/–	£19. 10. 0d	(£19.50p)
3 Bottles		Large	Hock at 3/–	9. 0d	(45p)
4 Bottles		Large	Claret at 2/6d	10. 0d	(50p)
2 Bottles		Small	Claret at 1/6d	3. 0d	(15p)
7 Bottles		Large	Burgundy at 3/–	1. 1. 0d	(£1.05p)
1 Bottles		Large	Port	4. 0d	(20p)
1 Bottles		Large	Sherry	3. 0d	(15p)
3 Bottles		Large	Cider at 6d	1. 6d	(7½p)
6 Bottles		Small	Burgundy at 1/9d	10. 6d	(52½p)
2 Bottles		Large	Beer at 8/–	16. 0d	(80p)
1 Bottles		Small	Beer	4. 0d	(20p)
1½ Bottles		Small	Lemonade at 2/–	3. 0d	(15p)
½ Bottles		Large	Lemonade at 4/–	2. 0d	(10p)
½ Bottles		Ginger	Beer at 2/–	1. 0d	(5p)
TOTAL				£23. 18. 0d	(£23.90p)

LIST OF INVITED GUESTS

Great Western Railway Management:-
Directors; General Manager; Superintendent of the line (T. I. Allen); Chief Engr (J. C. Inglis); Chief Civil Engr (F. Giles); New Works Engr (W. Y. Armstrong).

Earl & Countess of Morley, Saltram House, Nr. Plymouth.
Lord & Lady Auckland, Kitley, Yealmpton.
Lord Revelstoke, Membland, Noss Mayo.
Lord Rumbyson.
Sir Massey & Lady Lopes, Maristow, Roborough, Plymouth.
Sir John Aird.
Sir N. Kingcote.
Prince Sahu.
B. J. P. Bastard Esq & Mrs Bastard of Kitley, Buckland Court, Ashburton, Devon.
Rev W. P. & Mrs Bastard, Cofflete, Woodend Rd, Torquay.
Mr W. E. P. Bastard, Lyneham House, Yealmpton.
Rt Hon F. B. Mildmay M.P., GWR Director, Flete, Devon.
H. B. Mildmay Esq & Mrs Mildmay, 46, Berkley Square, London.

Thomas Bulteel Esq & Mrs Bulteel, Radford House, Nr. Plymouth.
John E. Yonge Esq, Puslinch, Yealmpton.
John Aird Esq, of London, Yealmpton Railway's Contractor.
J. T. Bond Esq, Solicitor, 2, Queen's Gate Villas, Plymouth.
H. Williams Esq & Mrs Williams, Gordon Hotels Ltd, London.
J. H. Ellis Esq, Town Clerk, Plymouth.
Col & Mrs Thompson.
Col Edgecombe.
Capt & Mrs Bainbridge & Family, Gnaton Hall, Yealmpton.
F. E. Burke, Dist Goods Manager Office, GWR, Plymouth.
P. A. Anthony Esq, District Engineers Office, GWR, Plymouth.
C. J. Owens Esq, Gen Managers Office, LSWR, Waterloo Station.
Vallance Esq, Dist Supt Office, LSWR, Queen St, Exeter.
White Esq, LSWR.
Mr William Grainger, Holsworthy & Bude Railway Works, LSWR, Bude, Cornwall.
J. R. Lake Esq, Chairman of Plymouth Inc Mercantile Association.
                    President of Chamber of Commerce.
J. Mc Andrew Esq, Lukesland, Ivybridge.
A. Kingston Esq.
Mr & Mrs H. Collins-Splatt, Brixton House, Brixton, Devon.
Mr W. King, Pitts, Son & King, Agricultural Merchs, Plymouth.
Mr W. Woolacombe, 2, Princess Sq, Plymouth.
Mr & Mrs Jameson, Torr House, Yealmpton.
Mr & Mrs Kerswill.
Mr & Mrs King.
Mr & Mrs Vaughan – Holberton, Newton Ferrers.
Mr & Mrs Lawson.
Mr & Mrs Robins.
Mr John Shelley, Princess House, Princess Sq, Plymouth.
Mr Law, Carhullen, Hartley, Plymouth.
Mr J. Bulteel.
Messrs Robinson; Fowler; Murdoch; Rooney; Compton; Avery; Waisher; Simpson;
Wootten; Elms; Gibbon; Adge; Brooke; Walby; Barker; Wilcox; Evea; Mc Pherson;
Hodge; Pethick.
Medames Warner; Quigley.
Press editors of:–
Daily Mercury; Independent; Western Morning News.
Committee of 10, Chairman W. E. P. Bastard Esq; Secretary Mr James Cross.
Band of 20 musicians.
Eighteen waiters.

SEATING OF GUESTS WITHIN THE GOODS SHED, AT THE OPENING CEREMONY OF THE LINE, 18 JANUARY 1898.

TABLE 1.   Mr Wilcox

Mr Radford	Mr M Williams
Mr Lake	Mr Bulteel
Mr W King	Mrs Bulteel

Miss Bainbridge	Capt Bainbridge
Miss Bainbridge	Mrs Bainbridge
Lord Auckland	Mr Murdock
Lady Auckland	Mr Wilkinson
Mr Owens, LSWR	Sir N Kingcote
Mr Law	Lord Emlyn
Mr Mc Andrew	Countess Morley
Mrs Thompson	W E P Bastard (Chairman)
Mr Holberton	Mrs Bastard
Mrs Holberton	Earl Morley
Col Thompson	Sir Massey Lopes
Mr Woolacombe	Mr Robinson
Mr Adge	Col Edgecombe
Mr Vallance, LSWR	Mr Ingles
Mr Collins-Splatt	Mr Allen
Mr Anthony	Mr. Giles
Mrs Jameson	Mr Armstrong
Mr J F Yonge	Mr Gibbon
Mrs Yonge	
Mr Jameson	

TABLE 2.   Mr Kingston

Mr W Cross	Mr J Cross
Mrs J Brown	Miss Snawdon
Mr J Brown	Mr M Snawdon
Mrs F Cross	Mrs Perring
Mr F Cross	Mr Perring
Mrs Ellis	Mr R Barker
Mr Ellis	Mr Avery
Miss Brooking	Mr Compton
Mr Brooking	Mr Fowler
Mrs Warner	Mr Jones
Mr Warner	Mr Quigley
	Press
	Press
	Press
	Mr Simpson
	Mr Wootten
	Mr Elms
	Mr Rooney
	Mr Evea
	Mr Grainger
	Mr W Snawdon
	Mr M Robins
	Mr Waisher
	Mr E Hodge
	Mr Burke

Below and overleaf: The GWR Company's official photographs of the stations along the branch taken just prior to, or just after, the opening, c1898.
British Railways Board

Billacombe.

Elburton Cross.

Brixton Road.

Steer Point.

Yealmpton.

The new line referred to in the *Railway Magazine* of February 1898 (see page 67) was a continuation of the LSWR from Plymstock. Although constructed by the GWR, both the Plymouth & Dartmoor and the LSW Railway Companies were interested in the line; but the peculiar circumstances that led to this three-sided arrangement are too lengthy for detail here.

The reference to the engine's name, *Lady Morley*, seems authentic, if temporary, and, in view of the services of the Countess of Morley, appropriate as a mark of respect, but in fact no such name was subsequently carried by a Great Western engine as far as can be proven.

However at this juncture, it is interesting to note another article which appeared in the *Railway Magazine*, eight years later in July 1906, *viz:-*

The new railway from Newton Ferrers to Yealmpton, the first sod of which has been recently cut by the Mayoress of Plymouth, is to be constructed by the Devon and South Hams Light Railway.

Although termed a light railway, it is to be of standard gauge and it is three miles long, branching the G.W.R.'s Yealmpton line at Puslinch, about a mile from Yealmpton, and running along the east bank of the river Yealm to Newton Ferrers and Noss Mayo.

The cutting of the first sod for the construction of the railway from Newton Ferrers by the Mayoress of Plymouth, Mrs J. F. Winnicott, on Saturday, May 30th 1906. Interestingly enough the ceremony took place some 200 yards above the proposed level of the line, on the western bank of Noss Creek, which suggests that this may have been the spot earmarked for the entrance to the station. In the centre of the photograph, just above the mayoress's head, can be seen the roof of Kiln Quay.

Courtesy of Mr Wilson, The River Yealm Hotel

Two photographs, taken on July 27th 1906, showing that although the proposed line from Newton Ferrers and Noss Mayo failed to become reality, work did commence on the project. *Above:* Excavation work in progress for Newton Ferrers Station building, adjacent to Kiln Quay. *Below:* Workmen preparing the trackbed in a southerly direction from the proposed station site towards The Pool (the confluence of Noss Creek and the River Yealm).

Courtesy of Mr P. H. Gatley

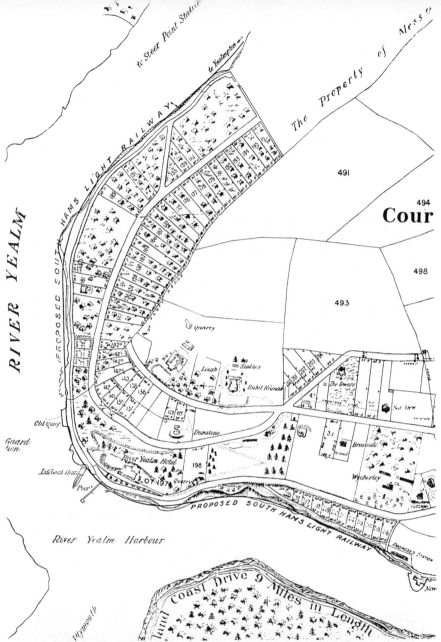

An architect's plan of the River Yealm building estate of 1910, showing the proposed route and station site of the South Hams Light Railway extension from Newton Ferrers. Although construction work started in 1906, the project was soon abandoned.

James Ford, CE (Courtesy of Mr C. Foster)

The order also provides for a railway from Salcombe, three and a half miles long, forming an extension of the G.W.R. Kingsbridge branch and running down the west side of the Kingsbridge estuary direct to Salcombe.

The third portion of the scheme is to construct a light railway of a 2' 6" gauge, seven miles long, from Kingsbridge station of the G.W.R. through Charleton, Frogmore, Chillington, Stokenham and Torcross to Slapton Sands, ending at the Royal Sands Hotel.

Had the line from Newton Ferrers and Noss Mayo become reality, and plans to continue the line to Modbury and, possibly, beyond (to connect with the Kingsbridge line) been fulfilled, Yealmpton Station would, of course, have become a junction. This, in turn, would also have given the station far greater importance and would, undoubtedly, have prolonged the line's life, particularly with regard to passenger traffic. However, not only did the line from Newton Ferrers and Noss Mayo fail to materialise, but the proposed extension (even to Modbury) fell by the wayside.

As regards the latter, mention should be made at this point that the projection of a line to Modbury had been part of an original plan by the Plymouth & Dartmoor Railway as a means of extending into the South Hams. Indeed, on June 28th 1888, and as agents for the LSWR, the company had secured parliamentary sanction for a line to leave the then proposed Plymouth to Turnchapel branch (later opened in 1897) and to proceed to Modbury via Yealmpton. At the time, not unnaturally, this had been of great concern to the GWR as it was feared that the LSWR would ultimately extend the Yealmpton branch to Torbay and Exeter. However, under a later Act of 1894 the rights for the Plymstock to Yealmpton section were transferred to the GWR and proviso made for each company to have running powers over the other as mutual checks. In the event, because the LSWR failed to build the Yealmpton to Modbury section, these running powers were never exercised.

The route that the extension was to have followed, incidentally, was, initially, from Yealmpton to a point just beyond Yealm Bridge. It was then to have proceeded up Longbrook Valley, cutting through the ridge of high ground between Clickland and Fleet Western Lodge and going across the River Erme at Groutsford, and continued onwards towards Fancy before terminating at Modbury, just below the church.

Returning now to the opening of the line, one immediate problem to come to light was that of access to and from Yealmpton Station – in two respects. Firstly, because it was situated at Torre and on the opposite side of the river to the village that it served, the nearby stone bridge spanning the river was found to be too narrow for wagons and horse-drawn buses, and had to be widened. Secondly, the steepness of Torre Hill proved to be too difficult for the horse-drawn buses, which were bound for Modbury (at this time also linked to Ivybridge Station by a similar means), and could only be overcome by the building of what, to this day, is still known as 'New Road', on the eastern side of the village.

Meanwhile, other matters of interest subsequent to the opening of the line are contained in the following minutes from G. W. Board Meetings:-

G.W. Board Meeting – 9th June 1898.

Minute 6: Referring to minute 39 in regard to the application of Messrs. John Aird and Co. for consideration in respect of the loss sustained by them on their contract for the Yealmpton line, the views of the Board were expressed for the Chairman's information and guidance, and it was agreed that the matter should be in his hands for settlement up to a sum not exceeding £2,000.

G.W. Board Meeting – 20th April 1899.

Minute 23: In reference to minute 23 of the meeting of the Board held on the 6th instant, the Chairman reported that the line from Plymstock to Yealmpton was opened on the 15th instant by the Countess of Morley, and that the ceremony was followed by a luncheon.
Upon the recommendations of the General Manager, the Board authorised the contribution of £20 towards the expenses incurred by the local committee on the occasion.

G.W. Board Meeting – 11th May 1899.

Minute 13: In reference to minute No. 6 of the meeting of the Board held on the 20th ultimo, the Chairman reported that he had discussed with Mr. John Aird the application made by his firm for assistance from the company to meet the loss sustained by them in carrying out their contract for the Yealmpton line and had disposed of the matter by a payment of £2,000 with which Mr. Aird had expressed himself perfectly satisfied.

During 1905, and despite having inaugurated its own road motor services between Modbury and Plymouth (via Yealmpton) in the previous year, the GWR considered that a halt was needed at Mount Gould. This was to be for rail motors on the branch, and was prompted by more and more residential development taking place in the Mount Gould area and also at nearby Tothill.

As the following communications indicate, the halt was subsequently erected later in that same year, although, contrary to expectations, it was to be little used and was subsequently closed on February 1st 1918 (after less than 13 years!):-

Paddington Station,
August 31st, 1905

Sir,
I send herewith a plan of a proposed halt for rail motor cars at Mount Gould, Plymouth; and shall be glad to receive provisional sanction from the Board of Trade to proceed with the works and bring them into use as and when required on the condition that they are submitted for inspection when complete.

I am Sir,
Your Obedient Servant,
James C. Inglis

_____

78

Board of Trade,
8, Richmond Terrace,
Whitehall,
London SW
8th January, 1906

Sir,

I have the honour to report for the information of the Board of Trade that in compliance with the instructions contained in your Minute of the 6th November last, I have inspected the new works at Mount Gould, Plymouth on the Great Western Railway.

At this point, which is between Mount Gould Jcn and Cattewater Jcn on the Plymstock Branch, a new stopping place for motor cars has been constructed. Two platforms have been erected, each of them being 150 yards long, 6 feet wide and 3 feet high: they are provided with shelter, name boards, lamps and a connecting overbridge.

The arrangements are satisfactory and I can recommend the Board of Trade to sanction the use of the new work being brought into use.

I have the honour
etc, etc, etc,
Col. Van Donops

Another proposal to be made in 1905, and of even greater significance, concerned the hitherto lowly Elburton Cross. Here, land was to be purchased to facilitate the provision of sidings for 20 wagons, complete with a mileage yard on the northern side of the station. It is believed that at the time new quarries were to have been opened in the vicinity but, apart from the existence of the engineering plan, no documentation has come to light; neither did anything come to fruition.

In the meantime, passenger traffic during these early years of the 20th century was growing steadily on the line, and goods traffic by an even greater extent. Moreover, this was a pattern that continued, including throughout the duration of World War I, until the start of the 1920s, at which point the branch reached its zenith. Up until then all of the intermediate stations had their own stationmasters, but these were now soon being systematically replaced by senior porters, and the stations themselves brought under the jurisdiction of the retained stationmaster at Yealmpton, who subsequently used to visit them daily.

The goods traffic over the branch included a daily coal service, considerable milk traffic (transported in 12-gallon churns), large hampers of rabbits, farm produce and animal feeding-stuffs, as well as general merchandise of widely varying types. All this originated from Yealmpton but, in addition, Steer Point (possibly the busiest station next to Yealmpton) provided very heavy traffic from the South Hams Brickworks, supplemented by large quantities of oysters from the nearby fishery, Brixton Road provided more coal and general traffic, while Billacombe added lime and quarry stone to the already wide range of freight being carried. Elburton, on the other hand, had no goods facilities.

Some milk traffic was carried by passenger trains as indicated in this photograph taken at Yealmpton Station in the early 1920s. Note the camera-conscious crew.

Lens of Sutton

During the early 1920s buses became well established and this, in turn, led to a steady decline in passenger traffic on the line until the situation became serious. By this time the tender locomotives that ran on the branch in earlier days had already given way to small pannier tank engines coupled to one or two pairs of auto coaches, while further efforts by the GWR to defray running expenses soon included the closing of Brixton Road signal box (during 1924/5) and later (in 1928/9) the introduction of steam railcars. Nevertheless, towards the end of the 1920s the situation had become critical, for motor cars, too, had begun to appear in competition with the railway and in 1928, despite the company's efforts, the following notice appeared in the local press as well as at local stations around Plymouth:-

'The Great Western Railway Co. give notice that they have in contemplation the closing of the Yealmpton branch between Plymstock and Yealmpton. The reason for this is that the revenue from the traffic on the branch does not meet the working expenses and the business is showing a definite downward trend. The Company appreciate that the closing of the branch will involve withdrawal of a facility which is of value to the public and traders of the district and they are prepared therefore to receive suggestions for increasing the passenger, parcels and merchandise traffic.
To this end they will defer coming to a definite decision to close the line until the 1st January next year but if the loss continues this will be inevitable. Meanwhile should there be a desire to discuss the matter with the company's officers, a public meeting will be arranged but if the various interests in the district wish the line to be kept open it should be recognised that it must be used more than has been the case during the last two years.'

G.W.R. Co. 1928

No suggestions for the increase in passenger and parcel traffic were forthcoming, however; indeed, the situation worsened and the passenger service that had existed for barely 32 years finally ceased on July 7th 1930. Meanwhile, in anticipation of this, the road services between Plymouth (Millbay) and Yealmpton (and beyond) had already been strengthened considerably as shown by the timetables reproduced in a later chapter. In fact, the bus service later became a through route from Millbay to Dartmouth and, eventually, came under the ownership of Western National because of an undertaking given by the Railways Companies' Association spokesman in the House of Lords. Interestingly enough, though, the bus crews retained their railway status for many years afterwards.

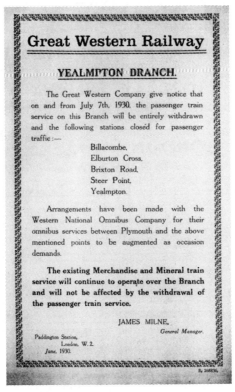

A reduced copy of the GWR Company's
'first' passenger closure notice.

(The seven superb and evocative photographs that appear on the next six pages were taken by G. N. Southerden on the day that the Yealmpton branch first closed to passengers (July 7th 1930) and are reproduced by kind permission of Wild Swan Publications Ltd)

Billacombe Station, viewed from Colesdown Hill road bridge.

Elburton Cross, viewed from Sherford Road bridge.

Two views of Brixton Road Station. *Above:* Looking northwards towards Billacombe. *Below:* Viewed from m.p. 2³/₄, showing the goods shed and yard.

Yealmpton Station, looking westwards from the platform end and showing Boldventure and J. F. Hollow's garage on either side of the line.

Another view of Yealmpton Station, as 0–6–0PT No. 738 and autocoach No.151 await the return trip to Plymouth.

A view looking eastwards from the platform edge at Yealmpton Station showing the 'double slip' into the goods yard and the 'through line' to Modbury that never was!

G.W.R.

G. W. R.

PLYMOUTH
(MILLBAY)

YEALMPTON

Phase 3 – 1930 to 1941: Goods traffic only

Despite much research, this period of decline does not reveal itself in any great detail. Nevertheless, without passenger services (except when the GWR experimented with 'Saturdays only' trains during the summers of 1931 and 1932), the appearance of the line, understandably, began to alter somewhat. For a start, its signalling was dramatically reduced due to the closing of the signal boxes at Brixton Road ('dead' since at least 1925) and Yealmpton (which was demolished) and, instead, the line was worked along the 'one train in motion' principle, the section from Plymstock to Yealmpton being controlled by Southern Railway electric train staff. At the same time newly-constructed 'ground frames' were brought into use, where required.

Other changes came about mainly as the result of stations beginning to take on different appearances. Those at Elburton Cross and Steer Point were partially recovered and left to fall into disrepair, but at Billacombe, Brixton Road and Yealmpton fate was a little kinder: whilst the station nameboards and all of the equipment for passenger running was recovered, the actual buildings were leased to the company's employees as dwelling places, remaining as such until the early 1960s. Furthermore, in order to provide extra accommodation, they were soon being extended by the addition of wooden structures that formed corridors below the canopy and between the doorways opening out onto the platform at each respective location. Outside, too, various lampmen's huts and other railway hutments became garden sheds and the like. At Yealmpton, for example, the base of the old signal box was initially turned into an outhouse-cum-workshop, while later it was converted to a chicken house by erecting a wooden top upon it.

Flower and vegetable gardens were also formed around the buildings, but with the passing of each successive year leading up to World War II, which erupted in the still autumn of 1939, a strange air of uncertainty hung over the branch. Even then this uncertainty remained for some time, and it was not until early 1941, when severe petrol rationing led to private cars starting to disappear from the roads and buses (many, by now, converted to gas propulsion) becoming far less frequent, that the situation looked like changing.

All the while, from 1930, the goods trains maintained a steady flow of merchandise to and from Yealmpton and the other stations on the branch. In fact, it differed little from that carried during the period described in phase 2. But now, in these early war years, the demands were suddenly becoming greater ...

Opposite: Three well known, but nevertheless rare, studies of the goods only period from 1930 to 1941. Shunting operations (*top*) and awaiting the 'off' (*centre*) are depicted at Yealmpton Station, whilst at Brixton Road Station (*lower*) there hangs an air of gloom and despondency as only a world war can bring back the passengers, c1933.

R. W. Kidner

Phase 4 – 1941 to 1947: Resurgam

After having received only one goods train each way per day for 11 years, the branch eventually took on a fresh lease of life during the latter half of 1941. First, on July 21st, a new passenger service for workmen was inaugurated and then, on November 3rd, and of far greater significance, came the re-introduction of a fully-fledged passenger service. Rather than being at Millbay, however, the terminus for these new services was the Southern Railway station at Friary, for the reasons stated in part (b) of the previous chapter. This, in turn, meant that whereas previously the trains had used the same route as their Southern Railway counterparts on the Turnchapel branch between Cattewater Junction and Plymstock, they now shared it over an even longer stretch; passing the SR Motive Power Depot, stopping at Lucas Terrace Halt and going over the former LSWR bridge that crossed The Embankment and led to Cattewater Junction, in the process.

The reason behind the resurrection of passenger services was that Yealmpton, along with its surrounding villages and adjacent parishes, had become a 'dormitory area' for much of the population of Plymouth as the result of the savage and intense bombing that the city had suffered during the previous March and April. Despite the five devastating raids that made up the Blitz, however, it seemed insufficient punishment for the local populace so far as the enemy was concerned, as the heavy aerial bombardment was still taking place and destined to continue for some considerable time.

The re-opening of the branch presented the GWR with problems, for, as already stated, on the previous closure to passengers the company had leased the station buildings at Billacombe, Brixton Road and Yealmpton to its employees. Therefore, prior to the new service beginning, the platforms at each of these locations had to be 'sealed off' by means of a concrete post and wire fencing so as to maintain the privacy of the families occupying the station buildings from the travelling public. Consequently, facilities for passengers waiting to board the trains were somewhat limited, while shelter from the elements was virtually non-existent due to the wooden structures that now existed below the station canopies.

Ticket offices were not deemed necessary at any station other than Yealmpton: tickets were, in fact, issued on the trains. But special treatment was dealt out at Yealmpton because, as a terminus, toilets were considered essential and a ticket office beneficial. As a result, a building (rather unsightly!) was constructed with cement blocks at the far, eastern end of the platform to serve as a toilet block, while at the western end a 'Pagoda'-type corrugated iron 'Ticket Office' was erected, thus enabling passengers starting their journeys from Yealmpton to buy tickets in advance. In later years it was converted into a small 'Waiting Room'.

The station building at Steer Point was renovated and re-used, but not so at Elburton Cross, where the low expected incidence of traffic predetermined this action. At the same time all the stations were 'renamed' by having their names painted in block capital letters on sections of the wooden structures (mentioned earlier) at the main ones, or on a convenient building at each of the others, using white paint on a black background. This was also done at a height designed to be easily seen by passengers sitting in the trains and was, of course, the means employed to replace the original nameboards that had been recovered after the former cessation of passenger services.

The Engineering Department had the largest task on the re-opening, that of upgrading the track maintenance from freight to passenger traffic standard. The motor trolley system, brought into service on October 12th 1931, was revised and re-employed, and the permanent way gangers' home base was at Yealmpton. From here, they examined 'the length' three times per week – on Mondays, Wednesdays and Fridays – using the motor trolley and its eight parking points along the branch. For their accommodation and messing facilities, they were provided with new Permanent Way huts built of brick to supplement, or replace, earlier ones constructed of old sleepers (see 'Engineering and Operating Data').

Early in the war the Luftwaffe succeeded in stopping traffic on the branch for a short time, when a lone bomber, carrying out a 'hit and run' attack, dropped a stick of bombs around the Puslinch area. One bomb scored a direct hit on Bridge Cottage, at the northern end of Puslinch Bridge, and blew out the rear of the building as well as leaving the first floor hanging perilously in mid air: the sole occupant who, it was said, was still in bed, was not injured! A second fell in Kilpark Orchard, on the far side of the line from the bridge, and exploded harmlessly, but a third hit the railway embankment and blew out all the ballast. In addition, a fourth bomb landed in marshland to the west of the line, near the weir, and failed to explode. Consequently, the Bomb Disposal Squad had to be called to the scene, but it is rumoured that they failed to recover it "because, as fast as they dug, the deeper it sank into the mud" – in which case it may still be there as I write! Meanwhile, a fifth bomb fell in the grounds of Puslinch House and, it is believed, killed a horse.

Passenger traffic during, and towards the end of, the war saw the restoration of the 1920s pattern. As well as the usual goods traffic common to that period, the Sunday School parties and various other childrens' outings to Yealmpton and Steer Point were, again, commonplace. However, one new source of unusual goods that the line found itself carrying was that of large quantities of Hydrogen gas cylinders for the RAF at Collaton Cross. Early in the war a barrage balloon repair station had been constructed at Collaton for the RAF, consisting of two large balloon hangers with workshops and all the ancillary accommodation supporting it. The full cylinders of gas were transported by train from Motherwell to Plymouth, and thence to Yealmpton, sometimes by night. At Yealmpton, much to the consternation of the residents of the station building, this highly explosive cargo would stand on the platform until it was shunted into the goods area for collection! The RAF collected the load with a lorry and trailer, both specially built for the task, while empty cylinders were despatched in the reverse order for refilling at the Motherwell factory. Yealmpton Station Yard, incidentally, also housed a searchlight battery site at this time.

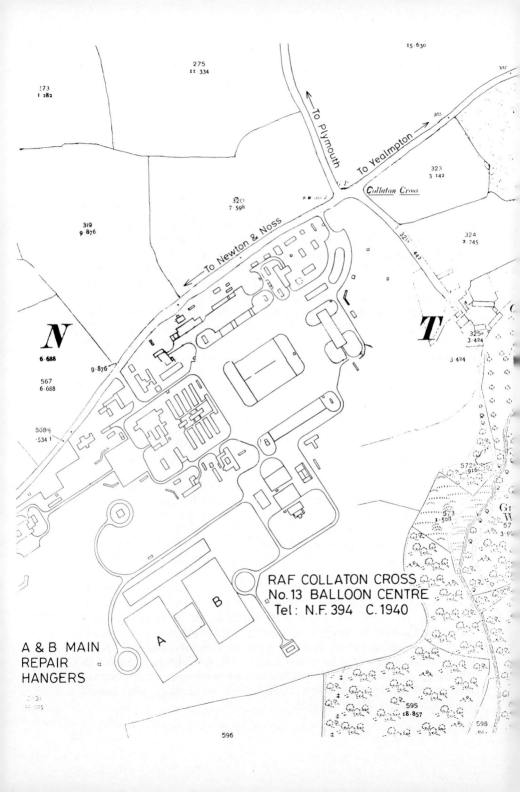

15·630

275
11·334

273
1·282

To Plymouth

To Yealmpton

305

307

323
3·142

Collaton Cross

320
7·598

R M ···2

319
9·876

To Newton & Noss

32··442

324
2·745

N

6·688

325··
3·424

T

3·424

9·876

567
6·688

568··
·534

572··
·916

573
1·508

595
18·857

G
W
57
3·99

RAF COLLATON CROSS
No. 13 BALLOON CENTRE
Tel: N.F. 394   C. 1940

A & B MAIN
REPAIR
HANGERS

A

B

598

596

The war in Europe finally drew to a close on May 8th 1945. Thereafter, the oil supply situation was gradually restored, and the buses began to retrieve the passengers that they had surrendered to the railway four years earlier as folk returned to their homes in the city. Indeed, many had already returned, and it consequently became apparent to both the GWR and the SR that a second closure to passengers was imminent.

A photograph taken at Friary Station (the new terminus for the passenger services re-instated in 1941) on August 30th 1945, with 0–6–0PT No. 3705 on a Yealmpton branch train and with a Turnchapel branch train partially hidden behind it.

H. C. Casserley

The 1.14pm ex-Plymouth (Friary) train waits at Yealmpton Station before the return journey on July 31st 1946.

S. C. Nash

It is interesting to note that during the final year of passenger operation it was noticed, upon line inspection, that water ingress into the rock face at the last cutting before Yealmpton Station had occurred. This had made overhanging rocks unstable, and the decision was taken to remove the same by blasting. The trains were temporarily suspended and the charges duly placed. When they exploded it transpired that someone had been over-zealous with their size and a sudden, very large explosion followed. Rock and debris were flung high into the air and, as the noise died away, rocks crashed down onto the line and, some, upon the houses in Boldventure. The surprised inhabitants had thought the third world war had broken out! There were, fortunately, no injuries and, later, compensation was paid.

During September 1947 the local press put out the following notice:-

> 'The Great Western and Southern Railway Companies give notice that, on and from the 6th October 1947, the passenger train service between Plymouth (Friary) and Yealmpton will be discontinued. Facilities will continue to be available for the conveyance of freight traffic. Dated the 4th September 1947. By order.'

This notice was not so polite as its 1928 predecessor, but, even so, it was worded less curtly than the many more closure notices that were to follow in later years nationwide. In the meantime, the last public passenger train ran on the branch on Saturday, October 4th 1947.

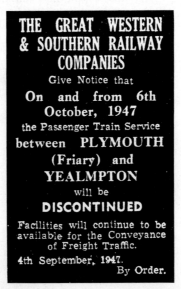

THE GREAT WESTERN
& SOUTHERN RAILWAY
COMPANIES
Give Notice that
On and from 6th
October, 1947
the Passenger Train Service
between PLYMOUTH
(Friary) and
YEALMPTON
will be
DISCONTINUED
Facilities will continue to be available for the Conveyance of Freight Traffic.
4th September, 1947.
By Order.

Opposite: Three studies during the period July 16th – 18th 1947 of 0–6–0PT No. 5412 and auto coaches Nos. 71 & 74 at Elburton Cross *(top),* Brixton Road *(centre)* and Steer Point *(lower)* respectively.

D. A. Thompson

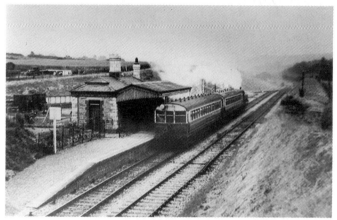

Phase 5 – 1947 to 1960: Good traffic only, again

Late 1947 saw the return of freight-line status once again and the recovery of all passenger service operating equipment and documentation, thus leaving the branch in much the same forlorn state as in the immediate pre-war years. In fact, if anything, the situation was even worse, and particularly so at the time when the line passed into the state ownership of British Railways (Western Region) following nationalisation on January 1st 1948: by then the deep inroads already made into passenger traffic by road competition had also begun to have its effect on freight traffic, especially with regard to branchlines.

The result was that the Yealmpton freight dwindled rapidly during the years following nationalisation, the service being cut back to one train each way per day in the early 1950s and to just three trains per week towards the end of the same decade. By that time only about 30 trucks of freight were passing over the branch each week, most of it consisting of coal and animal feeding-stuffs. Indeed, it was reported that during 1958 the branch carried only 4,487 tons of freight, 3,358 tons of which was coal.

Interestingly enough, during the years 1954 to 1960 (the final period of operation) detailed sightings were recorded of various goods trains along the branch, each numbering from one to eight wagons and a brake van. Occasionally as many as twelve to seventeen were recorded and on one particular sighting, on January 8th 1958, 0–6–0PT No. 9716 was seen climbing, with difficulty, to Elburton with a train of no less than thirty-five vans and two wagons, on its way to Yealmpton. What was more surprising was a sighting over a year earlier, on November 22nd 1956, when a P.W. train was seen relaying track on the Plymouth side of Elburton! On that occasion seventeen wagons, with a brake van at each end, were being loaded with old chairs and sleepers. The line then had just over three years to run!

The first recorded sighting of diesel-hauled freight on the line was on February 9th 1959, when a short train hauled by an 0–6–0 diesel shunter of the '112XX' class was seen between Elburton and Billacombe.

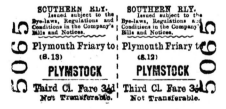

Opposite: Three studies of Yealmpton Station during the early years of the second goods traffic only period, showing the outside of the station and the 'Pagoda' ticket office *(top)*, a view eastwards from the platform, which includes part of the fenced-off main building and the 'new' toilet block *(centre)*, and a view westwards, which includes the parapets of the first over-bridge beyond the station *(lower)*.

J. H. Moss

97

Photographs taken along the branch during the 1950s by Charles Fennamore:-

Above: 0–6–0PT No. 3686 shunting at Billacombe goods yard.
Below: An unknown pannier tank with a train from Yealmpton at Brixton Road. Note that the loop has been removed.

Two more scenes at Brixton Road depicting 0–6–0PT No. 7726 *(above)* and 0–6–0 diesel shunter No. 11225 *(below)*. Whether it was steam or, later, diesel working it seems that the trains ran to timetable even if there was no freight!

Unusual inter-station views of steam-worked freight. *Above:* Nearing Cofflete Creek beyond Steer Point. *Below:* Between Warren Point and Cylinder Bridge.

Above and below: Shunting operations into the brickworks siding at Steer Point.

Above: A 'cinder train' unloading hot clinker from Laira MPD onto the embankment at Yealmpton 'Meadows' in order to kill weeds and control the undergrowth.

Below: 0–6–0PT No. 3629 departing from Yealmpton Station, with Hollow's Garage visible on the road below – at an unusual angle.

Passenger trains!

The only passenger traffic to traverse the line at this time were 'Enthusiasts Specials'. The first of these was on April 11th 1959, when the 'Railway Enthusiasts Club of Farnborough' ran a R.E.C. special three-car DMU, *The Devon Rambler*, from Marsh Mills to Yealmpton. (The Turnchapel branch was also covered.) At this time also, two 'chocolate & cream' camping coaches were noticed in the sidings at Yealmpton. They must have been there for temporary storage prior to scrapping, for no record exists of any being officially stationed at this spot.

This excursion was closely followed by another on May 2nd 1959, when the 'Railway Correspondence & Travel Society' ran a 'special' over the Yealmpton and Turnchapel lines as part of the 'Royal Albert Bridge Centenary Celebrations'. It consisted of an 0–6–0 PT, No. 6420, and two sets of auto coaches running in 'sandwich formation'.

Then, on February 27th 1960, came the last, which was run by 'The Plymouth Railway Circle' and consisted of 2–6–2T No. 4549 with nine goods brake vans (one GWR Toad and eight various double-verandah types from other companies). It ran to Yealmpton, stopping for photographs at each station site. On its return to Plymstock Station it then ran over the Turnchapel line to the terminus station at Turnchapel before returning to Friary. Thus the very last passenger train had traversed the Plymstock to Yealmpton section of the Yealmpton railway – some 62 years and 1½ months after the very first!

(Two additional passenger trains did subsequently cross the River Plym from Plymouth, on June 18th 1966 and on December 21st 1985 respectively, both calling at Plymstock Station. The first was a 'special' run by 'The Plymouth Railway Circle', of which, unfortunately, no details are recorded, while the second was when 'Hertfordshire Railtours' ran the *Gunnislake Goliath*, formed of a Hastings '6L' DEMU with one trailer removed. This was part of a more extended tour around the Plymouth area and, of course, included the Gunnislake branch: it was duly reported in the March 1986 issue of the *Railway Magazine*.)

An unusual view of Plymstock Station showing the Turnchapel branch veering off to the right of the Yealmpton branch, April 11th 1959.

E. R. Shepherd

103

Scenes at Elburton Cross *(top)*, Brixton Road *(centre)* and Yealmpton *(lower)* stations showing the only diesel passenger train ever to run on the branch – a R.E.C. special three-car DMU, *The Devon Rambler*, on April 11th 1959.

C. Fennamore

The second enthusiasts train to traverse the line was the R.C.T.S. 'special' on May 2nd 1959, consisting of 0–6–0PT No. 6420 and two pairs of auto coaches. The locations are Plymstock *(top)* and Yealmpton *(centre and lower)*.

W. E. Stevens, S. C. Nash & C. Fennamore

The last passenger train to cross the River Plym to Plymstock, long after the last train to Yealmpton did so, was the *Gunnislake Goliath* on December 21st 1985.

N. D. Darsley, courtesy of Railway Magazine

Phase 6 – 1960 to 1963: Complete closure, track lifting and demolition

Accountants were to declare that the final closure to goods traffic on February 29th 1960 was to save British Railways some £9,205 per annum, this sum being offset by only £1,000 loss of revenue from the freight being carried at this time. Road competition, by now having already caused the closure of a number of branchlines, and threatening the existence of many others remaining solvent through freight traffic alone, had, therefore, won the day `– a full two years before the implementation of the infamous Beeching Plan. (The results of this, 'the railways must pay their way' legislation, combined with a major shift of emphasis towards road transportation, have been the destruction of the countryside, with pastures having been turned into giant ribbons of tarmac, pollution of the atmosphere and horrific tolls from

Opposite: Three studies of the P.R.C. brake van 'special' which ran on February 27th 1960. Sadly everything depicted in these photographs has now passed into history: Friary Station *(top)* is now Friary Court, a housing development; the original 'Iron Bridge', seen here from the train *(centre)*, has been replaced by a new concrete road bridge which opened in 1962; and the last section of track leading into Plymstock Station *(lower)* was recovered in 1994. The CEGB 'A' and 'B' power stations, the Plymouth Destructor and the Glue Works, whose chimneys dominate the skyline in the lower photograph, have also long since been demolished. *R. C. Sambourne*

road traffic accidents. Little wonder, with such a strong 'road lobby' within successive parliaments, of all persuasion, that it is thought in some circles that our politicians have vested interests in the road haulage companies!)

Sadly the loss of all services from the line led to the inevitable decay – the rusting of rails, the ever-increasing ingress of vegetation and the destruction of the station buildings, through various means. Apart from the chief destroyer, the invading elements of the weather, the process was accelerated by small children and vandals as they paid their unwanted attentions.

The first recorded sign of 'life' returned to the line on June 1st 1960. At 1.30pm on that day 0–6–0 diesel No. 11225, complete with a guards van, was observed at Yealmpton Station standing on the line close to Forde Road over-bridge. The purpose of this visit is not recorded, but one may assume that it was to recover documents and fittings from station buildings and to serve as a planning visit for track-lifting operations which were still two years away.

The first of seven sad and conticent studies of the branch recorded by the camera of Michael Hale on August 28th 1960, whilst it was in a state of interregnum: Plymstock Station, still active with freight traffic at this time, looking westwards towards Plymouth.

Above: Plymstock Station, looking eastwards and showing evidence of local and Turnchapel freight activity.
Below: Billacombe, no longer occupied except by the ever-increasing weeds.

Above: Elburton Cross, with the station building and urinal already gone.
Below: Brixton Road Station, shown to be still in use as a residence but for nothing else.

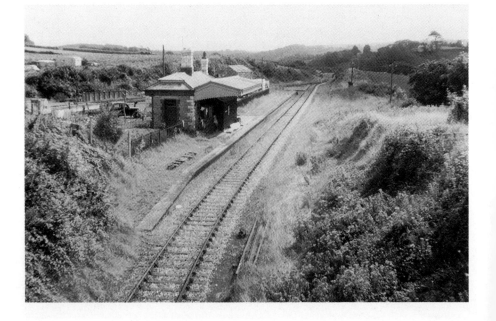

Above: Steer Point Station, where even the tide was out!
Below: Yealmpton Station, where the residents of the village had already removed curbing and masonry for their gardens.

On May 1st 1962, commensurate with the construction of new sidings into the cement works at Plymstock, the first casualty was observed being demolished at Brixton Road. This was the goods shed, built of limestone: the reason for its sudden demise is obscure, but it may have some bearing on the fact that a United Dairies refrigerated storage and distribution site served by road had been established there earlier, before closure to goods traffic.

Next, and after a sojourn of six months, came the arrival of the 'demolition train', hauled by diesel locomotive No. D2178. Needless to say, work now began in earnest: in fact, by November 12th all the track and signalling within the confines of Yealmpton Station had been recovered and track lifting was in progress at the rear of Boldventure, reaching Waltacre two days later.

At this juncture perhaps it should be explained how the recovery of the track was implemented. First of all a 'dismantling depot' was set up at the site of Steer Point Station, which included a converted Hawksworth coach (brought there by D2178) being stabled in a siding to act as the works department messing van. Secondly, the method of recovery involved lifting two or three lengths of track from the trackbed at a time by means of jacks. These were then lifted over the end of the existing track by chains attached to the locomotive and fitted with a number of small, single bogies, bolted onto the rail, prior to being lowered and towed away to Steer Point for dismantling.

A close-up of two small bogies bolted onto a section of track prior to it being towed away to a 'dismantling depot', November 1962. *A.R.K.*

Opposite: Three photographs taken by the author during November 1962 of the dismantling depot at Steer Point Station. *Top:* An overall view looking eastwards from the over-bridge, showing the 'dismantling depot' in the former goods yard and the Hawksworth messing coach in the brickworks siding. *Centre:* A length of track being towed by a diesel locomotive, using chains. *Lower:* Rails, chairs, fishplates and sleepers being sorted and loaded for despatch to various places, the rails being destined for Spain, the sleepers soon to be offered for sale to local farmers and the rest for scrap.

This process continued throughout the rest of November and into the following month, the track being lifted as far as Steer Point Station by December 14th. Thereafter, the work was concentrated on the Plymouth side of Steer Point, using Brixton Road Station as the new 'dismantling depot' (complete with the converted Hawksworth coach) and 0–6–0 diesel No. D2127 as the locomotive in charge of the train. Progress from this date was, naturally, impeded by the Christmas holiday, but the worst winter weather for many years was responsible for the greatest delay: heavy snow began to fall on December 29th and lasted, in places, until the following March. Nevertheless, by March 19th 1963 track lifting had been completed up to the site of the siding point at Brixton Road Station, and a month earlier the sidings at Billacombe Station had also been lifted in part, with 0–6–0 diesel No. D2197 observed in charge of the demolition train.

On April 30th of that year diesel locomotive No. D2175 was observed with its 'demolition train' at Billacombe Station, and this had now become the third site along the line for the 'dismantling depot'. It was also recorded that track lifting, by then, had reached a point on the Plymouth side of Elburton Cross, beyond the bridge over Stag Lane. However, along this stretch of line only the rails had been removed, which, with the sleepers and chairs still in situ, seemed to indicate that the previous method of recovery had been abandoned for some reason. In fact, sleepers were currently being lifted in the cutting to the east of Sherford Road.

Thereafter, there is little to record except to say that by June 12th 1963 all of the track had been lifted apart from one short section leading into Plymstock Station – some 11 chains, in fact!

Footnotes

1. In 1909 a grandiose (albeit abortive) scheme was proposed to construct a large commercial dock on what is now known as the Wembury beach and headland. It was to include the building of four huge breakwaters – from Wembury Point to the Great Mew Stone, from the Great Mew Stone towards Gara Point, from Gara Point towards the Great Mew Stone, and from the shore (to the east of the church) southwards – and involved enclosing an area of no less than 880 acres.
   To serve the dock, a railway from Wembury to Plymstock was also proposed. It was to run from a point to the west of the church at Wembury, up the valley on the eastern side of the Langdon Court Estate and on through Ranleagh, before passing under Staddiscombe by means of a long tunnel. Re-emerging from the tunnel at Goosewell, the line was then to continue past the western side of Plymstock Church and across Pomphlett to join the existing railway network at Plymstock Station. (Originally, two junctions were envisaged at Plymstock, one linking with the Turnchapel branch and the other with the Yealmpton branch, but this was opposed by both the LSWR and the GWR companies.)

2. Records show that the GWR bridge over The Embankment, together with the double track of the former Yealmpton branch in the vicinity, was not removed until late 1958, even though it had not been used for passenger trains for many years. The eastern abutment, incidentally, can still be seen adjacent to the high-level pavement on the opposite side of The Embankment from Heywood's Pavings Ltd.

TIME TABLES AND BRANCH WORKING

Branch Workings

Opening Ceremonies:-

Small-wheeled 4–4–0 of '3252' class.
'Duke', named *Lady Morley* for the occasion.

1900s/1910s:-

Passenger traffic   – 2–6–0s 'Aberdare' class.
0–6–0STs, double framed, of '1501' class.
0–4–2Ts of '517' class.
Steam Rail Motors, eg 22, 39, 47 and 76.
Auto Trains – 0–4–2Ts of '517' class, eg 205, 569 and 828.
0–6–0PTs of '2021' class, eg 2120 and 2140.

Goods traffic   – Dean 0–6–0 Tender engines.
0–6–0PTs of '1076', '1813' and '1854' classes.

1920s:-

Passenger traffic   – 0–6–0PTs, mainly '1076' class, *viz* 1165, 1252, 1265, 1269, 1271, 1284 and 1580.
0–6–0PT 738.
Auto Trailer Pairs 3 & 6, 2 & 26, 9 & 10, 71 & 74, 93 & 98, 126 & 127, and 134 & 135.

Summer Excursions– 'Bulldog' class 4–4–0 plus 10 coaches (termites, non-corridor).
'Aberdare' class 2–6–0 plus 4-coach corridor sets.

1929   – Steam Railmotor No. 72 (ex-Exeter/Christow/Heathfield).

1930   – 'Last train excursion' – 'Aberdare' class 2–6–0.

1930s:-

Goods traffic   – 0–6–0PTs of '1076' class.
(Experimental 'S.O.' passenger trains).

1940s:-

Passenger traffic   – 2–6–2T No. 4407 (ex-Princetown branch).
0–6–0PTs '54XX' & '64XX' classes, *viz* 5412, 6407, 6414 and 6421.
Auto Trailer Pairs 5 & 6.

Goods traffic   – 0–6–0PTs '57XX' class *viz* 3705.

1950s:-

Goods only traffic   – 0–6–0PTs of '57XX' class, *viz* 3629, 3639, 3686, 3790, 4656, 4658, 4679, 4693, 7762, 8719, 9716 and 9770.

1950 (June 20th)   – Noted: Scrap GWR coaches (No. 7469 and an un-identified one) are brought out of Yealmpton, observed at Plymstock behind 0–6–0PT No. 4693.

1956 (March 16th)   – Noted: Green camping coach stabled at end of goods shed siding.

1959 to 29.2.60:-

Goods traffic   – 0–6–0 Diesel shunters 11225, 11227, 11228 and 11229.

June 1st 1960   – Inspection train 11225 and brake van.

Specials

1959 (April 11th)   – *Devon Rambler.*
Railway Enthusiasts Club of Farnborough.
Diesel Multiple Units W51062, W59421 and W51090.
Noted: Two 'chocolate and cream' camping coaches in sidings (not in use).

1959 (May 2nd)   – Railway Travel & Correspondence Society Special with 0–6–0PT No. 6420.
Two pairs of auto coaches – W193 & W225 and W189 & W229.

1960 (February 27th) – Plymouth Railway Circle Special.
(Last passenger train)
Nine brake vans hauled by 2–6–2T No. 4549.
Nos. 310723, 954252, 17463 (GWR Toad), 952009,

953896, 187627, 950665, 287642 and 952760.

Recovery Trains

November 5th 1962 to
June 12th 1963   – Class 03 Diesel shunters Nos. D2127, D2175, D2178 and D2179.

Plymstock Station Only

Goods traffic:-
1966 to 1970s   – Liquefied petroleum gas (LPG) for Breakwater Works.

1963 to 1987
(February)*   – Bulk cement, coal, kiln bricks and paint for cement works.
Locos employed: 0–6–0 Diesel shunters, class 08 Nos. 08 394 and 08 576, also D4158.

*On April 26th 1987 a weed-killer train was operating, hauled by 37 196 'Tre-Pol-Pen' – two months after closure!

Specials

1966 (June 18th)   – Plymouth Railway Circle.
Plymouth Suburban Railtour.
Class 03 D2178.

1985
(December 21st)   – *Gunnislake Goliath.*
Hertfordshire Railtours.
Last passenger train over Laira rail bridge.
Hastings '6L' Diesel Electric Multiple Unit No. 1032 (less one car).

Final Recovery of Plymstock Station

1994 (late September
to October 12th)   – Road traffic only employed.
(Weaver Plant of Bristol recovered all remaining track at Plymstock Station site, the last rail being lifted at 3.50pm on Wednesday October 12th 1994.)

GWR Engine Restrictions, May 7th 1945.

Selected extract from Page 59 of the Great Western Freight Service Time Table for the period May 7th, 1945, (and until further notice).

ENGINE RESTRICTIONS

BRANCHES

Section of Line	Engines Authorised	Prohibitions
Mount Gould Jct. to Yealmpton	Uncoloured	+Specially authorised.
	"Yellow"	
	+"Blue" 4–4–0	Billacombe – 4–4–0 and 2–6–2T. Sidings leading to Goods Shed and Loading Bank.
	33XX and 34XX	Steer Point – 4–4–0 and 2–6–2T. Junction to Brickworks Siding.
	+"Blue" 2–6–2T	Yealmpton – 2–6–2T. Junction to Goods Yard Siding alongside Cattle Pens.
	41XX, 51XX	
	61XX, 81XX	

Selected extract from Page 55 of the Great Western Passenger Service Time Table for the period May 7th, 1945, (and until further notice).

ENGINE RESTRICTIONS

BRANCHES

Section of Line	Engines Authorised
Mount Gould Jct. to Yealmpton	Uncoloured ... ...
	Yellow ... ...
	Blue 4–4–0 Bulldogs 2–6–2T,
	41XX–61XX, 81XX for emergency only.

"Blue" engines not permitted:–
Billacombe – Sidings leading to Goods Shed and Loading Bank.
Steer Point – Junction to Brick Works Siding.
Yealmpton – 2–6–2T only. To Goods Yard and Siding alongside Cattle Pens.

PLYMOUTH AND YEALMPTON

A Road Motor Service is operated by the Western National Omnibus Company between Plymouth, Plymstock, Billacombe, Elburton, Brixton and Yealmpton. 'Buses leave as under:–

FROM PLYMOUTH (North Road Station)   **Service liable to alteration.**

Week Days:– 7B10, 7.15, 9.20, 10.10, 10.30, 11.5 a.m., 12G30, 1S15, 2.45, 5.15, 6.40, 7.0, 8.15, 9.0, 10.40, 11S5 p.m.
Sundays:– 10.45, 11.30 a.m., 2.45, 5.0, 8.50, 9.45 p.m.

FROM YEALMPTON

Week Days:– 8.0, 8.58, 9.52, 10.13, 11.48 a.m., 1.58, 3.18, 5.28, 5.42, 7.3, 8.3, 9.48, 10S33 p.m.
Sundays:– 9.3 a.m., 1.53, 2.58, 6.22, 8.8, 9.13 p.m.

B – Mondays only.   G – Saturdays excepted.   S – Saturdays only.

For intermediate times and other services between Plymouth (St. Andrew's Cross) and Yealmpton, see Western National Omnibus Company's time table.

Time Occupied 30 minutes.

Time Tables

A representative selection of public and working timetables from opening to closure of the branch:–

1898   – The first timetable.

1899   – The earliest WTT available.

1903   – WTT prior to the opening of Mount Gould & Tothill Halt.

1913   – PTT following the opening of the halt and also showing the connecting road services to Modbury, and beyond.

1924   – WTT showing the level of service when the competing road services were first introduced.

1928   – PTT showing the rail motor car services, just two years before the first closure to passengers.

1941   – PTT on the re-opening to passenger traffic during World War II.

1947   – WTT for the summer period and therefore the last before the second (and final) withdrawal of passenger services.

1959/60 – WTT for the last winter of operations on the branch, which it did not complete due to the termination of freight services in February 1960.

(A comprehensive set of bus timetables for 1928 follow, both for Great Western Road Motors and National (formerly Devon Motor Transport). These clearly indicate the level of road competition leading up to the first closure of the branch passenger service.)

Commencing on **Monday, January 17th, 1898,** the Great Western Company's service of trains between Plymouth and Yealmpton will be as follows:—

STATIONS.	1 Passenger.		2 Goods.		3 Passenger.		4 Passenger.		5 Passenger.	
	arr. a.m.	dep. a.m.	arr. a.m.	dep. a.m.	arr. a.m.	dep. a.m.	arr. p.m.	dep. p.m.	arr. p.m.	dep. p.m.
Plymouth (Millbay)	...	6 55	...	...	...	9 45	...	1 5	...	6 0
Plymouth (North Road)	6 58	7 0	...	...	9 48	9 50	1 8	1 10	6 3	6 5
Mutley	7 1	7 3	...	...	9 51	9 53	1 11	1 13	6 6	6 8
Laira Junction	...	...	...	8 30	...	...	...	...	...	...
Cattewater Junction	7	9	8 33		9	59	1	19	6	14
Plymstock	7 11	7 13	8 35	8 50	10 1	10 3	1 21	1 23	6 16	6 18
Billacombe	7 16	7 18	8 55	9 2	10 6	10 8	1 26	1 28	6 21	6 23
Elburton	CR	7 23			CR	10 13	CR	1 33		
Brixton Road	7 25	7 27	9 10	9 25	10 15	10 17	1 35	1 37	6 30	6 32
Sheer Point	7 30	7 32	9 30	9 40	10 20	10 22	1 40	1 42	6 35	6 37
Yealmpton	7 38	...	9 50		10 28	...	1 48	...	6 43	...

STATIONS.	1 Passenger.		2 Passenger.		3 Goods.		4 Passenger.		5 Passenger.	
	arr. a.m.	dep. a.m.	arr. a.m.	dep. a.m.	arr. a.m.	dep. a.m.	arr. p.m.	dep. p.m.	arr. p.m.	dep. p.m.
Yealmpton	...	7 50	...	10 55	...	11 25	...	2 30	...	7 5
Steer Point	7 56	7 58	11 1	11 3	11 35	11 45	2 36	2 38	7 11	7 13
Brixton Road	8 1	8 3	11 6	11 8	11 50	12 5	2 41	2 43	7 16	7 18
Elburton	CR	8 7	CR	11 12			CR	2 47	...	...
Billacombe	8 9	8 11	11 14	11 16	12 15	12 25	2 49	2 51	7 24	7 26
Plymstock	8 14	8 16	11 19	11 21	12 30	12 45	2 54	2 56	7 29	7 31
Cattewater Junction	8	18		11 23		12 47	2	58	7	33
Laira Junction	...	...	...	...	12 50	...	...	...	...	...
Mutley	8 24	8 26	11 29	11 31	...	...	3 4	3 6	7 39	7 41
Plymouth (North Road)	8 27	8 30	11 32	11 35	...	...	3 7	3 10	7 42	7 45
Plymouth (Millbay)	8 35	...	11 40	...	...	...	3 15	...	7 50	...

CR—Calls at Elburton when required.

GEO. T. WHITE,
Superintendent of the Line.
(2,000.)

WATERLOO STATION,
January 11th, 1898.
(A. 18,048.) (3/22099.)

Waterlow and Sons Limited, Printers, London Wall, London.

May 1899 until further notice.

YEALMPTON BRANCH.

Double Line between Mount Gould Junction and Cattewater Junction.
Single Line Cattewater Junction to Plymstock, worked by Electric Train Tablet.
Single Line between Plymstock and Yealmpton, worked by Electric Train Staff.

DOWN TRAINS.

NO SUNDAY TRAINS.

M.	C.	STATIONS.	1 A Passenger arr.	1 dep.	2 D Goods † arr.	2 dep.	3 A Passenger arr.	3 dep.	4 A Passenger arr.	4 dep.	5 A Passenger arr.	5 dep.	6 A Passenger arr.	6 dep.	7	8	9
			A.M.	A.M.	A.M.	A.M.	A.M.	A.M.	P.M.	NOON	P.M.	P.M.	P.M.	P.M.			
0	—	Plymouth		7 20		7‖ 0		8 45		12 0		2 10		6 0			
0	66	North Road	7 23	7 24	7 4		9 48	9 49	12 3	12 6	2 13	2 14	6 4	6 7			
1	13	Mutley	7 25	7 27	7 5		9 50	9 52	12 5	12 7	2 15	2 17	6 6	6 7			
2	29	Lipson Junction		7 30	7 8			9 55		12 10		2 20		6 10			
2	64	Laira Yard			7‖10	8 20											
		Mount Gould Junction		7 33		8 20		9 57		12 12		2 22		6 12			
3	18	Cattewater Junction	C7 35S		C8 22S		C9 58S		C12 13S		C2 23S		C6 15S				
3	66	Plymstock	7 35	7 36	8 25	8 45	10 0	10 4	12 15	12 16	2 25	2 26	6 15	6 16			
4	63	Billacombe	7 39	7 40	8 50	9 0	10 4	10 6	12 19	12 20	2 29	2 30	6 19	6 20			
5	65	Elburton Cross	7 43	7 45	9 0	9 25	10 8	10 10	12 23	12 25	2 33	2 35	6 23	6 25			
6	38	Brixton Road	7 47	7 49	9 30	9 40	10 12	10 14	12 27	12 29	2 37	2 39	6 27	6 28			
7	73	Steer Point	7 52	7 54	9 50		10 17	10 19	12 32	12 34	2 42	2 44	6 31	6 32			
10	23	Yealmpton	8 0				10 25		12 40		2 50		6 38				

† Engine and Guard to form Sutton Harbour Train at Laira.

UP TRAINS.

NO SUNDAY TRAINS.

M.	C.	STATIONS.	1 A Passenger arr.	1 dep.	2 A Passenger arr.	2 dep.	3 D Goods * arr.	3 dep.	4 A Passenger arr.	4 dep.	5 A Passenger arr.	5 dep.	6 A Passenger arr.	6 dep.	7	8	9
			A.M.	A.M.	A.M.	A.M.	A.M.	A.M.	P.M.	P.M.	P.M.	P.M.	P.M.	P.M.			
2	30	Yealmpton		8 20		10 40		11 15		1 0		4 40		6 50			
3	65	Steer Point	8 26	8 27	10 46	10 47	11 25	11 30	1 11	1 17	4 46	4 47	6 56	6 57			
4	38	Brixton Road	8 30	8 32	10 50	10 52	11 40		1 15	1 17	4 52	4 54	6 6	6 7			
5	40	Elburton Cross	8 34	8 36	10 54	10 56			1 20	1 22	4 56	4 58	7 8	7 9			
6	37	Billacombe	8 38	8 39	10 58	10 59	11 50	12 0	1 24	1 25	4 59	5 0	7	7			
7	5	Plymstock	8 42	8 44	11 2	11 3	12 5	12 30	1 29	1 31	5 2	5 4	7 12	7 14			
7	39	Cattewater Junction	C8 46S		C11 5S		C12 33S		C1 33S		C5 6S		C7 17S				
7	74	Mount Gould Junction	8 47				12 35		1 34		5 7		7 17				
7	74	Laira Yard					12 35	2‖ 0									
		Lipson Junction						2‖10		1 36				7 19			
9	10	Mutley	8 52	8 53	11 12	11 13			1 39	1 40	5 12	5 13	7 22	7 23			
9	37	North Road	8 54	8 57	11 14	11 17			1 41	1 44	5 14	5 17	7 24	7 27			
10	23	Plymouth	9 0		11 20				1 47		5 20		7 30				

* The Engine and Guard of this Train to shunt Laira Yard.

May 1903.

YEALMPTON BRANCH.

Double Line between Mount Gould Junction and Cattewater Junction. Single Line Cattewater Junction to Plymstock, worked by Electric Train Tablet.

Single Line between Plymstock and Yealmpton, worked by Electric Train Staff.

WEEK DAYS ONLY.

DOWN TRAINS.

Distance M. C.	STATIONS	1 B Passenger. arr.	dep.	2 K Goods. arr.	dep.	3 B Passenger. arr.	dep.	4 B Passenger. arr.	dep.	5 B Passenger. arr.	dep.	6 B Passenger. arr.	dep.	7 B Passenger. arr.	dep.	8	9
		A.M.	A.M.	A.M.	A.M.	A.M.	A.M.	P.M.	P.M.	P.M.	P.M.	P.M.	P.M.	P.M.	P.M.		
0 66	Plymouth	—	7 20	—	—	—	9 15	—	12 5	—	1 55	—	5 0	—	7 5		
1 13	North Road	7 23	7 24	—	—	9 18	9 19	12 8	12 9	1 58	1 59	5 4	5 5	7 8	7 10		
2 29	Mutley	7 25	7 27	—	—	9 20	9 22	12 10	12 12	2 0	2 2	5 6	5 7	7 11	7 12		
2 63	Lipson Junction	7 29	—	—	8 10	9 21	—	12 11	—	—	—	5 9	—	7 14	—		
2 63	Laira Yard	—	—	—	—	—	—	—	—	—	—	—	—	—	—		
3	Mount Gould Junction	7 31	—	8 11	—	9 24	—	12 16	—	2 6	—	5 11	—	7 16	—		
3	Cattewater Junction	C 7 35 S	—	C 8 13 S	—	C 9 27 S	—	C 12 17 S	—	C 2 7 S	—	C 5 12 S	—	C 7 17 S	—		
3 17	Plymstock	7 34	7 36	8 15	8 35	9 29	9 30	12 19	12 20	2 9	2 11	5 14	5 16	7 19	7 21		
4 64	Billacombe	7 39	7 40	8 40	8 50	9 32	9 33	12 22	12 23	2 14	2 15	5 19	5 20	7 24	7 25		
6 66	Elburton Cross	7 43	7 45	—	—	9 36	9 36	12 26	12 28	2 18	2 20	5 23	5 25	7 28	7 30		
6 67	Stop Board	—	—	8 54 P	8 57	—	—	—	—	—	—	—	—	—	—		
7 39	Brixton Road	7 47	7 48	8 59	9 5	9 40	9 41	12 30	12 31	2 22	2 23	5 27	5 28	7 32	7 33		
9 71	Steer Point	7 51	7 52	9 10	9 20	9 44	9 45	12 34	12 35	2 26	2 27	5 31	5 32	7 36	7 37		
10 24	Yealmpton	7 58	—	9 28	—	9 50	—	12 41	—	2 33	—	5 38	—	7 43	—		

+ Engine and Guard to form Sutton Harbour Train at Laira.

UP TRAINS.

STATIONS	1 B Passenger. arr.	dep.	2 K Passenger. arr.	dep.	3 K Goods. arr.	dep.	4 B Passenger. arr.	dep.	5 B Passenger. arr.	dep.	6 B Passenger. arr.	dep.	7 Passenger. arr.	dep.	8	9
	A.M.	A.M.	A.M.	A.M.	A.M.	A.M.	P.M.	P.M.	P.M.	P.M.	P.M.	P.M.	P.M.	P.M.		
Yealmpton	—	8 10	—	9 53	—	10 30	—	12 50	—	3 40	—	5 50	—	7 55		
Steer Point	8 16	8 17	10 3	10 4	10 40	11 0	12 55	12 56	3 46	3 48	5 56	5 57	8 1	8 3		
Brixton Road	8 20	8 22	10 7	10 8	11 0	11 15	12 59	1 0	3 51	3 52	6 0	6 4	8 5	8 7		
Elburton Cross	8 24	8 26	10 11	10 13	11 25	11 50	1 5	1 7	3 55	3 57	6 6	6 9	8 10	8 12		
Billacombe	8 28	8 29	10 15	10 16	11 55	x12 30	1 11	1 13	3 59	4 0	6 12	6 14	8 15	8 16		
Plymstock	C 8 36 S	—	C 10 22 S	—	C 12 35	—	C 1 15 S	—	C 4 5 S	—	C 6 15 S	—	C 8 23 S	—		
Cattewater Junction	8 47	—	10 25	—	12 33	—	1 18	—	4 8	—	6 17	—	8 23	—		
Mount Gould Junction	8 39	—	10 23	—	—	—	—	—	—	—	—	—	—	—		
Laira Yard	—	—	—	—	12 35	—	—	—	—	—	6 19	—	—	—		
Lipson Junction	8 42	8 43	10 28	10 30	—	—	1 21	1 22	4 10	4 16	6 22	6 23	8 28	8 30		
Mutley	8 44	8 47	10 31	10 35	—	—	1 23	1 26	4 13	4 19	6 24	6 27	8 31	8 35		
North Road	8 50	—	10 38	—	—	—	1 30	—	4 22	—	6 30	—	8 38	—		
Plymouth	—	—	—	—	—	—	—	—	—	—	—	—	—	—		

122

July 12th 1913 to September 30th 1913.

PLYMOUTH AND YEALMPTON.
Rail Motor Car. (one class only.)

Week Days.

		a.m.	a.m.	a.m.	p.m.	p.m.	p.m.	p.m.	p.m.	p.m.	p.m.	p.m.	p.m.	p.m.	p.m.
Plymouth	Millbay	dep.	7 22	9 9	10 50	1 0	2 50	5 5	6 35	8 33	9 55	11 17			
	North Road	,,	7 28	9 14	10 54	1 6	2 54	5 10	6 39	8 37	9 59	11 21			
	Mutley	,,	7 30	9 17	10 56	1 8	2 56	5 12	6 41	8 39	10 1	11 23			
Lipson Vale Halt		,,	7 33	9 19	10 59	1 11	2 59	5 15	6 44	8 33	10 4				
Mount Gould and Tothill Halt		,,	7 34	9 22	11 4	1 16	3 4	5 20	6 49	8 37	10 9				
Plymstock		,,	7 42	9 26	11 10	1 20	3 8	5 24	6 53	8 41	10 13	11 35			
Billacombe		,,	7 48	9 28	11 14	1 22	3 10	5 26	6 55	8 43	10 15	11 37			
Elburton Cross		,,	7 48	9 32	11 17	1 26	3 14	5 30	6 59	8 47	10 19	11 39			
Brixton Road		,,	7 51	9 35	11 17	1 29	3 17	5 33	7 2	8 50	10 22	11 42			
Steer Point		,,	7 55	9 39	11 21	1 33	3 21	5 37	7 6	8 54	10 26	11 46			
Yealmpton		arr.	8 0	9 44	11 26	1 38	3 26	5 42	7 11	8 59	10 31	11 51			

Sundays.

		a.m.	p.m.	p.m.	p.m.
Plymouth (Millbay) dep.		9 15	2 33		8 35
...		9 19	2 40		8 30
...		9 21	2 40		8 32
...		9 24	2 42		8 35
...		9 29	2 47		8 40
...		9 33	2 51		8 44
...		9 35	2 53		8 46
...		9 39	2 55		8 50
...		9 42	3 0		8 52
...		9 46	3 3		8 55
...		9 51	3 8		9 0

Week Days.

		a.m.	a.m.	a.m.	p.m.	p.m.	p.m.	p.m.	p.m.	p.m.	p.m.	p.m.
Yealmpton	dep.	8 15	10 0	11 32	0 3.45	5.50	7 18	9 0	10 27	11 55		
Steer Point	,,	8 20	10 5	11 37	3 50	5.55	7 23	9 5	10 42	12 0		
Brixton Road	,,	8 24	10 9	11 41	3 54	6.59	7 27	9 11	10 46	12 4		
Elburton Cross	,,	8 27	10 11	11 44	3 57	6 0	7 30	9 13	10 49	12 7		
Billacombe	,,	8 30	10 15	11 47	4 0	6 3	7 33	9 16	10 52	12 10		
Plymstock	,,	8 33	10 18	11 50	4 3	6 6	7 36	9 20	10 55	12 12		
Mount Gould and Tothill Halt	,,	8 37	10 22	11 54	4 7	6 12	7 40	9 24	10 59			
Lipson Vale Halt	,,	8 42	10 27		4 12	6 17	7 45	9 29	11 6			
Plymouth	Mutley	arr.	8 45	10 29	11 58	4 16	6 19	7 47	9 32	11 8		
	North Road	,,	8 47	10 31	12 0	4 18	6 21	7 49	9 34	11 10		
	Millbay	,,	8 52	10 36	12 5	4 26	6 26	7 56	9 39	11 14		

Sundays.

	a.m.	a.m.	p.m.	p.m.
...		10 0	4 1	9 6
...		10 5	4 4	9 11
...		10 9	4 4	9 14
...			4 12	9 18
...		10 13	4 15	9 21
...		10 16	4 18	9 24
...		10 18	4 18	9 31
...		10 22	4 22	9 38
...		10 27	4 32	9 40
...		10 29	4 34	9 42
...		10 36	4 41	9 47

ROAD MOTOR CARS AND OMNIBUSES.

YEALMPTON, MODBURY AND BIGBURY-ON-SEA.

Week Days.

	a.m.	a.m.	p.m.	p.m.	p.m.	p.m.
Yealmpton (Station) dep.		9 53	10 40	7 16		
Dunstone	,,		10 1	10 47	3 47	7 22
Western Lodge	,,		10 5	10 52	3 52	7 27
Flete (for Ermington)	,,		10 13	12 0 4	7 35	
Modbury (G. W. Hotel) arr. abt.	8G15	10 28	2 15	4 15	7 50	
Aveton Gifford	,,	8 45				
Harraton Cross	,,		10 38	2 25	8X 5	9X 40
Cumery Corner	,,		10 43	2 30	8X 5	9X
Seven Stones (for Kingston)	,,		10 48	2 35	8X 12	9X 47
St. Anne's Chapel (for Ringmore)	,,		10 55	2 42	8X 17	9X
Bigbury Village	,,		10 58	2 45	8X 20	9X 4
Folly Farm (for Bantham)	,,		11 10	2 57	8X 20	9X
Bigbury-on-Sea	,,		11 18	3 5	8X 30	9X 5

Sundays.

	a.m.	a.m.	p.m.	p.m.
...		9Y 5	10 7	9 7
...		9Y17	10 12	9 12
...		9Y17	10 20	9 20
...		9Y25	10 35	9 35
...		9Y40		
...	9Y40			
...	9X			
...	9X			
...	9X17			
...	9X17			
...	9X17			
...	9X17			
...	9X30			

Week Days.

	a.m.	a.m.	p.m.	p.m.	p.m.	p.m.	p.m.	p.m.	p.m.
Bigbury-on-Sea dep.	8 25			12 10		6X10 7Y25			
Folly Farm (for Bantham)	8 30			12 15		5X45 7Y30			
Bigbury Village	8 40			12 25		5X55 7Y40			
St. Anne's Chapel (for Ringmore)	8 45			12 30		6X 7Y45			
Seven Stones (for Kings-on)	8 52			12 37		6X 7 7Y52			
Cumery Corner	8 55			12 40		6X20 7Y57			
Harraton Cross				12 50		6X30 8Y 5			
Aveton Gifford	9T45								
Modbury (G. W. Hotel) dep.	9 15	10 45	1 0	3 10		6 30 8Y15 8T50		9 15	8D10
Flete (for Ermington) dep. abt.	9 25	10 55	1 10	3 10		6 40 8Y25		9 28	8D20
Western Lodge	9 35	11 5	1 20	3 20		6 50 8Y35		9 35	8D30
Dunstone	9 40	11 10	1 25	3 25		6 55 8Y40		9 40	8D35
Yealmpton (Station) arr.	9 50	11 20	1 35	3 35		7 5 8Y45		9 50	8D45

D—One car only with accommodation for 20 passengers will work this trip.
T—Thursdays and Saturdays only.
X—Wednesdays and Saturdays excepted up to September 13th, runs daily after this date.
G—Modbury dep. 8.15 a.m.
Y—Wednesdays and Saturdays only and not after September 13th.

123

ON THE WAY TO BIGBURY-ON-SEA. YEALMPTON STATION.

September 1924 until further notice.

YEALMPTON BRANCH.

Double Line between Mount Gould Jct. and Cattewater Jct.   Single Line Cattewater Jct. to Plymstock, worked by Electric Train Tablet.   Single Line between Plymstock and Yealmpton, worked by Electric Train Staff.   No Crossing place.

DOWN TRAINS.

			Time allowances for Ordinary Freight Trains (see page 2).		1 B	2 B	3 K		4 K	5 K	6	7 K	8 B	9 B	10 B	11 B	12	13
Distance from Millbay	STATIONS.	Ruling Gradient 1 in	Point to point times. Mins.	Allow for stop. Mins.	Allow for start. Mins.	Motor	Motor	Goods.		Motor	Motor		Motor	Motor	Motor	Motor	Motor		
M. C.						dep.	dep.	arr.	dep.	dep.	dep.		dep.	dep.	dep.	dep.	dep.		
						A.M.	A.M.	A.M.	A.M.	A.M.	P.M.		P.M.	P.M.	P.M.	P.M.	P.M.		
0	Plymouth	61 R	—	—		7 15	9 0	...	...	10 33	1 8		3 10	5 15	6 55	9 5	10 48		
0 68	North Road	77 R	—	—		7 21	9 5	...	...	10 38	1 15		3 15	5 21	7 1	9 10	10 53		
1 11	Mutley	72 F	—	—		7 23	9 7	...	...	10 41	1 15		3 17	5 23	7 3	9 12	10 55		
1 55	Lipson Vale Halt	83 F	—	—		7 26	9 10	...	...	10 44	1 17		3 20	5 25	7 5	9 14	...		
2 29	Lipson Junction		—	—		7 28	9 12	...	...	10 44	1 19		3 22	5 27	7 8	9 16	...		
2 69	Laira Yard	69	—	—				...	9 35										
3	Mount Gould Junc.	73 F	2	—		7 32	9 13	9 38	...	10 47	1 21		3 23	5 28	7 10	9 18	11 23		WEDNESDAYS, THURSDAYS & SATURDAYS ONLY.
3	Cattewater Junc.	90 F	2	—		7 32	9 14	9 40	10 12	10 51	1 24		3 26	5 31	7 12	9 21	11 25		
4 67	Plymstock	66 R	3	1		7 35	9 17	10 17	10 25	10 53	1 28		3 29	5 34	7 15	9 24	11 26		
5 69	Billacombe	70 R	—	—		7 40	9 24	10 58		10 58	1 32		3 31	5 39	7 17	9 27	11 12		
6	Elburton Cross	63 F	3	2															
6	Stop Board	60 F	2	—															
6 43	Brixton Road	60 F	3	—		7 44	9 28			11 2	1 36		3 38	5 43	7 21	9 33	11 16		
7 76	Steer Point	60 R	3	—		7 49	9 33			11 5	1 41		3 43	5 48	7 28	9 38	11 21		
10 25	**Yealmpton**	60 R	6	—		7 55	9 39	10 45		11 13	1 47		3 49	5 52	7 32	9 44	11 27		

SUNDAYS.

1 B	2 B	3 B	4
Motor	Motor	Motor	
dep.	dep.	dep.	
A.M.	P.M.	P.M.	
9 55	2 5	8 20	...
10 0	2 10	8 25	...
10 2	2 12	8 27	...
10 5	2 15	8 30	...
10 7	2 17	8 32	...
10 8	2 18	8 33	...
10 9	2 20	8 35	...
10 11	2 21	8 36	...
10 14	2 24	8 39	...
10 19	2 29	8 44	...
10 23	2 33	8 48	...
10 28	2 38	8 53	...
10 34	2 44	8 59	...

UP TRAINS.

			Time allowances for Ordinary Freight Trains (see page 2).		1 B	2 B	3		4 K	5 K	6	7 B	8 B	9 B	10 B	11 B	12	13
	STATIONS.	Ruling Gradient 1 in	Point to point times. Mins.	Allow for stop. Mins.	Allow for start. Mins.	Motor	Motor	Motor		Goods.	Motor		Motor	Motor	Motor	Motor	Motor		
						dep.	dep.	dep.		arr.	dep.		dep.	dep.	dep.	dep.	dep.		
						A.M.	A.M.	A.M.		A.M.	A.M.		A.M.	P.M.	P.M.	P.M.	P.M.		
	Yealmpton	60 F	—	—		8 10	9 51	11 20			11 45	1 53		3 55	6 10	7 40	9 50	11 35		
	Steer Point	60 R	6	—		8 16	9 55	11 26		11 55	12 25	1 59		4 1	6 16	7 46	9 56	11 39		
	Brixton Road	68 F	3	—		8 21	10 0	11 31		12 30	12 40	2 4		4 6	6 21	7 51	10 1	11 44		
	Elburton Cross	68 F	—	—		8 25	10 4	11 35				2 8		4 10	6 25	7 55	10 5	11 48		
	Billacombe	70 F	3	—		8 29	10 8	11 39		12 50	1 6	2 12		4 14	6 29	8 0	10 9	11 52		
	Plymstock	72 F	1	—		8 33	10 11	11 43		1 10	1 35	2 16		4 18	6 32	8 4	10 13	11 56		
	Cattewater Junction	66 F	2	—		8 35	10 13	11 44				2 19		4 21	6 36					WEDS., THURS. AND SATURDAYS ONLY.
	Mount Gould Junction	73 R	—	—						1 30	1 42									
	Laira Yard		—	—															
	Lipson Junction	60 F	—	—		8 37	10 14	11 47				2 20		4 25	6 38	8 6	10 17	11 58		
	Lipson Vale Halt	60 R	1	—		8 40	10 17	11 50						4 28	6 11	8 8	10 20	12 1		
	Mutley	68 F	3	—		8 43	10 20	11 53				2 24		4 31	6 13	8 11	10 23	12 4		
	North Road	66 F	1	—		8 47	10 23	11 55				2 27		4 34	6 15	8 14	10 25	12 7		
	Plymouth	73 R	2	—		8 51	10 27	12 3			1 42	2 31		4 39	6 50	8 20	10 30	12 10		

Motors must pass Cattewater Junction at a speed not exceeding 4 miles an hour.

SUNDAYS.

1 B	2 B	3 B	4
Motor	Motor	Motor	
dep.	dep.	dep.	
A.M.	P.M.	P.M.	
10 45	2 30	9 10	...
10 51	2 36	9 16	...
10 56	2 41	9 21	...
11 0	2 45	9 25	...
11 4	2 49	9 29	...
11 8	2 53	9 33	...
11 10	2 55	9 35	...
11 12	2 57	9 37	...
11 15	3 0	9 40	...
11 18	3 3	9 43	...
11 21	3 6	9 46	...
11 25	3 10	9 50	...

F To commence May 31st.

September 24th 1928.

90 PLYMOUTH AND YEALMPTON. (Rail Motor Car, one class only.)

Week Days only.

Down Trains.

M'ls		a.m.	a.m.	p.m.	p.m.	p.m.	p.m.	p.m.
—	Plymouth { Millbay ... dep.	7 15	9 0	10 35	1 8	3 8	5 10	6 38	9 5
¾	North Road "	7 19	9 4	10 38	1 12	3 12	5 13	6 42	9 9
1¼	Mutley "	7 21	9 6	10 40	1 14	3 14	5 15	6 44	9 11
1½	Lipson Vale Halt "	7 24	9 9	10 43	1 17	3 17	5 18	6 47	9 14
4	Plymstock ... "	7 30	9 15	10 50	1 23	3 23	5 25	6 53	9 19
4½	Billacombe "	7 33	9 18	10 53	1 26	3 26	5 28	6 56	9 22
5½	Elburton Cross "	7 37	9 22	10 57	1 30	3 30	5 32	7 0	9 26
6¼	Brixton Road "	7 41	9 26	11 1	1 34	3 34	5 36	7 4	9 30
8	Steer Point "	7 45	9 30	11 5	1 38	3 38	5 40	7 8	9 34
10¼	Yealmpton ... arr.	7 51	9 36	11 11	1 44	3 44	5 46	7 14	9 40

	a.m.	a.m.	a.m.	p.m.	p.m.	p.m.	p.m.	p.m.
Yealmpton ... dep.	8 5	9 39	11 17	1 55	3 55	5 50	7 44	9 52
Steer Point "	8 11	9 45	11 23	2 1	4 1	5 56	7 50	9 58
Brixton Road "	8 15	9 49	11 27	2 5	4 5	6 0	7 54	10 2
Elburton Cross "	8 19	9 53	11 31	2 9	4 9	6 4	7 58	10 6
Billacombe "	8 22	9 56	11 34	2 12	4 12	6 7	8 1	10 9
Plymstock "	8 26	10 0	11 38	2 16	4 16	6 11	8 5	10 13
Lipson Vale Halt "	8 32	10 6	11 45		4 23	6 18	8 11	10 19
Plymouth { Mutley ... arr.	8 34	10 9	11 48		4 26	6 21	8 14	10 22
North Road "	8 37	10 13	11 51		4 26	6 21	8 17	10 25
Millbay "	8 41	10 17	11 55		4 30	6 25	8 22	10 30

November 3rd 1941 until further notice.

YEALMPTON BRANCH.   Week Days only   (Commences November 3rd, 1941)

THE SPEED OF TRAINS OVER THE BRANCH MUST NOT EXCEED 30 MILES PER HOUR.

Double Line between Friary "A" and "B" Boxes. Single Line between Friary "A" Box and Plymstock worked by Southern Railway Electric Train Tablet. Single Line between Plymstock and Yealmpton worked by Electric Train Token. No crossing place.

Down Trains.

STATIONS.	B Motor dep.	B Motor dep.	Motor dep.	Motor dep.	B Motor dep.	B Motor dep.	B Motor dep.
	a.m.	a.m.	a.m.	a.m.	p.m.	p.m.	p.m.
FRIARY (S.R.) ...	7 18	CS	CS	CS	2 50	4 50	6 10
Friary "A" Box...	CS	9 0	10 33	CS	2 52	CS	CS
Lucas Terrace Halt ...	7 20	9 2	10 35	CS	2 52	4 52	6 12
Cattewater Junction	CS	CS	CS	CS	2×58	CS	CS
Plymstock ...	7 24	9 6	10 39	1 14	2 59	4 56	6 16
Billacombe ...	7 27	9 9	10 42	1 17	3 2	4 59	6 19
Elburton Cross ...	7 31	9 13	10 46	1 21	3 6	5 3	6 23
Brixton Road ...	7 35	9 17	10 50	1 25	3 10	5 7	6 27
Steer Point ...	7 39	9 21	10 54	1 31	3 14	5 11	6 31
YEALMPTON ...	7 45	9 27	11 0	1 37	3 17	5 17	6 37

Up Trains.

STATIONS.	B Motor dep.	Motor dep.	Motor dep.	B Motor dep.	Motor dep.	Motor dep.	B Motor dep.	B Motor dep.
	a.m.	a.m.	a.m.	a.m.	p.m.	p.m.	p.m.	p.m.
YEALMPTON ...	8 0	8 11	9 39	11 17	1 30	3 30	5 23	8 45
Steer Point ...	CS	8 17	9 45	11 23	1 36	3 36	5 31	8 51
Brixton Road ...	8 13	9 27	9 49	11 27	1 40	3 40	5 35	6 55
Elburton Cross ...	8 23	9 31	9 53	11 31	1 44	3 44	5 39	7 0
Billacombe ...	8 27	10 9	9 56	11 34	1 47	3 47	5 42	7 5
Plymstock ...	CS	10 2	10 0	11×39	2 17	3 59	5 47	7 7
Cattewater Junction	CS	CS	CS	CS	CS	CS	CS	CS
Lucas Terrace Halt	8 30	10 4	10 42	11 42	2 20	3 55	5 50	7 10
Friary "A" Box	CS	10 6	10 44	11 44	2 22	3 57	5 52	7 12
FRIARY (S.R.) ...	8 32							

June 16th 1947 to October 5th 1947.

PLYMOUTH AND YEALMPTON.

Double Line between Mount Gould Junction and Cattewater Junction and between Friary "A" and "B" Boxes. Single line between Friary "A" Box and Cattewater Junction, and between Cattewater Junction and Plymstock worked by Southern Railway Electric Train Tablet. Single Line between Plymstock and Yealmpton, worked by Electric Train Token.

THE SPEED OF TRAINS OVER THE BRANCH MUST NOT EXCEED 30 MILES PER HOUR.

When absolutely necessary two Freight Trains or a Passenger and a Freight Train may cross at Brixton Road on the understanding that the Passenger Train is always kept on the running line.

Down Trains.

Week Days only.

M.P. Mileage.		Distance from Millbay.		STATIONS.	Ruling Gradient 1 in	Time Allowances for Ordinary Freight Trains. See page 5.			B Motor. dep.	B Motor. dep.	B Motor. dep.	B Freight. arr. dep.	E Motor. dep.	B Motor. dep.	B Freight. arr. dep.	B Motor. dep.	B Motor. dep.	B Motor. dep.	B SO dep.	B Motor. dep.
M.	C.	M.	C.			Point to point times. Mins.	Allow for Stop. Mins.	Allow for Start. Mins.	a.m.	a.m.	a.m.	a.m.	a.m.	a.m.	p.m.	p.m.	p.m.	p.m.	p.m.	p.m.
			69	Laira Yard								11 30								
			75	Mount Gould Junction	73 F			7 0	8 53	10 33		1 14	2 50		5 20	6 40	9 45
		2		FRIARY (S.R.)				CS	CS	CS		CS	CS		CS	CS	CS
				Friary "A" Box				7 2	8 55	10 35		1 16	2 52		5 22	6 42	9 47
			22	Lucas Terrace Halt	90 F		2	CS	CS	CS		CS	2X56		CS	CS	CS
		3	71	Cattewater Junction	66 R		2	7 6	8 59	10 39		1 23	2 59		5 26	6 46	9 51
0	0		68	Plymstock	70 R		6	7 9	9 2	10 42	11 50	1 27	3 7		5 29	6 49	9 53
0	77		68	Billacombe	68 F			7 13	9 6	10 46	12 15	1 29	3 9		5 33	6 53	10 5
1	52		43	Elburton Cross	60 F		5	7 17	9 10	10 50	12 30	1 35	3 11		5 37	6 57	10 2
2	76			Brixton Road	60 F		3	7 21	9 14	10 54	12 35	1 37	3 11		5 41	7 1	10 6
4	33		24	Steer Point	60 R		1	7 24	9 18	11 0	12 50	1 39	3 14		5 45	7 5	10 9
6				YEALMPTON	60 R		6	7 27	9 20	11 0	12 58	1 41	3 17		5 47	7 7	10 12

Up Trains.

Week Days only.

STATIONS.	Ruling Gradient 1 in	Time Allowances for Ordinary Freight Trains. See page 55.			B Motor. dep.	B Motor. dep.	K Freight. arr. dep.	B Motor. dep.	K Freight. arr. dep.	B Freight. RR arr. dep.	B Motor. dep.	Motor. dep.	Motor. SO dep.
		Point to Point times. Mins.	Allow for Stop. Mins.	Allow for Start. Mins.	a.m.	a.m.	p.m.	p.m.	p.m.	p.m.	p.m.	p.m.	p.m.
YEALMPTON					7 46	9 28	2 18	1 55	2 35		3 30	5 55	7 15
Steer Point	60 F	6	1		7 50	9 34	Z	CS	CS	3 55	3 36	CS	7 21
Brixton Road	60 R	3	1		7 54	9 38		2 9	2 53X		3 40	6 9	7 25
Elburton Cross	60 R		1		7 57	9 42		2 12	C3		3 44	6 12	7 29
Billacombe	68 F	6	1		8 2	9 45		2 17	7S	4 12	3 47	CS	7 32
Plymstock	70 F	3	1		8 5	9 50	2 48	CS		C4 34S	3 52	6 17	7 37
Cattewater Junction	66 F	1	1		CS	CS	3 5	2 30		C4 38S	CS	CS	CS
Lucas Terrace Halt					8 5	9 53	7S	CS			3 55	6 20	7 40
FRIARY "A" Box					CS	CS		2 22	3 53X		3 57	CS	CS
FRIARY (S.R.)			1		8 7	9 55						6 22	7 42
Mount Gould Junction	90 R	2	1				3 9		3				
Laira Yard	73 R						3 12			4 40			11 10

A—Runs on Market Days only.   Z—Does not run on Market Days.   SO—Saturdays only.   SX—Saturdays excepted.
‡—Engine to proceed to Laira for coal at 12.5 p.m. and return. thence at 12.50 p.m. and return. 12.58 p.m., Friary arrive 1.14 p.m. Friary to Yealmpton.
†—Engine depart Laira 6.25 a.m., Friary arrive 6.41 a.m. (To convey Trailers on Mondays.)
N—Engine and Trailers to Laira 11.10 p.m.

PLYMOUTH FRIARY, CATTEWATER, TURNCHAPEL AND YEALMPTON

WEEKDAYS   **D47**

DOUBLE LINE between Friary "A" and "B" Boxes.
SINGLE LINE between Friary "A" Box and Cattewater Junction and between Cattewater Junction and Plymstock, worked by Southern Region Electric Train Tablet.
SINGLE LINE between Plymstock and Yealmpton, worked by Wooden Train Staff under "One Engine in Steam" Regulations.
The speed of Up and Down Trains between Friary and Turnchapel, Cattewater Junction and Cattewater Harbour not to exceed 15 m.p.h.
The speed of Up and Down Trains between Plymstock and Yealmpton not to exceed 30 m.p.h.

Mileage from Friary			Ruling Gradient 1 in	9317	9317	9317	9391	9391	0317	9317	9396
											From Baylys Siding
										L E	
M	C									SX Q	MWF
				am	am	am	am	am	am	PM	PM
0	0	PLYMOUTH FRIARY dep	—	6 25	8 5	9 0	9 15		10‖45	12 30	12 40
0	75	Cattewater Jn.	66 F	6 30	8 10	9 3	9 20	..	10 48	12 35	12 45
2	19	CATTEWATER...... arr	66 F	6 37	8 17	9 6			10‖51	12 42	
1	44	Plymstock ... ... arr	66 R	..	..	..	9 24	10 17		..	
		.... dep					9 38	10 32			R
2	0	Oreston	50 R	..		..	9 45				
2	26	Baylys Sidings .... arr	35 F								
2	45	TURNCHAPEL... ... arr	50 F					10 40			
2	41	Billacombe	70 R								R
4	16	Brixton Road	60 F								R
5	49	Steer Point.................	60 F								R
7	77	YEALMPTON ... ... arr	60 R	..	..	..	..	..		..	1 45

			9317	0317		9391		9317	9317	9317	
				L E							
			SX	SX Q		SX		SX	SX	SX Q	
			PM	PM		PM		PM	PM	PM	
PLYMOUTH FRIARY dep			2 15	2‖55		3 20		4 0	5 0	6 35	
Cattewater Jn.			2 20	2 58		3 25		4 5	5 5	6 40	
CATTEWATER...... arr			2 27	3‖ 1	Applies also on Saturdays during Manure Season			4 12	5 12	6 47	
Plymstock ... ... arr			..			3 29		..	..	..	
.... dep						3 41					
Oreston			..			..		..	..	..	
Baylys Siding ... ... arr			..			3 48		..	..	..	
TURNCHAPEL... ... arr			..					..	..	..	

	Ruling Gradient 1 in	To Turnchapel	9364	9391	9364	9364	9364	0364	9364	9364	9364
									L E		
								SO		SX	MWF
			Q					PM	PM	PM	PM
YEALMPTON .... dep	—		am	am	am	am				2 15
Steer Point...	60 F		..	..	..	..	To be retained at Cattewater Harbour during Manure Season and work until finish	..	..	R
Brixton Road..............	60 R									R
Billacombe ... ... arr	60 R									R
TURNCHAPEL ...... dep	70 F		..	..	11 10			..	..	
Baylys Siding ... ... dep	50 R		10 10		11 15			..		
Oreston .... arr	35 R		..		11 25			..		
... ... dep			..		11 30			..		
Plymstock .... arr	50 F		10 17		11 40			..		
... ... dep			10 32					..		2 50
CATTEWATER...... dep	66 F	10 30		11 15		1 45	12‖30	12 50	1 30	..
Cattewater Jn.	66 R	10 33		11 18		11 45	12 36	12 57	1 33	2 55
PLYMOUTH FRIARY arr	66 R	10 36		11 21		11 50	12‖39	1 2	1 36	3 0

	9364	9364	9364	9364	9364	9364	9364
	SX Q	SX	SX	SX	SX	SX Q	SX
	PM	PM	PM	PM	PM	PM	PM
TURNCHAPEL........ dep							
Baylys Siding........ dep	..	..	..	4 10	..	..	..
Oreston .... arr	..	..	..	4 15	..	..	..
... ... dep	..	..	..	4 23	..	..	..
Plymstock .... arr	..	..	..	4 28	..	..	..
... ... dep	..	..	..	4 32	..	..	..
CATTEWATER...... dep	3 30	4 25		5 25	6 0	7 40	8 40
Cattewater Jn.	3 33	4 32	4 37	5 32	6 7	7 47	8 47
PLYMOUTH FRIARY arr	3 36	4 37	4 42	5 37	6 12	7 52	8 52

(Applies also on Saturdays during Manure Season)

KINGSBRIDGE, MODBURY, YEALMPTON AND PLYMOUTH.

	Market Day.	Early Closing.
MODBURY	2nd Monday in the month.	Wednesday.
YEALMPTON	4th ,, ,, ,,	Wednesday.
PLYMOUTH	Tues., Thurs. and Sat.	Wednesday.

WEEK DAYS.

		a.m.	a.m.	a.m.	a.m.	a.m.	a.m.	p.m.	p.m.	p.m	p.m.	p.m.	p.m.	p.m.
KINGSBRIDGE (Station) .. .. dep.		..	8* 0	..	9 10	..	11 5	..	..	1 15	..	3 10	4*15	..
CHURCHSTOW (Church House Inn) ,,		..	8*10	..	9 20	..	11 15	..	..	1 25	..	3 20	4*25	..
AVETON GIFFORD (P.O.) .. ,,	From Noss Mayo.	..	8*20	B	9 30	From Noss Mayo.	11 25	..	B	1 35	..	3 30	4*35	B
HARRATON CROSS .. .. ,,		..	..	8 33	9 43		11 38	..	12Y48	1 48	..	3 43		4 58
TURNPIKE .. .. ,,		..	..	8 36	9 46		11 41	..	12Y51	1 51	..	3 46		5 1
MODBURY .. .. { arr.		..	..	8 39	9 49		11 44	..	12Y54	1 54	..	3 49		5 4
{ dep.		..	..	8 40	9 50		11 45	..	12Y55	1 55	..	3 50		5 5
FANCY .. .. ,,		..	..	8 42	9 52		11 47	..	12Y57	1 57	..	3 52		5 7
FLETE .. .. ,,		..	..	8 45	9 55		11 50	..	1Y 0	2 0	..	3 55		5 10
WESTERN LODGE .. .. ,		..	..	8 52 10 2			11 57	..	1Y 7	2 7	..	4 2		5 17
DUNSTONE .. .. .. ,,		..	..	8 56 10 6			12 1	..	1Y11	2 11	..	4 6		5 21
YEALMPTON .. .. { arr.		..	..	9 4 10 14			12 9	..	1Y19	2 19	..	4 14		5 29
{ dep.		7 55	8 25	9 5 10 15	10 55 12 10			1 10	1Y20	2 20	3 20	4 15		5 30
BRIXTON .. .. .. ,,		8 1	8 31	9 11 10 21	11 1 12 16			1 16	1Y26	2 26	3 26	4 21	5 31	5 36
ELBURTON (Hotel) .. .. ,,		8 5	8 35	9 15 10 25	11 5 12 20			1 20	1Y30	2 30	3 30	4 25	5 35	5 40
BILLACOMBE .. .. .. ,,		8 10	8 40	9 20 10 30	11 10 12 25			1 25	1Y35	2 35	3 35	4 30	5 40	5 45
PLYMSTOCK .. .. .. ,,		8 15	8 45	9 25 10 35	11 15 12 30			1 30	1Y40	2 40	3 40	4 35	5 45	5 50
PLYMOUTH (Millbay Station) .. arr.		8 30	9 0	9 40 10 50	11 30 12 45			1 45	1Y55	2 55	3 55	4 50	6 0	6 5

18

KINGSBRIDGE, MODBURY, YEALMPTON AND PLYMOUTH (continued).

		WEEK DAYS—continued.					SUNDAYS.					
		p.m.	p.m.	p.m	p.m.	p.m.	a.m.	a.m.	p.m.	p.m.	p.m.	p.m.
KINGSBRIDGE (Station) .. .. dep.		5 35	..	7 0	9V10	..	8 50	..	1 25	..	6 45	8 15	..
CHURCHSTOW (Church House Inn) ,,		5 45	..	7 10	9V20	..	9 0	..	1 35	..	6 55	8 25	..
AVETON GIFFORD (P.O.) .. ,,	From Noss Mayo.	5 55	..	7 20	9V30	..	9 10	..	1 45	..	7 5	8 35	..
HARRATON CROSS .. .. ,,		6 8	..	7 33	9V43	..	9 23	..	1 58	6R 3	7 18	8 48	..
TURNPIKE .. .. ,,		6 11	..	7 36	9V46	..	9 26	..	2 1	6R 6	7 21	8 51	..
MODBURY .. .. { arr.		6 14	..	7 39	9V49	..	9 29	..	2 4	6R 9	7 24	8 54	..
{ dep.		6 15	..	7 40	9V50	9S55	9 30	..	2 5	6R10	7 25	8 55	..
FANCY .. .. ,,		6 17	..	7 42	9V52	9S57	9 32	..	2 7	6R12	7 27	8 57	..
FLETE .. .. ,,		6 20	..	7 45	9V55	10S 0	9 35	..	2 10	6R15	7 30	9 0	..
WESTERN LODGE .. .. ,,		6 27	..	7 52	10V 2	10S 7	9 42	..	2 17	6R22	7 37	9 7	..
DUNSTONE .. .. .. ,,	From Noss Mayo.	6 31	..	7 56	10V 6	10S11	9 46	..	2 21	6R26	7 41	9 11	..
YEALMPTON .. .. { arr.		6 39	..	8 4	10V14	10S20	9 54	..	2 29	6R34	7 49	9 19	..
{ dep.		6 40	7 45	8 5	10V15	..	9 55	10R45	2 30	6R35	7 50	9 20	..
BRIXTON .. .. .. ,,		6 46	7 51	8 11	10V21	..	10 1	10R51	2 36	6R41	7 56	9 26	..
ELBURTON (Hotel) .. .. ,,		6 50	7 55	8 15	10V25	..	10 5	10R55	2 40	6R45	8 0	9 30	..
BILLACOMBE .. .. .. ,,		6 55	8 0	8 20	10V30	..	10 10	11R 0	2 45	6R50	8 5	9 35	..
PLYMSTOCK .. .. .. ,,		7 0	8 5	8 25	10V35	..	10 15	11R 5	2 50	6R55	8 10	9 40	..
PLYMOUTH (Millbay Station) .. arr.		7 15	8 20	8 40	10V50	..	10 30	11R20	3 5	7R10	8 25	9 55	..

S—Saturdays only.　　V—Thursdays only.　　Y—Thursdays and Saturdays only.
* Not on Saturdays nor during School vacations.
B—From Bigbury-on-Sea, see page 31.　　R—Not during December, 1928, and January and February, 1929.
For Train Service see pages 37, 33 and 39.

129

PLYMOUTH, YEALMPTON, MODBURY AND KINGSBRIDGE.

Market Day. Early Closing.
YEALMPTON 4th Monday in the month. Wednesday.
MODBURY   2nd ,, ,, ,, Wednesday.
KINGSBRIDGE Wednesday. ,, Thursday.

WEEK DAYS.

	a.m.	a.m.	a.m.	a.m.	a.m.	a.m.	p.m.	p.m.	p.m.	p.m.	p.m.	p.m.	p.m.
PLYMOUTH (Millbay Station) dep.		9 5	9 25	10 0	11 5	11 45	1 5	1 50	2Y10	3 15	4 0	5 0	6 10
PLYMSTOCK ,,		9 15	9 35	10 10	11 15	11 55	1 15	2 0	2Y20	3 25	4 10	5 10	6 .0
BILLACOMBE ,,		9 18	9 38	10 13	11 18	11 58	1 18	2 3	2Y23	3 28	4 13	5 13	6 23
ELBURTON (Hotel) ,,		9 23	9 43	10 18	11 23	12 3	1 23	2 8	2Y28	3 33	4 18	5 18	6 28
BRIXTON ,,		9 28	9 48	10 23	11 28	12 8	1 28	2 13	2Y33	3 38	4 23	5 23	6 33
YEALMPTON { arr.		9 36	9 56	10 31	11 36	12 16	1 36	2 21	2Y41	3 46	4 31	5 31	6 41
YEALMPTON { dep.		9 37	To Noss Mayo	10 32	11 37	To Noss Mayo	1 37	To Noss Mayo	2Y42	3 47		5 32	To Noss Mayo
DUNSTONE ,,		9 41		10 36	11 41		1 41		2Y46	3 51		5 36	
WESTERN LODGE ,,		9 45		10 40	11 45		1 45		2Y50	3 55		5 40	
FLETE ,,		9 49		10 44	11 49		1 49		2Y54	3 59		5 44	
FANCY ,,		9 54		10 49	11 54		1 54		2Y59	4 4		5 49	
MODBURY { arr.		9 59		10 54	11 59		1 59		3Y 4	4 9		5 54	
MODBURY { dep.		10 0		10 55	12 0		2 0		3Y 5	4 10		5 55	
TURNPIKE ,,		10 4		10 59	12 4		2 4		3Y 9	4 14		5 59	
HARRATON CROSS ,,		10 8		11 3	12 8		2 8		3Y13	4 18		6 3	
AVETON GIFFORD (P.O.) ,,	8*25	10 22			12 22		2 22					6 17	
CHURCHSTOW (Church House Inn) ,,	8*37	10 34		B	12 34		2 34		B	4 44	4*52	6 29	
KINGSBRIDGE (Station) arr.	8*48	10 45			12 45		2 45			4 55	5* 3	6 40	

PLYMOUTH, YEALMPTON, MODBURY AND KINGSBRIDGE (continued)

	WEEK DAYS—continued.					SUNDAYS.						
	p.m.	p.m.	p.m	p.m	p.m	a.m.	a.m.	p.m.	p.m.	p.m.	p.m.	p.m.
PLYMOUTH (Millbay Station) dep.	6 30	7 30	8 30	9 0	11V 0	10 45	11R30	4 40		7R15	8 30	10 0
PLYMSTOCK ,,	6 40	7 40	8 40	9 10	11V10	10 55	11R40	4 50		7R25	8 40	10 10
BILLACOMBE ,,	6 43	7 43	8 43	9 13	11V13	10 58	11R43	4 53		7R28	8 43	10 13
ELBURTON (Hotel) ,,	6 48	7 48	8 48	9 18	11V18	11 3	11R48	4 58		7R33	8 48	10 18
BRIXTON ,,	6 53	7 53	8 53	9 23	11V23	11 8	11R53	5 3		7R38	8 53	10 23
YEALMPTON { arr.	7 1	8 1	9 1	9 31	11V31	11 16	12R 1	5 11		7R46	9 1	10 31
YEALMPTON { dep.	7 2	8 2	To Noss Mayo	9S32	11V32	11 17	12R 2	5 12	7 0		9 2	
DUNSTONE ,,	7 6	8 6		9S36	11V36	11 21	12R 6	5 16	7 4		9 6	
WESTERN LODGE ,,	7 10	8 10		9S40	11V40	11 25	12R10	5 20	7 8		9 10	
FLETE ,,	7 14	8 14		9S44	11V44	11 29	12R14	5 24	7 12		9 14	
FANCY ,,	7 19	8 19		9S49	11V49	11 34	12R19	5 29	7 17		9 19	
MODBURY { arr.	7 24	8 24		9S54	11V54	11 39	12R24	5 34	7 22		9 24	
MODBURY { dep.	7 25	8 25			11V55	11 40	12R25	5 35	7 23		9 25	
TURNPIKE ,,	7 29	8 29			11V59	11 44	12R29	5 39	7 27		9 29	
HARRATON CROSS ,,	7 33	8 33			12V 3	11 48	12R33	5 43	7 31		9 33	
AVETON GIFFORD (P.O.) ,,		8 47			12V17	12 3		5 57	7 45		9 47	
CHURCHSTOW (Church House Inn) ,,		8 59		B	12V29	12 9	B	6 9	7 57		9 59	
KINGSBRIDGE (Station) arr.		9 9			12V40	12 25		6 20	8 8		10 10	

21

B—To Bigbury-on-Sea, see page 31. R—Not during December, 1928, and January and February, 1929.
S—Saturdays only. V—Thursdays only. Y—Thursdays and Saturdays only. * Not on Saturdays
nor during School vacations. For Train Services see pages 37, 38 and 39.

A GWR rear entry bus waits outside The Great Western Hotel, Modbury in March 1915. Now demolished, it was more recently called The Red Devon Hotel.

H. Pitts

A fine example of a 30 cwt Thornycroft bus of the type that ran from Newton & Noss to Yealmpton in the 1920s. This photograph shows No. 914 which was actually allocated to Newbury, Berkshire, and is seen outside the works at Slough.

British Railways Board

A GWR Maudsley Type ML3, No. 1201, waiting outside The Yealmpton Hotel in 1927. This bus, together with others of its type, had been allocated to Kingsbridge in 1926.

H. Pitts

National (formerly Devon Motor Transport), September 1st 1928.

92

SERVICE 214, 215, 216, 216A & 217.

PLYMOUTH, ELBURTON, WEMBURY, BRIXTON, YEALMPTON, RIVER YEALM, ERMINGTON and IVYBRIDGE.

		*	K*	*	*	*	SO	*				*	
		a.m	a.m.	a.m.	a.m.	a.m.	a.m.	a.m.	a.m.	a.m.	a.m.	a.m.	a.m. a.m.
Plymouth	dep.	7 0	7 30	7 40	8 45	8 55	9 30	9 30	9 45	1015	1030	1045	1115
Billacombe	,,	7 12	7 42	7 52	8 57	9 7	9 42	9 42	9 57	1027	1042	1057	1127
Elburton	,,	7 16	7 46	7 56	9 1	9 11	9 46	9 46	10 1	1031	1046	11 1	1131
Wembury	,,				9 16		10 1				11 1		1138
Brixton	,,	7 23		8 3		9 18		9 53	10 8	1038		11 8	1145
Yealmpton	,,	7 30		8 10		9 25		10 0	1015	1045		1115	
Yealm Bridge	,,							10 4					12 0
River Yealm	,,	7 45		8 25		9 40			1030	11 0		1130	
Flete Weston Lodge	.							1010					
Ermington	,,							1017					
Caton	,,							1022					
Ivybridge	arr.							1030					

CONTINUED :—		p.m.	p.m.	p.m.	p.m.	p.m.	p.m.	p.m.	p.m.	p.m.	p.m.	p.m.	p.m.
Plymouth	dep.	1145	12 0	1215	1230	1245	1 15	1 45	2 5	2 15	2 45	3 15	3 30
Billacombe	,,	1157	1212	1227	1242	1257	1 27	1 57	2 17	2 27	2 57	3 27	3 42
Elburton	,,	12 1	1216	1231	1246	1 1	1 31	2 1	2 21	2 31	3 1	3 31	3 46
Wembury	,,		1231					2 36					
Brixton	,,	12 8		1238	1253	1 8	1 38	2 8		2 38	3 8	3 38	3 53
Yealmpton	,,	1215		1245	1 0	1 15	1 45	2 15		2 45	3 15	3 45	4 0
Yealm Bridge	,,				1 4								4 4
River Yealm	,,	1230		1 0		1 30	2 0	2 30		3 0	3 30	4 0	
Flete Weston Lodge	,,				1 10								4 10
Ermington	,,				1 17								4 17
Caton	,,				1 22								4 22
Ivybridge	arr.				1 30								4 30

CONTINUED :—		p.m.	p.m.	p.m.	p.m.	p.m.	p.m.	p.m.	p.m.	p.m.	p.m.	p.m.	p.m.
Plymouth	dep.	3 45	4 0	4 15	4 45	5 15	5 40	5 55	6 30	6 55	7 30	7 40	7 55
Billacombe	,,	3 57	4 12	4 27	4 57	5 27	5 52	6 7	6 42	7 7	7 42	7 52	8 7
Elburton	,,	4 1	4 16	4 31	5 1	5 31	5 56	6 11	6 46	7 11	7 46	7 56	8 11
Wembury	,,		4 31			6 11				8 1			
Brixton	,,	4 8		4 38	5 8	5 38		6 18	6 53	7 18		8 3	8 18
Yealmpton	,,	4 15		4 45	5 15	5 45		6 25	7 0	7 25		8 10	8 25
Yealm Bridge	,,							7 4					
River Yealm	,,	4 30		5 0	5 30	6 0		6 40		7 40		8 25	8 40
Flete Weston Lodge	,,							7 10					
Ermington	,,							7 17					
Caton	,,							7 22					
Ivybridge	arr.							7 30					

For continuation see Page 93.

National (formerly Devon Motor Transport), September 1st 1928 (continued).

SERVICE 214, 215, 216, 216A & 217.

PLYMOUTH, ELBURTON, WEMBURY, BRIXTON, YEALMPTON, RIVER YEALM, ERMINGTON and IVYBRIDGE.

CONTINUED :—		p.m.	NS	p.m.	S	p.m.	p.m.					
Plymouth	dep.	8 55	9 15	9 30	10 0	1010	11 0					
Billacombe	,,	9 7	9 27	9 42	1012	1022	1112					
Elburton	,,	9 11	9 31	9 46	1016	1026	1116					
Wembury	,,		9 46		1031							
Brixton	,,	9 18		9 53		1033	1123					
Yealmpton	,,	9 25		10 0		1040	1130					
Yealm Bridge	,,			10 4								
River Yealm	,,	9 40				1055	1145					
Flete Weston Lodge	,,			1010								
Ermington	,,			1017								
Caton	,,			1022								
Ivybridge	arr.			1030								

*—Not Sundays. SO Sundays only. K Arrives Knighton Hill 7.58 a.m. Weekdays only. NS—Not Saturdays. S Saturdays only.

		*	K*	*		*	*	*	SO		*		
		a.m.	a.m.	a.m.	a.m.	a.m.	a.m.	a.m.	a.m.	a.m.	a.m	a.m.	a.m.
Ivybridge	dep.		7 35									11 5	
Caton	,,		7 43									1113	
Ermington	,,		7 48									1118	
Flete Weston Lodge	,,		7 55									1125	
River Yealm	,,	7 0		8 0	8 45		9 45		1045		1115		
Yealm Bridge	,,			8 1								1131	
Yealmpton	,,	7 15		8 5	8 15	9 0		10 0		11 0		1130	1135
Brixton	,,	7 22		8 12	8 22	9 7		10 7		11 7		1137	1142
Wembury	,,					9 45			1015		1115		
Elburton	,,	7 29	8 14	8 19	8 29	9 14	10 0	1014	1030	1114	1130	1144	1149
Billacombe	,,	7 33	8 18	8 23	8 33	9 18	10 4	1018	1034	1118	1134	1148	1153
Plymouth	arr.	7 45	8 30	8 35	8 45	9 30	1016	1030	1046	1130	1146	12 0	12 9

CONTINUED :—		a.m.	p.m.	p.m.	p.m.	p.m.	p.m.	p.m.	p.m.	p.m.	p.m.	p.m.	p.m.
Ivybridge	dep.								2 15				
Caton	,,								2 23				
Ermington	,,								2 28				
Flete Weston Lodge	,,								2 35				
River Yealm	,,	1145	1215	1245		1 15	1 45	2 15			2 45	3 15	3 45
Yealm Bridge	,,								2 41				
Yealmpton	,,	12 0	1230	1 0		1 30	2 0	2 30	2 45		3 0	3 30	4 0
Brixton	,,	12 7	1237	1 7		1 37	2 7	2 37	2 52		3 7	3 37	4 7
Wembury	,,				1 15					2 55			
Elburton	,,	1214	1244	1 14	1 30	1 44	2 14	2 44	2 59	3 10	3 14	3 44	4 14
Billacombe	,,	1218	1248	1 18	1 34	1 48	2 18	2 48	3 3	3 14	3 18	3 48	4 18
Plymouth	arr.	1230	1 0	1 30	1 46	2 0	2 30	3 0	3 15	3 26	3 30	4 0	4 30

CONTINUED :—		p.m.		p.m.	p.m.	p.m.	p.m.	p.m.	p.m.	p.m.	p.m.	p.m.	p.m.
Ivybridge	dep.					5 15							8 0
Caton	,,					5 23							8 8
Ermington	,,					5 28							8 13
Flete Weston Lodge	,,					5 35							8 20
River Yealm	,,	4 15		4 45	5 15		5 45		6 15	6 55	7 55		
Yealm Bridge	,,					5 41							8 26
Yealmpton	,,	4 30		5 0	5 30	5 45	6 0		6 30	7 10	8 10		8 30
Brixton	,,	4 37		5 7	5 37	5 52	6 7		6 37	7 17	8 17		8 37
Wembury	,,		4 55				6 20					8 15	
Elburton	,,	4 44	5 10	5 14	5 44	5 59	6 14	6 35	6 44	7 24	8 24	8 30	8 44
Billacombe	,,	4 48	5 14	5 18	5 48	6 3	6 18	6 39	6 48	7 28	8 28	8 34	8 48
Plymouth	arr.	5 0	5 26	5 30	6 0	6 15	6 30	6 51	7 0	7 40	8 40	8 46	9 0

CONTINUED :—		p.m.	p.m.	NS	p.m.	S	p.m.						
Ivybridge	dep.												
Caton	,,												
Ermington	,,												
Flete Weston Lodge	,,												
River Yealm	,,	8 35	8 55		9 50		11 0						
Yealm Bridge	,,												
Yealmpton	,,	8 50	9 10		10 5		1115						
Brixton	,,	8 57	9 17		1012		1122						
Wembury	,,			9 55		1035							
Elburton	,,	9 4	9 24	1010	1019	1050	1129						
Billacombe	,,	9 8	9 28	1014	1023	1054	1133						
Plymouth	arr.	9 20	9 40	1026	1035	11 6	1145						

*—Not Sundays. SO—Sundays only. K—Leave Knighton Hill 8.0 a.m. Week days only. NS—Not Saturdays. S—Saturdays only.

FARE TABLE. **PLYMOUTH, ERMINGTON, IVYBRIDGE** SERVICE 217.

Plymouth									Returns. direct.		
3d	Plymstock								Plymouth to Ermington ..	2/3	
4d	2d	Billacombe							,, Flete Weston	2/-	
5d	3d	2d	Elburton Cross						,, Yealmpton	1/3	
6d	4d	2d	2d	Brixton Road Station					,, Brixton ..	1/-	
7d	5d	3d	2d	2d	Brixton				,, Elburton ..	9d	
9d	7d	5d	3d	3d	2d	Kitley Lodge			,, Billacombe	6d	
9d	9d	6d	4d	3d	2d	2d	Yealmpton				
1/-	10d	8d	6d	4d	4d	3d	2d	Dunstone Cross			
1/1	1/-	10d	8d	7d	6d	4d	4d	2d	Flete Weston Lodge		
1/2	1/-	10d	9d	8d	7d	6d	5d	3d	2d	Modbury Cross	
1/3	1/2	1/-	11d	10d	9d	7d	6d	5d	3d	2d	Ermington
1/6	1/4	1/2	1/1	1/-	11d	9d	8d	7d	5d	4d	2d Caton
1/9	1/6	1/4	1/3	1/2	1/1	11d	10d	9d	7d	6d	5d 3d **Ivybridge**

133

Composite Time Tables (GWR/National), September 1928.

YEALMPTON TO PLYMOUTH ROAD SERVICES OPERATED BY THE GREAT WESTERN AND BY NATIONAL IN SEPTEMBER 1928

WEEK DAYS.

Operator	NAT	GW	NAT	NAT	GW	GW	NAT	GW	NAT	GW	NAT	GW	GW
Origin	New	Noss	Ivy	New	Yeal	New	New	Bigb	New	King	New	Ivy	Noss
	am	am	am	am	am	am	am	am	am	am	am	am	am
Yealmpton	7 15	7 55	8 15	8 25	9 0	9 5	9 30	9 40	10 15	10 55	11 0	11 30	11 35
Plymouth	7 45	8 30	8 35	8 45	9 0	9 30	9 40	10 30	10 50	11 30	11 30	12 0	12 5

Operator	NAT	NAT	GW	GW	NAT	GW	GW	NAT	NAT	NAT	GW	NAT	NAT
Origin	New	King	New	Bigb (ThSO)	Noss	New	King	New	Ivy	New	King	New (ThSO)	Ivy
	am	am	pm	pm	pm	pm	pm	pm	pm	pm	pm	pm	pm
Yealmpton	11 30	11 30	12 0	12 5	12 10	12 30	12 45	1 0	1 10	1 20	1 30	2 0	2 20
Plymouth	12 10	12 12	12 30	12 45	1 0	1 10	1 20	1 30	1 45	1 55	2 0	2 30	2 55

Operator	GW	NAT	NAT	NAT	GW	GW	NAT	GW	NAT	NAT	GW	NAT	GW
Origin	King	New	Noss	New	Noss	Bigb	New	New	King	New	Noss	New	Bigb
	pm	pm	pm	pm	pm	pm	pm	pm	pm	pm	pm	pm	pm
Yealmpton	2 30	2 45	3 0	3 20	3 30	3 55	4 0	4 15	4 30	4 50	5 0	5 25	5 30
Plymouth	3 0	3 15	3 30	3 55	4 0	4 30	4 50	5 0	5 30	6 0	6 6	6 0	5 56

Operator	NAT	NAT	NAT	GW	NAT	NAT	NAT	GW	GW	NAT	NAT	NAT	NAT	GW
Origin	Ivy	New	New	King	Ivy	New	New	New	King (ThSO)	Ivy	New	New	New	New (Bigb)
	pm	pm	pm	pm	pm	pm	pm	pm	pm	pm	pm	pm	pm	pm
Yealmpton	5 45	6 0	6 15	6 30	7 10	7 15	7 40	7 45	8 10	8 20	8 40	8 50	9 10	9 20
Plymouth	6 15	6 30	6 30	7 0	7 15	7 40	8 10	8 20	8 40	8 40	9 9	9 20	9 40	10 5

Operator	GW	NAT	NAT
Origin	King (ThSO)	New	Ivy
	pm	pm	pm
Yealmpton	10 5	10 35	10 50
Plymouth	10 15	10 50	11 15

SUNDAYS.

Operator	NAT	GW	GW	NAT	NAT	NAT	GW	NAT	NAT	NAT	NAT
Origin	New	King	Yeal	New	Ivy	New	New	New	Ivy	New	New
	am	am	am	am	am	am	pm	pm	pm	pm	pm
Yealmpton	8 15	9 55	10 30	11 0	11 30	12 0	12 0	12 30	1 0	1 30	2 0
Plymouth	8 45	10 30	11 20	11 30	12 0	12 5	12 30	1 0	1 30	2 0	2 30

Operator	NAT	GW	NAT	GW	GW	NAT	NAT	NAT	GW	NAT	NAT	GW
Origin	New	King	New	Ivy	King	New	New	New	King	New	New	Bigb
	pm	pm	pm	pm	pm	pm	pm	pm	pm	pm	pm	pm
Yealmpton	2 0	2 30	3 0	3 15	4 0	4 30	5 0	5 30	5 45	6 0	6 30	6 35
Plymouth	2 30	3 3	3 30	3 30	4 30	5 0	5 30	6 0	6 15	6 30	7 0	7 10

Operator	NAT	GW	NAT	NAT	NAT	GW	NAT	NAT	NAT
Origin	New	King	New	Ivy	New	King	New	New	New
	pm	pm	pm	pm	pm	pm	pm	pm	pm
Yealmpton	7 10	7 50	8 10	8 30	8 50	9 10	9 20	10 5	11 15
Plymouth	7 40	8 25	8 40	9 0	9 20	9 40	9 55	10 35	11 45

Great Western Road Motors terminated at Plymouth Millbay Station.
National Road Motors terminated at Plymouth St. Andrew's Church.

Both operators' services passed near Brixton Road, Elburton Cross, Billacombe and Plymstock Stations, and served Yealmpton and Brixton village centres. Steer Point was the only station without nearby road services.

NAT - National (previously Devon Motor Transport). GW - Great Western Road Motor. ThSO - Thursdays and Saturdays only.
New - Newton Ferrers. King - Kingsbridge. Bigb - Bigbury-on-Sea. Yeal - Starts from Yealmpton.
Noss - Noss Mayo. Ivy - Ivybridge.

Composite Time Tables (GWR/National), September 1928 (continued).

PLYMOUTH TO YEALMPTON ROAD SERVICES OPERATED BY THE GREAT WESTERN AND BY NATIONAL IN SEPTEMBER 1928

WEEK DAYS.

Operator	Destination	Plymouth	Yealmpton
NAT	New	7 0 am	7 30 am
NAT	New	7 40 am	8 10 am
NAT	New	8 55 am	9 25 am
GW	King	9 5 am	9 36 am
GW	Noss	9 25 am	9 56 am
NAT	Ivy	9 30 am	10 0 am
NAT	New	9 45 am	10 15 am
GW	Bigb	10 0 am	10 15 am
NAT	New	10 15 am	10 31 am
NAT	New	10 45 am	11 15 am
GW	King	11 5 am	11 36 am
GW	Noss	11 45 am	1216 am
NAT	New	1145 am	1215 am
NAT	Ivy	1215 pm	1245 pm
NAT	New	1230 pm	1 0 pm
NAT	New	1245 pm	1 15 pm
GW	King	1 5 pm	1 36 pm
NAT	Ivy	1 15 pm	1 45 pm
GW	Yeal	1 45 pm	2 15 pm
GW	New	1 50 pm	2 12 pm
GW	Noss	2 10 pm	2 41 pm
NAT	New	2 15 pm	2 45 pm
GW	King (ThSO)	2 45 pm	3 15 pm

Operator	Destination	Plymouth	Yealmpton
NAT	New	3 15 pm	3 45 pm
NAT	New	3 30 pm	3 46 pm
GW	King	3 45 pm	4 0 pm
NAT	Ivy	4 0 pm	4 15 pm
GW	Bigb	4 15 pm	4 31 pm
NAT	New	4 45 pm	4 45 pm
NAT	New	5 0 pm	5 15 pm
NAT	Ivy	5 15 pm	5 31 pm
GW	Bigb	5 31 pm	5 45 pm
GW	Noss	5 55 pm	6 25 pm
NAT	New	6 10 pm	6 30 pm
NAT	New	6 30 pm	6 30 pm
NAT	Ivy	6 55 pm	7 0 pm
NAT	New	7 30 pm	7 17 pm
NAT	Ivy	7 40 pm	7 30 pm
GW	New	7 55 pm	7 55 pm
GW	King	8 30 pm	8 18 pm
NAT	New	8 55 pm	8 25 pm
NAT	New	9 0 pm	8 59 pm
GW	Noss	9 30 pm	9 19 pm
GW	Bigb (ThSO)	1010 pm	9 25 pm
NAT	New	11 0 pm	10 0 pm
NAT	New	1130 pm	1040 pm
GW	King (ThSO)	1131 pm	—

SUNDAYS.

Operator	Destination	Plymouth	Yealmpton
NAT	New	9 45 am	1015 am
NAT	Ivy	1015 am	1045 am
GW	Bigb	1045 am	1116 am
NAT	New	1115 am	1145 am
NAT	New	1130 am	12 1 pm
NAT	Ivy	1215 pm	1245 pm
GW	King	1230 pm	1 0 pm
NAT	New	1245 pm	1 15 pm
NAT	New	1 15 pm	1 45 pm
NAT	Ivy	1 45 pm	2 15 pm
NAT	New	2 15 pm	2 45 pm
NAT	New	2 45 pm	3 15 pm
NAT	New	3 30 pm	3 45 pm
GW	King	3 45 pm	4 0 pm
NAT	New	4 15 pm	4 45 pm
GW	New	4 45 pm	5 15 pm
GW	King	5 15 pm	5 45 pm
NAT	New	5 55 pm	6 25 pm
NAT	Ivy	6 30 pm	6 55 pm
NAT	New	6 55 pm	7 25 pm

Operator	Destination	Plymouth	Yealmpton
GW	Bigb	7 15 pm	7 46 pm
NAT	New	7 40 pm	8 10 pm
NAT	New	7 55 pm	8 25 pm
GW	King	8 30 pm	9 1 pm
NAT	New	9 30 pm	9 25 pm
NAT	King	10 0 pm	10 0 pm
NAT	New	1010 pm	1031 pm
NAT	New	11 0 pm	1040 pm
NAT	New	—	1130 pm

Great Western Road Motors started from Plymouth Millbay Station.
National Road Motors started from Plymouth St.Andrew's Church.

Both operators' services passed near Plymstock, Billacombe, Elburton Cross and Brixton Road Stations, and served Brixton and Yealmpton village centres. Steer Point was the only station without nearby road services.

NAT - National (previously Devon Motor Transport).   GW - Great Western Road Motor.   ThSO - Thursdays and Saturdays only.
New - Newton Ferrers.   King - Kingsbridge.   Ivy - Ivybridge.   Noss - Noss Mayo.   Bigb - Bigbury-on-Sea.   Yeal - Terminates at Yealmpton.

ENGINEERING AND OPERATING DATA

(a)   Pages 137 to 143 are reproduced from LSWR Instruction No. 16, 1898.

(b)   Pages 144 to 147 are reproduced from the Appendix to No. 6 Section of the Service Time Tables. GWR – April 1939.

(c)   Pages 149 to 151 are reproduced from the Alterations and Additions to the Appendix to No. 6 Section of the Service Time Tables, fifth supplement. GWR Instruction No. 2395, Plymouth, October 1941.

(d)   Pages 152 to 155 are reproduced from the District Traffic Managers & Divisional Engineers Instruction and Appendix No. 2528. GWR – Tuesday 27th November 1945.

(e)   Pages 156 to 157 are reproduced from the Alterations and Additions to the Appendix to No. 6 Section of the Service Time Tables, ninth supplement. GWR Instruction No. 2544, Plymouth, February 1946.

(f)   Pages 159 to 162 contain signal box diagrams of all stations on the Plymouth (Friary) to Yealmpton route of the 1941–1947 passenger era. They are not exclusively of this era, for signalling of this type was recovered from Plymstock to Yealmpton after the first closure to passengers in 1930. The signal box diagrams were specially prepared for this book by G. A. Pryer Esq. and L Crosier Esq. of the Historical Signalling Society.

(g)   Details of the Mount Gould Junction, Cattewater Junction and Plymstock signal boxes, and the signalling between Plymstock and Yealmpton, appear on pages 163 to 173.

Photographs of luggage labels and tickets appear on various pages throughout the book.

(Items (a) to (e) in this chapter are reproduced by kind permission of British Railways Board and, irrespective of dates, remain its exclusive copyright.)

LONDON & SOUTH WESTERN RAILWAY.

OPENING of a NEW SIGNAL BOX
AT
CATTEWATER JUNCTION,
WITH NEW AND ALTERED SIGNALS,
On THURSDAY, JANUARY 13th, 1898.
ALSO
OPENING of the SOUTH HAMS RAILWAY,
AND BRINGING INTO USE THE
NEW AND ALTERED SIGNALS
IN CONNECTION THEREWITH,
On SATURDAY, JANUARY 15th, 1898.

Instructions to District Superintendents, Station Masters,
Inspectors, Enginemen, Guards, Signalmen, and all others concerned.

STATION MASTERS are required personally to distribute this Notice to their Staff, and every person supplied with a copy is held responsible to read it carefully through, to note the general information it contains and to act up to and obey the instructions particularly applicable to himself. No excuse of want of knowledge of these Special Arrangements can be admitted for any failure or neglect of duty.

The South Hams Railway will be opened to the public on Monday, January 17th, when the Service of Trains contained in this Notice will commence, but Passenger Trains in connection with the opening ceremony will run over the Line on Saturday, 15th January.

The South Hams Railway runs out of the Eastern end of Plymstock Station and it will be worked by the Great Western Railway Company.

The Line is 6¼ miles in length from Plymstock to Yealmpton, and there will be Stations at Billacombe, Elburton, Brixton Road, Steer Point and Yealmpton.

The Line from Plymstock to Yealmpton will be worked under the Electric Train Staff System.

The Great Western Company's Trains to and from Yealmpton will run over a New Curve Line which the Great Western Company have constructed between Mount Gould Junction and Cattewater Junction, passing thence over this Company's Line between Cattewater Junction and Plymstock.

CATTEWATER JUNCTION.

A New Signal Box has been erected on the Up Line side at **Cattewater Junction**, and in preparation for the opening of the New Line this Box will be brought into use commencing Thursday, January 13th, and out-door Signals will be worked therefrom, as shown in the following list.

A **Three-armed bracket Signal** on the Down Line side, 640 yards from the Signal Box towards Friary, which will apply as shown on Diagram No. 1.

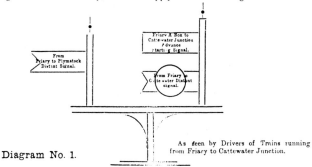

From Friary to Plymstock Distant Signal.

Friary A Box to Cattewater Junction Advance starting Signal.

From Friary to Cattewater Distant Signal.

As seen by Drivers of Trains running from Friary to Cattewater Junction.

Diagram No. 1.

CATTEWATER JUNCTION.
NEW AND ALTERED SIGNALS—*continued*.
To be brought into use on **Thursday, January 13th.**

A two-armed bracket Signal Post on the Down Line side, 180 yards the Friary side of the Cattewater Junction Signal Box. See Diagram No. 2.

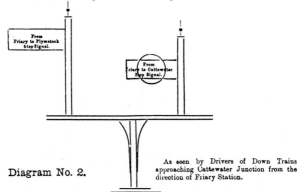

Diagram No. 2.

As seen by Drivers of Down Trains approaching Cattewater Junction from the direction of Friary Station.

The **Distant Signals** for trains to Plymstock and Cattewater from the Great Western Line are on the **Mount Gould Junction Starting Signal Post.** See Diagram No. 3.

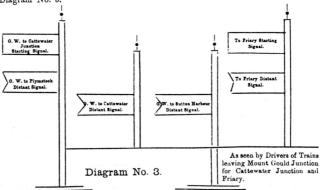

Diagram No. 3.

As seen by Drivers of Trains leaving Mount Gould Junction for Cattewater Junction and Friary.

A two-armed bracket Signal Post on the Great Western Line, 88 yards from Cattewater Junction Signal Box towards Mount Gould Junction will apply as shown on Diagram No. 4.

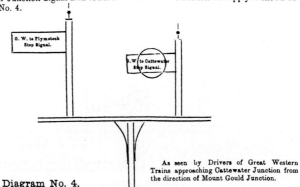

Diagram No. 4.

As seen by Drivers of Great Western Trains approaching Cattewater Junction from the direction of Mount Gould Junction.

CATTEWATER JUNCTION.
NEW AND ALTERED SIGNALS—*continued.*
To be brought into use on **Thursday, January 13th.**

A three-armed bracket Signal Post on the Plymstock Line, 285 yards from Cattewater Junction Signal Box, will apply as shown on Diagram No. 5.

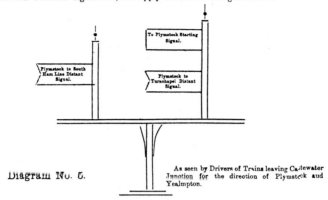

Diagram No. 5.

As seen by Drivers of Trains leaving Cattewater Junction for the direction of Plymstock and Yealmpton.

A two-armed Signal Post on the South Western Line, 197 yards from Cattewater Junction Signal Box towards Friary, will apply as shown on Diagram No. 6.

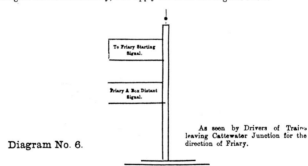

Diagram No. 6.

As seen by Drivers of Trains leaving Cattewater Junction for the direction of Friary.

A two-armed Signal on the Great Western Line, for Great Western Trains leaving Cattewater Junction in the direction of Mount Gould Junction, about 260 yards from Cattewater Junction Signal Box towards Mount Gould Junction, will apply as shown on Diagram No. 7.

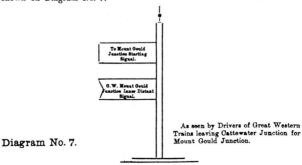

Diagram No. 7.

As seen by Drivers of Great Western Trains leaving Cattewater Junction for Mount Gould Junction.

CATTEWATER JUNCTION.
NEW AND ALTERED SIGNALS—*continued.*
To be brought into use on **Thursday, January 13th.**

A three-armed bracket Signal on the Cattewater Line, 128 yards from Cattewater Juncion Signal Box, will apply as shown on Diagram No. 8.

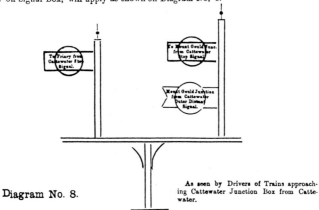

Diagram No. 8.

As seen by Drivers of Trains approaching Cattewater Junction Box from Cattewater.

A two-armed bracket Signal on the Cattewater Line, 150 yards from the Stop Signals, will apply as shown on Diagram No. 9.

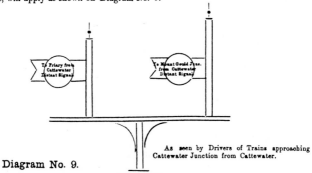

Diagram No. 9.

As seen by Drivers of Trains approaching Cattewater Junction from Cattewater.

A three-armed bracket Signal Post on the Plymstock Line, 190 yards from Cattewater Signal Box towards Plymstock, will apply as shown on Diagram No. 10.

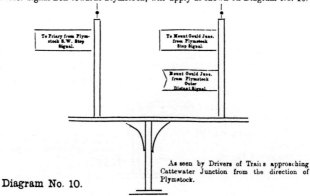

Diagram No. 10.

As seen by Drivers of Trains approaching Cattewater Junction from the direction of Plymstock.

CATTEWATER JUNCTION.
NEW AND ALTERED SIGNALS—*continued.*
To be brought into use on **Thursday, January 13th.**

A three-armed bracket Signal Post on the Plymstock Line, 573 yards from Cattewater Junction Stop Signals, and 289 yards the Cattewater Junction side of Plymstock Signal Box. See Diagram No. 11.

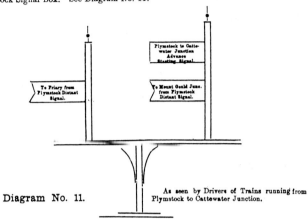

Plymstock to Cattewater Junction Advance Starting Signal.

To Friary from Plymstock Distant Signal.

To Mount Gould June. from Plymstock Distant Signal.

Diagram No. 11.

As seen by Drivers of Trains running from Plymstock to Cattewater Junction.

FRIARY "A" SIGNAL BOX.
The new **Distant Signal** for trains from Cattewater Junction is on the Cattewater Junction Starting Signal Post. See Diagram No. 6.

The new **Advance Starting Signal** for trains going towards Cattewater Junction is on the Cattewater Junction Distant Post. See Diagram No. 1.

SIGNALS TO BE REMOVED.
The existing Advance Starting Signal to Plymstock and Cattewater.

The existing Distant Signal from Plymstock and Cattewater.

PLYMSTOCK STATION.
New and **Altered Signals.** To be brought into use on **Thursday, January 13th.**

A **Starting Signal** has been provided at the Yealmpton end of the platform for trains going to Yealmpton.

The **Facing Points** at the Yealmpton end of the Station have been moved to a point about 60 feet nearer Yealmpton.

A **Stop Signal** has been provided for Up Yealmpton Trains about 135 yards from the Signal Box, and close to the above mentioned facing Points.

A **Distant Signal** has been provided for Up Yealmpton Line Trains about 900 yards from the Up Stop Signal.

The new **Up Advance Starting Signal** is on the Cattewater Junction Distant Signal Post. See Diagram No. 11.

The **Down Distant Signals** are on the Cattewater Junction Starting Post. See Diagram No. 5.

SIGNALS TO BE REMOVED.
The existing Up Advance Starting Signal.

The existing Down Distant Signals.

In connection with the opening of the South Hams Railway, the Train Staff and Ticket arrangements between Friary " A " Box and Plymstock will be abolished, and the Line between **Friary " A "** Box and **Plymstock** will be worked under **Tyers** (New) **Train Tablet System** as described in Instruction No. 17, 1898.

This Tablet Instruction will be supplied to all concerned, including Enginemen and Guards, and must be exhibited in the Station Master's Offices at Friary and Plymstock, also in Friary " A," Cattewater Junction and Plymstock Signal Boxes.

The **Train Tablet sections** will be as follows :

Friary " A " Box and **Cattewater Junction.**
Cattewater Junction and **Plymstock.**

Instructions as to Single Line Working by a Pilotman on Lines during the failure or breakdown of Tablet System :—

The working of the Traffic on Single Lines during a failure or breakdown of the Tablet Instruments, **when the Telegraph Speaking Instruments are not affected, must be by means of a Pilotman,** which is the only method sanctioned by the Board of Trade.

In order to minimise the delay to traffic, which must almost necessarily follow a breakdown, the method of establishing Pilot-working when only the Tablet Apparatus has failed will be different (with certain exceptions) to that when both the Tablet Apparatus and the Telegraph Speaking Instruments also have failed, according to the following particulars.

For example, assume that a Tablet cannot be obtained for a Down Train to proceed from Cattewater Junction to Plymstock.

FAILURE OF TABLET INSTRUMENT ONLY.

The Signalman at Cattewater Junction to immediately telegraph to the Station Master at Plymstock advising him of the failure and requesting him to establish Pilot-working for the Down Train, by filling in the necessary Pilot-working forms and sending a Pilotman as quickly as possible along the line (to ascertain that the section is clear) to Cattewater Junction.

FAILURE OF TABLET AND SPEAKING INSTRUMENTS.

The working must be in accordance with the following, viz. :—

The Station Master at Plymstock (having an Up Train to proceed to Cattewater Junction and being unable to obtain a Tablet) would fill in the requisite forms for Pilot-working and must himself proceed (or send a duly appointed Pilotman) to Cattewater Junction, and having left the necessary forms at the Signal Box there and ascertained that the Section is clear, return as quickly as possible to Plymstock Station for the Up Train.

Should it be expected that a Down Train would be due to leave Cattewater Junction during the interval that the Up Train would be detained at Plymstock, and which would enable the Pilotman to reach Plymstock sooner than by walking the distance or by conveyance, it would be his duty to wait and Pilot the Down Train.

These instructions apply to any two Tablet Stations and it is thus evident that the responsibility for safe working rests entirely with the Station Masters without communicating with a Crossing Agent, which cancels previous orders as to Crossing Agents on the Friary and Plymstock Line.

The Lineman for the Train Tablet Stations, Friary " A " Box to Plymstock inclusive, whose name is Woollacott, lives at Tavistock, and upon any irregularity or failure of the instruments occurring he must be communicated with immediately. In addition to the Lineman at Tavistock being advised, a wire must also be sent to **Mr. Watkins, Exeter,** and to **Mr. Vallance, Exeter,** giving particulars of the irregularity or failure, but the first care must be to secure the attendance of the resident Lineman, who must always leave word with the Station Master at Tavistock where he is to be found.

FRIARY " A " BOX AND CATTEWATER JUNCTION.

All Trains **must** slacken at Friary " A " Box and Cattewater Junction to receive or deliver up the **Train Tablet.**

CATTEWATER BRANCH.

On and after Thursday, January 13th, 1898, the Cattewater Branch will be worked under the **Absolute Train Staff System.** For full particulars see Instruction No. 15, 1898.

Commencing on **Monday, January 17th, 1898,** the Great Western Company's service of trains between Plymouth and Yealmpton will be as follows:—

STATIONS.	1 Passenger.		2 Goods.		3 Passenger.		4 Passenger.		5 Passenger.	
	arr. a.m.	dep. a.m.	arr. a.m.	dep. a,m.	arr. a.m.	dep. a.m.	arr. p.m.	dep. p.m.	arr. p.m.	dep. p.m.
Plymouth (Millbay)	...	6 55	...	...	...	9 45	...	1 5	...	6 0
Plymouth (North Road)	6 58	7 0	...	...	9 48	9 50	1 8	1 10	6 3	6 5
Mutley	7 1	7 3	...	...	9 51	9 53	1 11	1 13	6 6	6 8
Laira Junction	...	...	...	8 30	...	...	...	...	...	...
Cattewater Junction	7	9	8 33		9 59		1 19		6 14	
Plymstock	7 11	7 13	8 35	8 50	10 1	10 3	1 11	1 18	6 16	6 19
Billacombe	7 16	7 18	8 55	9 2	10 6	10 8	1 26	1 28	6 21	6 23
Elburton	CR	7 23	...	...	CR	10 13	CR	1 33	...	...
Brixton Road	7 25	7 27	9 10	9 25	10 15	10 17	1 35	1 37	6 30	6 32
Sheer Point	7 30	7 32	9 30	9 40	10 20	10 22	1 40	1 42	6 35	6 37
Yealmpton	7 38	...	9 50	...	10 28	...	1 48	...	6 43	...

STATIONS.	1 Passenger.		2 Passenger.		3 Goods.		4 Passenger.		5 Passenger.	
	arr. a.m.	dep. a.m.	arr. a.m.	dep. a.m.	arr. a.m.	dep. a.m.	arr. p.m.	dep. p.m.	ar. p.m.	dep. p.m.
Yealmpton	...	7 50	...	10 55	...	11 25	...	2 30	...	7 5
Steer Point	7 56	7 58	11 1	11 3	11 35	11 45	2 36	2 38	7 11	7 13
Brixton Road	8 1	8 3	11 6	11 8	11 50	12 5	2 41	2 43	7 16	7 18
Elburton	CR	8 7	CR	11 12	...	...	CR	2 47	...	...
Billacombe	8 9	8 11	11 14	11 16	12 15	12 25	2 49	2 51	7 24	7 26
Plymstock	8 14	8 16	11 19	11 21	12 30	12 45	2 54	2 56	7 29	7 31
Cattewater Junction	8	18	11	23	12	47	2	58	7	33
Laira Junction	...	...	...	...	12 50	...	...	...	...	...
Mutley	8 24	8 26	11 29	11 31	...	...	3 4	3 6	7 39	7 41
Plymouth (North Road)	8 27	8 30	11 32	11 35	...	...	3 7	3 10	7 42	7 45
Plymouth (Millbay)	8 35	...	11 40	...	...	...	3 15	...	7 50	...

CR—Calls at Elburton when required.

Page 124 of the Main Line Service Book, so far as it relates to the Friary, Cattewater, Plymstock and Turnchapel Branches, will be re-issued for the opening of the South Hams Railway.

The **District Inspector** to report to me, through the District Superintendent, on the working of the New and Altered Signals.

GEO. T. WHITE,
Superintendent of the Line.
(2,000.)

WATERLOO STATION,
January 11th, 1898.
(A. 18,048.) (3/22099.)

Waterlow and Sons Limited, Printers, London Wall, London.

YEALMPTON BRANCH.
Mount Gould Junction—Working Tram Wagons over the Dartmoor Tramway.

1. The Dartmoor Tramway passes across the Yealmpton Branch at the junction of the latter with the Sutton Harbour Branch, and Safety Apparatus has been provided to ensure that no obstruction from Tram Wagons shall affect Yealmpton Branch Trains. This has been fixed at the junction of the Yealmpton Branch, and in the Mount Gould Signal Box ; and the Signalman there has control over the arrangement.

The appliances are as follows :—

2. Locking Frame Lever, No. 12.—This lever, when drawn from the back to the front position of the Locking Frame, locks all signals leading to or from the Yealmpton Branch, and at the same time is locked itself by the electric lock, and closes two Throw-off points on the Sutton Harbour side, and two on the Laira side of the Yealmpton Branch line.

3. Electric Lock Box.—Immediately behind No. 12 lever, and secured to the floor, is an iron box containing the electric lock. The cover of this Box is padlocked, and the key of the padlock is held by the District Lineman. At the top of this box is the Emergency Lever.

4. Emergency Lever.—This is a small brass lever, standing when in its normal position at an angle of about 45 degrees to the top of the box and padlocked, the Signalman holding the key of the padlock.

When necessary, the Signalman can release this padlock and move the lever to the vertical position and padlock it there, this movement having the effect of switching the electric lock, and consequently the Safety Apparatus out of use.

The key of this padlock must be kept in a place of security where each Signalman in turn can obtain it when wanted.

5. Electric Lock Indicator.—This is placed on a shelf behind No. 12 lever, and its use is to indicate to the Signalman when the electric lock is on or off.

The instrument shows three indications, one at a time, as follows :—

"Lock on"	"Wrong"	"Lock off"
(Red disc)	(Black disc)	(White disc)

When No. 12 lever is in the forward position, the red disc shews
"Lock on."

When No. 12 lever is in the back position, the white disc should shew
"Lock off."

which is the normal indication when the Safety Apparatus is not in use.

Should anything be wrong with the apparatus within the "Electric Lock Box," or the batteries relating thereto, the black disc showing
"Wrong"

will be visible, and the Signalman will then know that the instrument is out of order, and requires attention. If the difficulty be one the Signalman cannot rectify, he must send for the Lineman.

6. Foot Plunger.—In front of No. 12 lever, and projecting only slightly above the floor level is the brass top of the foot plunger, the object of which is to enable the Signalman, by placing his foot upon it, to release the electric Lock from No. 12 lever, so that at the proper moment, which will be described hereafter, he may move that lever from the front to the back position.

7. Fouling Bars and Contact Boxes.—Between the two Throw-off points on the Sutton Harbour side, and the two on the Laira side of the Yealmpton Branch, flat bars of iron, counterweighted, are placed close to, and parallel with, one rail of the Tramway.

These flat bars are continuous, but made in several sections, and each section is coupled to a "Contact Box" placed by the side of the Tramway.

8. The mode of procedure for passing Tram Wagons and using the Safety Apparatus, is as follows :—

When a train of Tram Wagons is being horsed from Prince Rock to Lee Moor, or from Lee Moor to Prince Rock, the Signalman at Mount Gould Junction Box, must, before giving the Driver permission to cross the Yealmpton Branch line, draw over No. 12 lever to the forward position. This will have the effect of locking all the points and signals leading to or from the Yealmpton Branch line, and at the same time the lever is itself automatically locked, and closes the four Throw-off points before referred to, so that the Tramway may be continuous for the Tram Wagons to pass.

As soon as one of the wheel tyres of the first Tram Wagon, and of the succeeding ones, touches the flat iron bar referred to, the bar will be depressed, and will cause the electric circuit to be broken in the first of the contact boxes referred to.

As the Tram Wagons proceed over each succeeding Section of the iron bar arrangement, the contact becomes broken in like manner in the contact box relating to each of the several sections.

Breaking contact in this way causes the electric lock in the Signal Cabin to remain locking No. 12 lever to the forward position until the rear Tram Wagon has passed over the last flat bar of the series, and is clear of the Junction, when the Signalman must place his foot on the foot plunger, which will release the electric lock, and cause "Lock-off" to appear on the electric lock indicator. He can then move No. 12 lever to the back of the frame, thereby placing the four Throw-off points in the Tramway line to the open position, and unlocking the signals and points relating to the Yealmpton Branch. The Signalman must not move No. 12 lever from the forward position until he sees "Lock-off" on the indicator.

The primary object of the apparatus described is that so long as a wheel tyre of any Tram Wagon is touching either of the fouling bars referred to, and consequently fouling the Branch line, the Signalman is prevented from working the signals or the points for a train to pass to or from the Yealmpton Branch.

9. The emergency lever referred to in Clause 4, is provided in case any of the appliances should fail, and so interrupt the working of the Branch.

This, however, is a rare contingency, but if it should happen, the Signalman must unlock the padlock, place the lever in the vertical position, and padlock it there. He must also, at once, advise the Lineman.

This will switch out the electric lock, and the Signalman will have to work without the security of the Safety Apparatus.

He must then take particular care in working the trains of Tram Wagons to satisfy himself by observation that the Yealmpton Branch line is clear of obstruction before allowing any train to or from Yealmpton to approach the Junction.

When at any time the Signalman finds the electric locking apparatus defective, he must, if it be broad daylight, at once satisfy himself by observation from the Signal Box that there is no obstruction on the Yealmpton Branch line as would arise from a Tram Wagon having been accidentally left, fouling the line.

If it be not broad daylight, or the atmospheric conditions prevent a clear view from the Signal Box of the two sets of Throw-off points in the Tramway, he must at once leave his Box and walk to the place referred to and not return until he has satisfied himself by inspection that there is no obstruction.

Under no circumstances must the "Emergency lever" be brought into use until the Signalman first personally satisfies himself that the line at the Junction with the Yealmpton Branch is clear.

Occupation of the Yealmpton Branch by Permanent Way Department.

The Motor Trolley System of Maintenance is in operation on this Branch, and the instructions on page 69 of the General Appendix as far as they apply, must be observed. The Home Station of the gang is Yealmpton. Telephones are fixed as under :—

	Miles.	Chains.		Miles.	Chains.
Plymstock Station	—	—	Hut No. 2	3	32
Hut No. 1	—	38	Steer Point	4	7
Billacombe	1	0	Hut No. 3	4	79
Elburton Cross	2	0	,, ,, 4	5	59
Brixton Road	2	55	Yealmpton	6	34

The telephone code calls are as follows :—

Plymstock, 3-2 ; Yealmpton 4.

1. The Ganger examines the length three times weekly, i.e., on Mondays, Wednesdays, and Fridays, using the inspection car for the purpose.

2. The Engineering Department have absolute occupation of the line between Plymstock and Yealmpton from 12.30 p.m. after the arrival of the Freight train at Plymstock on the return journey from Yealmpton, until shortly before the Freight train is due to leave Plymstock for Yealmpton the following morning. If any work is taken in hand during that interval and it cannot be completed, or the car is on the line, and will not be removed shortly before the Freight train is due to leave Plymstock for Yealmpton, the Ganger must act in accordance with Rules 215 and 217, of the Book of Rules and Regulations, and also telephone to Plymstock Signal Box. In such a case the train must be detained at Plymstock Station until the Ganger advises the Signalman, by telephone or otherwise, that the line is clear.

3. No special train must be run during the time the Engineers have absolute occupation between the hours mentioned in Clause 2, unless written notice has been previously given to the Ganger, and his receipt held by the Plymstock Signalman for it. If it should be necessary to run a special train over the Branch without notice, between the hours of 12.30 p.m. and 9.50 a.m., Plymstock and Yealmpton must be advised by telephone, and an acknowledgment received before the special is run.

MOUNT GOULD JUNCTION.

Instructions for Working Engines and Freight Trains from Friary, and from Sutton Harbour to Laira Yard, and vice versa.

1. Immediately any engine or train leaves Friary or Sutton Harbour for Laira Yard, a message must be sent on the telephone from Sutton Harbour, or from Friary, as the case may be, to Friary Junction, Mount Gould Junction and the Laira Inspector. On arrival at Mount Gould, the engine or train, as the case may be, must stop dead at the signal governing the Facing points leading to the Yard.

2. The Shunter at Laira must meet all engines and trains going into the Yard, and he is responsible for their safe entry to the Yard, and also for the engines or trains leaving the Yard for Friary or Sutton Harbour. He is likewise responsible for seeing that no engines or vehicles are standing at or approaching the Mount Gould end of the Yard, that will interfere with any shunting operations that may be necessary to enable the engine or train to enter or leave the Yard.

3. The Signalman at Mount Gould Junction, on receipt of the advice referred to in Clause 1, must inform the Shunter the time the train left, and it will be the duty of the Shunter to be present at the entrance to the Yard, and not keep the engine or train waiting.

4. Any engine or train running via Lipson Junction going to Laira Yard over No. 1 curve, must be met at the entrance to the Yard by the Shunter, as provided for in Clause 2.

DISTANT SIGNALS WHICH STAND AT CAUTION WHEN THE SIGNAL BOXES ARE SWITCHED OUT OF CIRCUIT.

Station or Signal Box.	Signal.	Station or Signal Box.	Signal.
Mount Gould Junction	All Distant Signals.	St. Budeaux West	Down Distant.
Friary Junction	Up Distant (S.R.)	Penwithers Junction	Up Distant.
Mannamead	Down Distant.	Carn Brea	Up Distant.
Devonport	Up Distant.	North Crofty	Up Distant.
Trenance Junction	Up, Outer and Inner Distants.	Gwinear Road East	*Down Distant.

* Slotted with West Box.

Runaway Loose Catch Points—continued.

Between what Stations.		Up or Down Lines	Where situated.	If connected with and worked from the Signal Box.	Gradient 1 in	Signal Box when Lever Clip and Padlock are kept.	REMARKS.
From	To						
			—Yealmpton Branch.				
Mount Gould Junction	Lipson Junction.	Up	294 yards Mount Gould side of Lipson Junction Up Home Signal.	No	81	Mount Gould Junction.	Only one engine in steam or two coupled together allowed on this Section.
"	Cattewater Junction	Down to Yealmpton	486 yards Mount Gould side of Cattewater Junction Down Home Signal.	No	66	"	

WORKING OF SINGLE LINES.

FROM	TO	Where Electric Train Token or Train Staff and Tickets are kept.	Description of Staff, etc.		Persons at Station or Junction responsible for exchanging Token or Ticket when on duty.	Person responsible when aforesaid man is not on duty.
			Colour.	Shape.		
Cattewater Junction ..	Plymstock ..	Signal Box, Cattewater Junction	—	Electric Tablet S.R.	S.R. Signalman	..
Plymstock ..	Yealmpton ..	Plymstock Booking Office	Black	Square	..	..

GROUND FRAMES AND INTERMEDIATE SIDINGS.

Name of Station or Siding.	Where Situated.	By whom Attended.	How Locked.
Plymstock	West end of Station ..	Guard of Train ..	Key on T.S.
Billacombe	One each end of Station ..	" " " ..	" "
Brixton Road	At Station	" " ..	" "
Steer Point	" "	" " ..	" "
Yealmpton	" "	" " ..	" "

WHISTLING AT LEVEL CROSSINGS.

Drivers of all trains must sound their whistles when approaching the following places :—

Where Whistles **must** be sounded.	Position, and whether Whistle Boards provided.
Yealmpton Branch.	
When passing 6 m.p.	Between Elburton Cross and Brixton Road.
When leaving Yealmpton Station ..	
When Up trains pass through Cutting	6¼ m.p.

Instructions and Restrictions—*continued.*

Station.	Line over which 70 foot stock must not pass.	Lines over which 70 foot stock must pass with caution.
	Yealmpton Branch.	
Billacombe	Loading Bank Sidings.	
Steer Point	All Sidings.	
Yealmpton	Crane and Outer Mileage Sidings.	Crossover from Loop to Branch.

Inclines steeper than 1 in 200—*continued.*

Incline situated between	Length of Incline.	Gradient one foot in	Falling towards	Places at which Notice Boards have been fixed and at which trains must stop to put down brakes.	Modifications of or additions to the Standard Instructions for working Inclines.
			Yealm	pton Branch.	
Lipson Junction and Mount Gould Junction	¼ m.	73 and 81	Mount Gould Junction		
Mount Gould Junction and Cattewater Junction	12 ch.	66	Mount Gould Junction		
Plymstock and Elburton Cross	2 m.	90 / 68	Cattewater Junction / Plymstock		
Elburton Cross and Steer Point	2 m.	60	Steer Point		
Steer Point and Yealmpton	2¼ m.	60 for 35 chains	Steer Point		

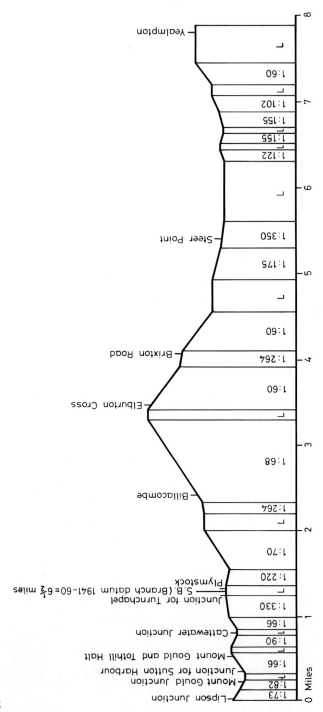

The Plymouth to Yealmpton Railway (Gradient Chart)

Page 4

GROUND FRAMES AND INTERMEDIATE SIDINGS
Amend as follows :

Name of Station or Siding	Where situated	By whom Attended	How locked
Billacombe	West end of Station	Guard ..	E.T. Token Key
Brixton Road ..	One each end of Station	Guard ..	E.T. Token Key
Steer Point ..	One each end of Loop	Guard ..	E.T. Token Key
Yealmpton	On Platform	Signalman ..	Operated by Signalman
Yealmpton	One each end of Station	Signalman or Guard	E.T. Token Key
Delete			
Plymstock	At Station	Guard ..	E.T. Token Key

Page 7

WORKING OF SINGLE LINES
Entry re Yealmpton Branch to be altered to read :

From	To	Description of Staff, etc. Colour	Shape	Where Electric Train Token or Train Staff and Tickets are kept	Persons at stations or Junction responsible for exchanging Token or Ticket when on duty	Person responsible when aforesaid man is not on duty	Remarks
Plymstock	Yealmpton	—	Electric Token	Signal Box—Plymstock Goods Office Yealmpton	Signalman Signalman	— —	An Intermediate Token Instrument is provided at Brixton Road. See page 79. To be worked by 64xx (0-6-0) class engine and two trailers. See page 49.
Add : Cattewater Junction	Friary "A" Box	—	Electric Tablet S.R.	Signal Box Friary "A"	S.R. Signalman	—	Exchange of the S. Rly. Electric Tablet is made by hand at Plymstock Station, Cattewater Junction and Friary "A" Signal Boxes.

Page 49

RESTRICTIONS ON WORKING OF COACHING STOCK OVER CERTAIN BRANCH LINES
Add :

Branch	Restriction
Yealmpton	70-feet trailers fitted with centre folding steps must not be worked in this service nor must 70-feet trailers be shunted into the sidings at Friary.

Page 50

HALTS AT WHICH STAFF IS NOT KEPT
Add :

Name of Halt	Station Supervising Halt
Mary Tavy	Tavistock
Steer Point	Yealmpton
Brixton Road	Yealmpton
Elburton Cross	Yealmpton
Billacombe	Yealmpton (for Traffic Dept. purposes)

149

PAGE 79

YEALMPTON BRANCH.
Occupation by Permanent Way Department.

To be amended as shewn:

1. The instructions on pages 65–68 of the General Appendix apply. The Home Station of the Ganger is Yealmpton. Telephone and Key Boxes are fixed as under:

One Key.

	m.	c.
Plymstock Signal Box	0	0
Hut No. 1		19
„ „ 2	1	0
„ „ 3	1	69
„ „ 4	2	55
„ „ 5	3	32
„ „ 6	4	7
„ „ 7	4	79
„ „ 8	5	59
Yealmpton	6	33

Note.—The telephones communicate with the Signalmen at Plymstock Signal Box and Yealmpton.

2. It will only be possible for the Ganger to obtain occupation of the Branch under these instructions when the Branch is open. If occupation is required at any other times, Handsignalmen must be sent out in accordance with Rules 215 and 217.

3. Notice No. 2215 (Introduction of Motor Economic System of Maintenance—Yealmpton Branch) dated October 5th, 1931, is hereby cancelled.

PAGE 79

PLYMSTOCK.

When Trains from Yealmpton are accepted by Plymstock under the "Warning" Signal (3-5-5), such trains must be brought to a stand at the Up Home Signal before being admitted to the station in accordance with the special instructions issued to the Signalman at Plymstock.

BILLACOMBE.

The Ground Frame is released by means of the E.T.T. Key and Electric Train Token Block Regulation 34 applies.

BRIXTON ROAD.
Intermediate Train Token Instrument.

1. An Intermediate Token Instrument is provided at the Yealmpton end of Brixton Road Platform and should it be necessary for an engine or engine and vehicles to be crossed to the Loop or put into a siding to permit another train to enter the Section, a complete understanding must be arrived at with the Plymstock Signalman by means of the telephone provided, and after the engine or engine and vehicles have been placed in clear of the catch point, and the points replaced to normal, the Token must be inserted in the Intermediate Token Instrument by the Guard, who must advise the Plymstock Signalman on the telephone that he has restored the Token, and give him an assurance that the Line is clear. The Plymstock Signalman will then advise the Yealmpton Signalman and send the "cancelling" signal to Yealmpton in the case of Down trains. For Up trains the Yealmpton Signalman must send the "cancelling" signal to Plymstock on receipt of the advice from the Plymstock Signalman that the engine or engine and vehicles are in clear of the main line and the Main Line is clear.

When the time arrives for the engine or engine and vehicles to leave for Yealmpton or Plymstock the Guard must communicate with the Plymstock Signalman on the telephone, and the Signalman there will telephone the Yealmpton Signalman, and if it is agreed that the engine or engine and vehicles may leave Brixton Road, the Signalman at Yealmpton or Plymstock, as the case may be, must ask "Is Line Clear?" and when this has been accepted the Plymstock Signalman must so inform the Guard. The Guard must then lift the Token from the column to the centre opening of the instrument, press the Token forward, as if using an ordinary key in a lock (the key end of the Token must engage on the centre pin of the instrument), then turn the Token from right to left as far as possible. The Guard must then wait until both indicators operate, this being done by both Signalmen holding down on their respective Token ringing keys, and afterward continue to turn the Token from right to left until the Token is free, when it can be withdrawn from the Instrument. A bell will ring in the Intermediate Token Instrument to indicate that the Token can be withdrawn. He must then inform the Signalman that the Token has been withdrawn, and lock the hut door with the Token. The Ground Frame may then be operated, and after the engine or engine and vehicles has drawn clear on to the Main Line the points must be re-set to normal, and the Token handed to the Driver for the engine or engine and vehicles to proceed.

In the event of a Pilotman being appointed owing to failure of apparatus, the Pilotman when distributing the Pilot Working Forms must satisfy himself that all points are locked in the normal position, and if an engine or train is in a siding or in the Loop at Brixton Road at the time, see that the Token is properly locked in the Intermediate Instrument. If, however, the Pilotman is able to withdraw the Token from the Intermediate Token Instrument, this must be done and the Token retained by the Pilotman until normal working is resumed.

A Token can be placed in the Intermediate Instrument at any time, but one can only be withdrawn by co-operation between the Plymstock and Yealmpton Signalman.

2. The line is on a falling gradient towards Steer Point and the Instructions on Page 157 of the General Appendix re "Shunting on Inclines" will apply.

STEER POINT.

The Ground Frames are released by means of the E.T.T. Key and Electric Train Token Block Regulation 34 applies.

YEALMPTON.

PAGE 79

Add:

1. A "Stop" Lamp has been provided at the "Dead End" end of the platform and loaded Passenger Trains must not under any circumstances proceed beyond that point.

2. The position occupied by the "Stop Lamp" must be regarded as the authorised "clearing point."

3. After "Line Clear" has been given for a Passenger Train no movement must be made with an engine or engine and vehicles in the loop or which would foul the Branch Line in advance of the clearing point until the Passenger train has left Yealmpton on its return journey to Plymouth.

4. The E.T.T. Key releases the ground frames situated at each end of the station. The two-lever ground frame on the platform operates the Down Home signal and the Up Starting signal and must be operated only by the Yealmpton Signalman. The Electric Train Token Instrument is fixed in the Goods Office.

5. The line is on a falling gradient towards Steer Point and the instructions on page 157 of the General Appendix re "Shunting on Inclines" will apply. No shunting movement must be made beyond the Starting signal.

6. Use of the loop can be made, if necessary, for empty passenger trains.

7. Catchpoints at the "dead-end" end of the platform are trailing and before an engine is allowed to proceed beyond the "stop lamp" for the purpose of taking water at the water column the Signalman must take the Token Key from the Engineman and close the catch points, and when this is done give the Driver a hand signal to proceed past the "stop lamp" for the purpose of taking water.

WORKING OF PASSENGER TRAINS.

The Passenger services on this Branch are worked without Guards, but a Woman Porter will be provided to issue tickets to Passengers joining at Lucas Terrace Halt, Billacombe, Elburton Cross, Brixton Road, and Steer Point, and also to collect tickets from Passengers alighting at those places, but will not act in the same capacity as a Guard so far as Guard's duties are concerned regarding the protection of the train (as provided for in Electric Train Token Regulations 14, 14B, 14C or Rule 179) and the following instructions will apply :

1. As a general principle the service will be worked by an Auto engine of the 64XX (0-6-0) class and two trailers, but trailers fitted with centre folding steps must not be used in this service.

2. The Woman Porter will be responsible for seeing that all doors are secured when leaving Lucas Terrace Halt, Billacombe, Elburton Cross, Brixton Road and Steer Point.

3. If more than three trailers are used at any time a Guard must be provided.

4. Auto trains working on this Branch without Guards must not convey more than one four-wheeled vehicle as tail traffic unless a Guard is provided and such vehicles must, in all cases, be vacuum fitted and connected. The Station Master or person in charge must see that such vehicles are properly attached or detached by the Shunter or Porter, and that the tail lamp is transferred to the proper position in each case.

5. In the event of the engine becoming disabled in the section, and the application of Electric Train Token Regulation 14 becoming necessary, the Fireman, before proceeding to the nearest Token Station for assistance must protect the train in the opposite direction by putting down three detonators, 10 yards apart, at least 300 yards from the train.

6. Special attention is directed to the instructions on page 132 of the General Appendix re "Working Auto Trains on Branch Lines without Guards."

7. Tail traffic must not be detached at any of the stations between Plymstock and Yealmpton.

WORKING OF TRAINS BETWEEN PLYMSTOCK AND FRIARY.

There is a permanent speed restriction of 15 m.p.h. when crossing from one line to another or when entering or leaving Loop or Slow lines, Platform or Bay lines.

WORKING OF FREIGHT TRAINS.

Up and Down Freight Trains must be dealt with under E.T.T. Regulation 8.

J. H. PARKER,
Plymouth, October 1941.   809—4300   **District Traffic Manager.**

- -

Received District Traffic Manager's Instruction No. 2395 re 5th Supplement to the Appendix to No. 6 Section of the Service Time Table.

Date.................... Station.................... Signature..................

GREAT WESTERN RAILWAY

(For the use of the Company's Employees only)

PLYMOUTH DISTRICT

YEALMPTON BRANCH

Blasting at Messrs. F. J. Moore Ltd.'s New Quarry

Motor Trolley System of Maintenance— Re-arrangement of and Revised Occupation Key Control System

TUESDAY, NOVEMBER 27th, 1945.

The section Plymstock—Yealmpton will be divided into two groups each group being provided with one key, as follows:

Group No. 1 (One Key)	M.	C.	Group No. 2 (One Key)	M.	C.
Plymstock Signal Box	o	o	Hut No. 3	1	30
Hut No. 1		19	Hut No. 4	2	55
Hut No. 2	1	o	Hut No. 5	3	32
Hut No. 3	1	30*	Hut No. 6	4	7
			Hut No. 7	4	79
			Hut No. 8	5	59
			Yealmpton	6	33

*—This Hut has been moved from 1m. 69c.

The Occupation Control Instrument at Yealmpton will be taken out of use.

Occupation Key Release Instruments controlling the revised groups as shewn above will be provided at Plymstock Signal Box. These Key Release instruments will be of a new type fitted with a commutator handle and involve a modification of paragraphs (b) and (e) of Clause 7 of the instructions appearing on page 66 of the General Appendix to the Rule Book under heading "Instructions in connection with motor trolley system of maintenance on single lines." The modified instructions are shewn in the Appendix to this Instruction.

Telephonic communication will be provided between Messrs. F. J. Moore Ltd.'s office at the site of the new Quarry and No. 3 Occupation Key Hut.

The Occupation Keys will not be available for use on November 27th, 1945.

The District Inspector must be prepared to arrange working by Pilotman if necessary in accordance with E.T.T. Regulation 25.

This work will be carried out on **Tuesday, November 27th, 1945**, between the hours of 9.0 a.m. and 4.0 p.m., or until the work is completed, and all arrangements for safe working must be made by the District Inspector.

BLASTING AT MESSRS. F. J. MOORE LTD.'s QUARRY.

The above-mentioned firm is opening a new Quarry in land situated on the Down side of the line between 1m. 0c. and 1m. 26c., between Billacombe and Elburton Cross. Excavations will commence on land situated approximately 25 yards from the line at 1m. 25c.

Commencing on **Wednesday, November 28th, 1945,** blasting may take place between the following agreed times:

> 10.0 a.m. to 10.30 a.m. (Mondays to Saturdays inclusive).
> 3.55 p.m. to 4.25 p.m. (Mondays to Fridays inclusive).

To enable the Engineering Department to obtain occupation of the major portion of the Branch simultaneously with the blasting operations, the Occupation Key System has been re-arranged as shewn above.

The particulars shewn on page 79 of the Appendix to the No. 6 Section of the Service Time Tables are hereby amended accordingly.

Telephonic communication is provided between Messrs. F. J. Moore Ltd.'s office at the site of the new Quarry and No. 3 Occupation Key Hut.

The following instructions must be observed by all concerned:

1. The Permanent Way Length Ganger must arrange for the Occupation Key for group No. 1 to be in No. 3 Key Box before the times shewn above, on the days specified above. He must also arrange for a Lengthman acquainted with these instructions to be in attendance at No. 3 Occupation Key Box by these times.

2. The Quarry Foreman in charge of the blasting operations will telephone the Lengthman at No. 3 Hut asking permission to blast, the following words being used:

"May blasting commence?"

3. Before giving the Quarry Foreman permission to blast, the Lengthman must place a red flag on each post situated 100 yards on each side of 1m. 25c. He must then telephone the Plymstock Signalman and obtain permission to withdraw the Occupation Key for Group No. 1 in accordance with the instructions on pages 65—68 of the General Appendix to the Rule Book, as modified in the Appendix to this Instruction, and if occupation can be granted and the Lengthman has withdrawn the Occupation Key, he must telephone the Quarry Foreman and give permission for blasting to take place, the message to be given being:

"Yes, you may blast."

In the event of the Signalman at Plymstock not being in a position to grant the occupation the Lengthman must immediately advise the Quarry Foreman, the message being "No" on the telephone and the red flags must be removed from each of the posts.

4. Immediately the Quarry Foreman is satisfied that all the charges have been detonated, he must telephone the Lengthman and give him an assurance that all charges have been exploded, the following words being used:

"Blasting completed, all charges exploded."

The Lengthman must then examine the line and satisfy himself that it is not obstructed and is safe for the passage of trains. If so, he must remove the red flag from each of the posts and replace the Occupation Key in the Key Box at No. 3 Hut, in accordance with the instructions on pages 65—68 of the General Appendix to the Rule Book, as modified in the Appendix to this Instruction.

In the event of the line having been damaged or obstructed, the Lengthman must not remove the red flags or restore the Occupation Key until the line is clear and safe for the passage of trains. He must advise the Plymstock and Yealmpton Signalmen of the position and take all necessary steps to have the line repaired or cleared of any obstruction with the utmost promptitude.

5. The Station Master or person in charge at Plymstock must advise the Permanent Way Length Ganger and Messrs. F. J. Moore Ltd., in the event of any special trains being arranged at short notice which would interfere with the intervals agreed upon for blasting.

6. Permission must not be given to blast during fog or falling snow.

ALL CONCERNED TO NOTE AND ACKNOWLEDGE RECEIPT.

E. LAKE,   **J. S. P. PEARSON.**
    Divisional Engineer.   **District Traffic Manager.**

Plymouth.
    November 20th, 1945.   810—500

- -

Received District Traffic Manager's and Divisional Engineer's Instruction No. 2528 *re* Yealmpton Branch—Blasting Operations.

Date........................ Station............................. Signature........................

Supplement to Instructions as shewn on page 66 of the General Appendix
to the Rule Book under Heading:

MOTOR TROLLEY SYSTEM OF MAINTENANCE ON SINGLE LINES.

(b) Token Section in which Control Instrument and two or more Occupation Keys are provided.

Immediately the Occupation has been agreed the Signalman to whom the Ganger has applied for occupation must turn the commutator of the key control instrument from No. 1 (normal) to No. 2 position and the Signalman at the other end of the section must press the bell key of his Token Instrument. This will unlock the commutator of the Key Control instrument, which must then be turned to the No. 4 position.

The Signalman who is giving the occupation must ask the Ganger concerned, or the Signalman at the other end of the section (if the Occupation Key is at that signal box) to press the plunger to enable the applicable Key Control instrument to be operated from the No. 4 position to No. 6 position, in which position the Signalman can release the key. The press button associated with the Key Control instrument must be pushed in, thus allowing the Ganger (or Signalman if the key is at the signal box) to withdraw the key.

The Signalman at the other end of the section must press the bell key of his Token Instrument for each occupation given.

(e) Giving up occupation.

The Ganger, when he has obtained occupation of the line, must so arrange his work as to be able to put back the Occupation Key at the appointed time. He may put the key into any instrument in the group to which it belongs as it will fit all the instruments in the group, and will restore the Token working equally well in any Key Instrument.

When putting back the key he must turn it until the Indicator shews No. 1. Having restored the Occupation Key, the Ganger must call up the Signalman on the telephone and notify him that he has restored the key (giving the number of the key instrument) and that the line is safe for the passage of the trains over the section. Should he not receive any reply after a reasonable time the Ganger must proceed on foot to the nearest telephone, or signal box, and establish communication.

Where "Key Control Instruments" are provided, the Ganger after restoring the key must press the plunger provided in connection with the Key Instrument until notified by the Signalman that the Key Control apparatus has been properly reset. The Signalman must then turn the Commutator of Key Control Instrument from No. 6 to No. 5 position when, if the Ganger is pressing the plunger at the Key Instrument the commutator of the "Key Control Instrument" can be turned to No. 1 (Normal position) restoring the electric train token working. The Signalman will then notify the Signalman at the other end that the Occupation Key has been replaced.

PAGE 79. **YEALMPTON BRANCH.**

Occupation by Permanent Way Department.

Amend :

The existing instructions to be amended as follows :

The instructions on Pages 65–68 of the General Appendix to the Rule Book apply, subject to the modifications of paragraphs (b) and (e) thereof as set out below. The Home station of the Ganger is Yealmpton. Telephones and key boxes are fixed as under :

Group No. 1 (One Key)	M.	C.	Group No. 2 (One Key)	M.	C.
Plymstock Signal Box	0	0	Hut No. 3 ..	1	30
Hut No. 1		19	Hut No. 4 ..	2	55
Hut No. 2	1	0	Hut No. 5	3	32
Hut No. 3	1	30	Hut No. 6 ..	4	7
			Hut No. 7 ..	4	79
			Hut No. 8 ..	5	59
			Yealmpton ..	6	33

The telephones communicate with the Signalman at Plymstock.

Occupation Key Release Instruments controlling the groups as shewn above are provided in Plymstock Signal Box. These Key Release instruments are fitted with a commutator handle and involve a modification of paragraphs (b) and (e) of Clause 7 of the instructions appearing on Page 66 of the General Appendix to the Rule Book under heading "Instructions in connection with motor trolley system of maintenance on single lines." The modified instructions are shewn below :

(b) Token Section in which Control Instrument and two or more Occupation Keys are provided.

Immediately the Occupation has been agreed the Signalman to whom the Ganger has applied for occupation must turn the commutator of the key control instrument from No. 1 (normal) to No. 2 position and the Signalman at the other end of the section must press the bell key of his Token Instrument. This will unlock the commutator of the Key Control instrument, which must then be turned to the No. 4 position.

The Signalman who is giving the occupation must ask the Ganger concerned, or the Signalman at the other end of the section (if the Occupation Key is at that signal box) to press the plunger to enable the applicable Key Control instrument to be operated from the No. 4 position to No. 6 position, in which position the Signalman can release the key. The press button associated with the Key Control instrument must be pushed in, thus allowing the Ganger (or Signalman if the key is at the signal box) to withdraw the key.

The Signalman at the other end of the section must press the bell key of his Token Instrument for each occupation given.

(e) Giving up occupation.

The Ganger, when he has obtained occupation of the line, must so arrange his work as to be able to put back the Occupation Key at the appointed time. He may put the key into any instrument in the group to which it belongs as it will fit all the instruments in the group, and will restore the Token working equally well in any Key Instrument.

When putting back the key he must turn it until the Indicator shews No. 1. Having restored the Occupation Key, the Ganger must call up the Signalman on the telephone and notify him that he has restored the key (giving the number of the key instrument) and that the line is safe for the passage of the trains over the section. Should he not receive any reply after a reasonable time the Ganger must proceed on foot to the nearest telephone, or signal box, and establish communication.

Where "Key Control Instruments" are provided, the Ganger after restoring the key must press the plunger provided in connection with the Key Instrument until notified by the Signalman that the Key Control apparatus has been properly reset. The Signalman must then turn the Commutator of Key Control Intrument from No. 6 to No. 5 position when, if the Ganger is pressing the plunger at the Key Instrument the commutator of the "Key Control Instrument" can be turned to No. 1 (Normal position) restoring the electric train token working. The Signalman will then notify the Signalman at the other end that the Occupation Key has been replaced.

PAGE 79. **YEALMPTON BRANCH.**

Insert :

BLASTING AT MESSRS. F. J. MOORE LTD.'s QUARRY.

The following to be inserted after the entry "Occupation by Permanent Way Department":

The above-mentioned firm has opened a Quarry in land situated on the Down side of the line between 1m. 0c. and 1m. 26c., between Billacombe and Elburton Cross.

Blasting may take place between the following agreed times :

10-0 a.m. to 10-30 a.m. (Mondays to Saturdays inclusive).

3-55 p.m. to 4-25 p.m. (Mondays to Fridays inclusive).

4

Telephonic communication is provided between Messrs. F. J. Moore Ltd.'s office at the site of the Quarry and No. 3 Occupation Key Hut.

The following instructions must be observed by all concerned:

1. The Permanent Way Length Ganger must arrange for the Occupation Key for Group No. 1 to be in No. 3 Key Box before the times shewn above, on the days specified above. He must also arrange for a Lengthman acquainted with these instructions to be in attendance at No. 3 Occupation Key Box by these times.

2. The Quarry Foreman in charge of the blasting operations will telephone the Lengthman at No. 3 Hut asking permission to blast, the following words being used:

"May blasting commence?"

3. Before giving the Quarry Foreman permission to blast, the Lengthman must place a red flag on each post situated 100 yards on each side of 1m. 25c. He must then telephone the Plymstock Signalman and obtain permission to withdraw the Occupation Key for Group No. 1 in accordance with the instructions on pages 65–68 of the General Appendix to the Rule Book, as modified in the instructions under the heading above "Occupation by Permanent Way Department" and if occupation can be granted and the Lengthman has withdrawn the Occupation Key, he must telephone the Quarry Foreman and give permission for blasting to take place, the message to be given being:

"Yes, you may blast."

In the event of the Signalman at Plymstock not being in a position to grant the occupation the Lengthman must immediately advise the Quarry Foreman, the message being " No " on the telephone and the red flags must be removed from each of the posts.

4. Immediately the Quarry Foreman is satisfied that all the charges have been detonated, he must telephone the Lengthman and give him an assurance that all charges have been exploded, the following words being used:

"Blasting completed, all charges exploded."

The Lengthman must then examine the line and satisfy himself that it is not obstructed and is safe for the passage of trains. If so, he must remove the red flag from each of the posts and replace the Occupation Key in the Key Box at No. 3 Hut, in accordance with the instructions on pages 65–68 of the General Appendix to the Rule Book, as modified in the instructions under the heading above "Occupation by Permanent Way Department".

In the event of the line having been damaged or obstructed, the Lengthman must not remove the red flags or restore the Occupation Key until the line is clear and safe for the passage of trains. He must advise the Plymstock and Yealmpton Signalman of the position and take all necessary steps to have the line repaired or cleared of any obstruction with the utmost promptitude.

5. The Station Master or person in charge at Plymstock must advise the Permanent Way Length Ganger and Messrs. F. J. Moore Ltd., in the event of any special trains being arranged at short notice which would interfere with the intervals agreed upon for blasting.

6. Permission must not be given to blast during fog or falling snow.

J. S. P. PEARSON;

Plymouth, February 14th, 1946.   907—4,300.   **District Traffic Manager.**

Received District Traffic Manager's Instruction No. 2544 *re* Alterations and Additions to the Appendix to No. 6 Section of the Service Time Tables (Ninth Supplement).

Date.................. Station......................... Signature..........................

WESTERN OPERATING AREA

TEMPORARY SPEED RESTRICTIONS PERMANENT WAY OPERATIONS SIGNAL ALTERATIONS, APPENDIX INSTRUCTIONS, ETC.

SATURDAY, 15th MARCH
to
FRIDAY, 21st MARCH (inclusive) 1952

Enginemen and Guards must pay particular attention to works contained in this notice and keep a good look out for hand signals, which will be exhibited at the various localities in accordance with the Rules and Regulations. Work at places other than those mentioned may be in progress, of which it may not have been possible to give previous notice, and enginemen must be on the look-out and be prepared to stop or run at reduced speed when and where hand signals may be exhibited

---

Brixton Road.—The Loop Line has been taken out of use. The West Ground Frame (2 levers) has been recovered. Levers (Nos. 3 and 4) working the Loop connection have been recovered from the East Ground Frame leaving two levers. This Ground Frame has been renamed " Brixton Road Ground Frame ".

Plymstock—Yealmpton.—The old Electric Token Instruments between Plymstock and Yealmpton and the Intermediate Token Instrument at Brixton Road have been taken out of use.

A Wooden Staff (shape—square; colour—black) fitted with Annett's Key has been provided between Plymstock and Yealmpton.

The Ground Frames at Billacombe, Brixton Road, Steer Point and Yealmpton have been fitted with Annett's locks, which are released by the Key on the new Wooden Staff.

Occupation Key Boxes have been taken out of use from Plymstock Signal Box, Huts 1 to 8, inclusive, and Yealmpton Station.

The occupation Control Instruments have been taken out of use at Plymstock Signal Box.

CATTEWATER JCN.

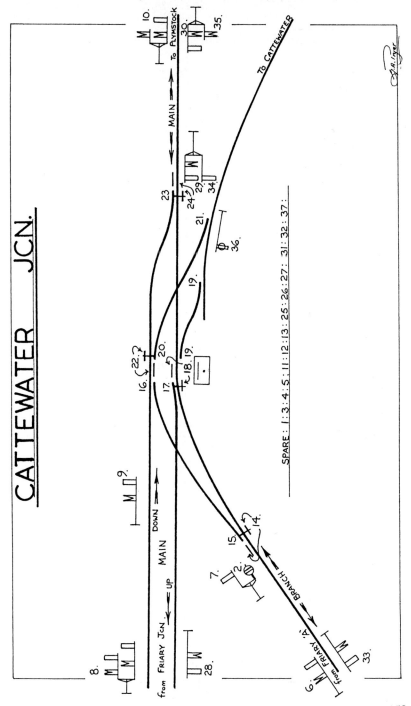

SPARE : 1 : 3 : 4 : 5 : 11 : 12 : 13 : 25 : 26 : 27 : 31 : 32 : 37 :

159

PLYMSTOCK

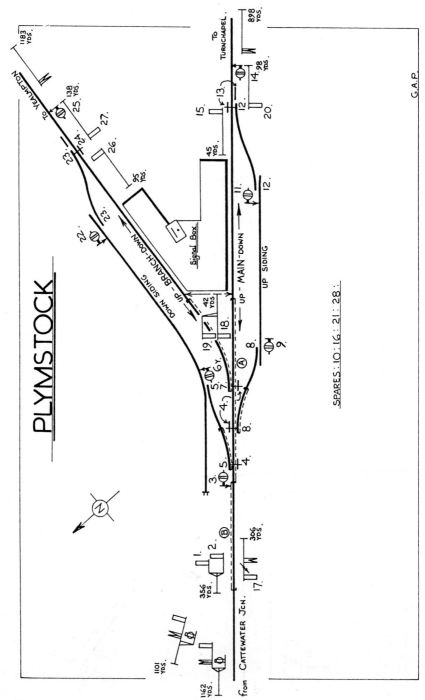

SPARES: 10: 16: 21: 28:

160

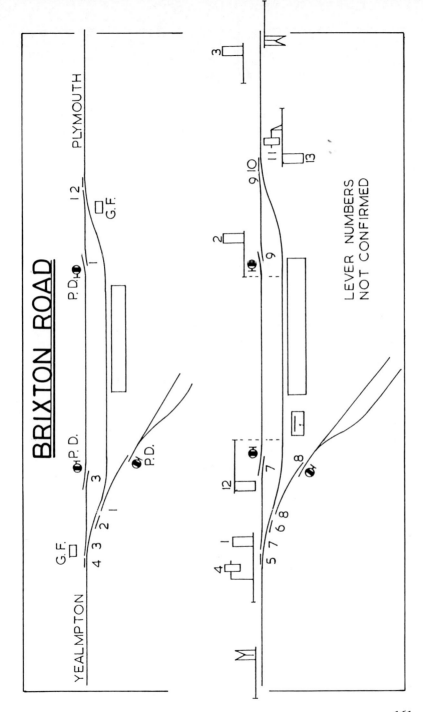

BRIXTON ROAD

YEALMPTON   PLYMOUTH

LEVER NUMBERS
NOT CONFIRMED

161

YEALMPTON

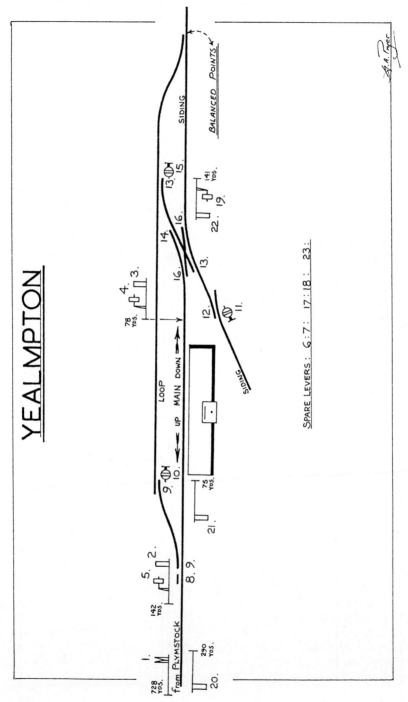

SPARE LEVERS: 6:7: 17:18: 23:

Mount Gould Junction Signal Box

Opened	Closed	Type	Frame
03.1891	10.11.1973	5	DT
			VT 5 BAR

The box opened circa March 1891 and contained a frame of 15 working levers and 10 spare levers. It controlled the Laira to Sutton Harbour branch and the Plymouth No. 1 Curve (a new line to allow the LSWR Company to reach its new Friary terminus from the recently opened Lydford to Devonport line).

Plymouth No. 2 Curve was constructed in order to allow the GWR Company access to its Yealmpton branch, which was opened in 1898. To control the junction leading to the new line, the existing frame was extended to 31 levers, of which 29 were working. In addition, because the Plymouth & Dartmoor Railway ran parallel to the Sutton Harbour line and had to cross the No. 2 Curve on the level, the box controlled catch points installed (and maintained) by the GWR so as to prevent that company's horses and wagons from fouling the No. 2 Curve. As an added precaution, electric depression bars were installed, which prevented the Mount Gould Junction signalman from restoring the lever working the catch points if wagons were on the crossing.

Apart from the 'distants' for the No. 2 Curve being permanently fixed at 'danger' c1918, and 'up' and 'down' detonator machines being provided, there was little in the way of alteration at Mount Gould Junction until 1958, when No. 2 Curve was closed to all traffic. This then meant that the 'Westcountry' class engines, which previously turned via this line because the Friary turntable was too small to accommodate them, now had to turn via Lipson and Laira Junctions.

During the following year the floor of the box and its windows were lowered about three feet, giving it a rather peculiar appearance. At the same time the old double twist frame was replaced by a 45-lever, 5-bar VT frame: the new frame was required in connection with the new carriage sidings in Laira Yard, it included 26 working and 10 spare levers and was placed at the back of the box. The work also included the closure of Friary Junction box, so access to the Sutton Harbour branch was provided by means of a new ground frame released from Mount Gould Junction.

Some of the resultant spare levers were subsequently brought into use in 1960, when Mount Gould Junction became a fringe box for Plymouth Panel, while the remainder of them were linked up to the new connections for the Diesel Depot in 1961.

In 1962 an additional lever was required in order to release lifting barriers at the entrance to the Diesel Depot. However, what must surely have been unique was the installation, in 1969, of a new carriage-washing machine on the 'down' main line between Mount Gould Junction and Friary Junction. A switch was provided in Mount Gould Junction box to operate the washing

163

G. W. R.

Billacombe

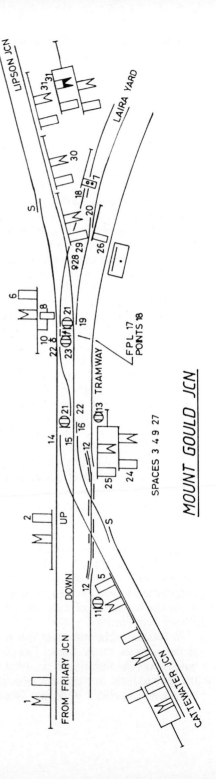

G. W. R.

NORTH ROAD
(PLYMOUTH)

164

machine, and care had to be taken to ensure that it was switched off before signalling a freight train destined for Friary or Sutton Harbour!

ADDITIONAL INSTRUCTIONS FOR MOUNT GOULD JUNCTION SIGNAL BOX

Regulation 3
"Is Line Clear?" must be sent for Down and Up trains as soon as "Is Line Clear?" is received.

Regulation 4A
The Distant signal for Friary Junction for trains from Sutton Harbour and the Distant signal for Cattewater Junction for trains from Plymstock being permanently fixed at Caution, Regulation 4A will not apply to trains from Sutton Harbour and Plymstock. When Friary Junction is out of circuit Regulation 4A will not apply to Up trains from Friary.

GREAT WESTERN RAILWAY
NOTICE
NO UNAUTHORIZED PERSON ALLOWED IN THIS BOX
BY ORDER

Cattewater Junction Signal Box

Opened	Closed	Type	Frame	Levers
13.01.1898	1.10.1963	LSWR	Stevens	37
			Stevens	25 from 1938

From September 5th 1892, when passenger trains commenced running on the Plymstock branch, the points providing access to the Cattewater Harbour branch were controlled by a ground frame released by Annett's Key attached to the Friary A – Plymstock Train Staff. This, however, proved to be only a rather short-lived arrangement because, in connection with the opening of the

GWR Company's line from Mount Gould Junction to Cattewater Junction (to allow that company access to its new branch from Plymstock to Yealmpton), a new signal box was required at the latter location. This would be built by the LSWR Company, but at the GWR Company's expense as part of the Agreement for the construction of the Yealmpton branch.

The resultant box was grossly over-signalled, with no less than 29 of its 37 levers working what could only be described as a small, non-crossing junction. In fact, during June 1906 these working levers were already being reduced to 24, when the 'stop' signals between Mount Gould Junction and Cattewater Harbour were removed, along with the four 'distant' signals to and from the latter. This was then followed, in September 1922, by a further reduction, when the layout was modified without losing any of the existing facilities.

In June 1938 switching-out apparatus was installed so as to allow the box to close after the day's freight service at Cattewater Harbour had been completed, until just before the first train for Cattewater was due to leave Friary on the following morning. The existing frame now contained 25 levers, of which only 15 were working.

At this point it needs to be stated that Cattewater Junction box was the classic example of how much consideration railway companies had for their employees. It had been built at another company's expense and had signals everywhere, yet no proper sanitation despite the fact that dwellings with such facilities were less than 250 yards away. Furthermore, up until at least the early 1950s a Tilley paraffin lamp was the only lighting, a chemical toilet had to suffice for personal needs, and water was delivered by churn on the afternoon freight train to Cattewater Harbour.

Another drawback at Cattewater Junction was that the signalmen at Friary A and Plymstock had to 'hold in' on their Electric Train Tablet instruments so as to enable the Cattewater Junction signalman to switch out (see above). This, for example, was particularly apparent during what was commonly referred to as the 'manure season', when the Fison's factory at Cattewater was despatching seemingly endless bags of fertiliser for about two months (March and April) each year, and extra trains ran between Cattewater Harbour and Laira Yard until late at night. Normally the Cattewater Junction box closed at 8.20pm, and once the last railcar had cleared the branch by about 10.40pm the Plymstock signalman could go home. On these occasions, however, it was not unusual for him to be waiting until after midnight before the Cattewater Junction signalman could switch out as he, in turn, had to wait until after the last 'manure train' had left Cattewater Harbour and the points leading from there to Mount Gould Junction had been changed for through running between Friary and Plymstock.

(The switching-out apparatus was taken out of use after the Turnchapel passenger train service ceased in September 1951 because Plymstock box was reduced to a 'middle turn only' for the freight trains and remained as such until being closed in 1963.)

Plymstock Signal Box

Opened	Closed	Type	Frame	Levers
5.9.1892	14.7.1935	LSWR	Stevens	19
14.7.1935	1941		Stevens	21 from 1898
12.10.1941	1.5.1963		Westinghouse	28

Plymstock signal box was constructed in order to control the Plymstock terminus of the new branchline from Friary, and contained a frame of 15 working and 4 spare levers. The line was worked by Train Staff only.

The branch was extended from Plymstock to Turnchapel in 1896. However, whilst the line was seemingly ready for opening in May of that year, it failed to meet the requirements of the Inspecting Officer (Lt Col Addison, R.E.). In fact, such was the state of its signalling that it was possible to open the swing bridge at Turnchapel when a train was approaching it!

To overcome this problem the Plymouth & Dartmoor Railway Company (acting as agents for the LSWR) subsequently gave an undertaking to the Board of Trade that the line would be worked by the Electric Train Tablet system as from August 12th 1896 (the date on which the line was passed subject to the undertaking being given) and by Annett's Key electrically locked with the Tablet machine in the Plymstock box. In this manner, if the key was withdrawn, it would break the Tablet circuit: conversely, if a tablet was withdrawn it would break the Annett's Key circuit. This, of course, was also the case when a second Annett's Key was needed for a connection to a short branch opened from a point approximately 200 yards on the Plymstock side of the swing bridge to Bayly's Wharf.

There seemed to be no hurry to open the new line; in fact, it was delayed until January 1st 1897. At the same time the section between Friary A and Plymstock would be worked by the Train Staff and Ticket method, the notice for the change from the Staff system being dated December 1896. Also included in this notice was a set of instructions for sending a train from Plymstock to Friary if a 'down' train was late and the Staff was at the Friary end of the section. Interestingly enough, these instructions were identical to proposals that the Board of Trade had refused to allow on the Tavistock branch in 1876.

When the Yealmpton branch of the GWR opened on January 17th 1898, the frame contained 21 levers, including 4 push-pull ones. At the same time Cattewater Junction box came into use, and the Train Staff and Ticket system between Friary and Plymstock was replaced by Tyers Electric Train Tablet system. The Yealmpton branch, on the other hand, was controlled by the Electric Train Staff system.

The GWR Company withdrew passenger trains from its Yealmpton branch on July 7th 1930. As a result, the Train Staff and 'one engine in steam' system replaced the Electric Train Staff on January 23rd 1931, and the 'distant' signals were fixed at 'danger' on June 27th 1933. Meanwhile, in July 1931, a siding opened at Oreston (on the Plymstock to Turnchapel section) which had its points controlled by a 2-lever ground frame released by the Tablet machine in Plymstock box. Consequently, there were now two ground frames in the section locked by different methods. Apart from almost certainly making the working on this section unique, it also meant that only freight trains from Turnchapel could call at the Oreston siding.

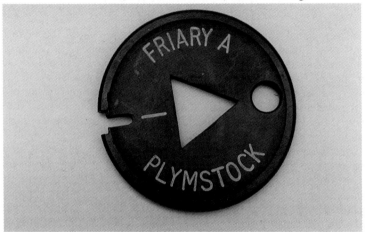

Long section tablet (reduced size), used only between Friary 'A' and Plymstock signal boxes when the Cattewater Junction box was switched out. This is a modern 'fibre' tablet which dates from 1938 and replaced the old steel and aluminium tablets of the early 1930s.

The triangular centre was known as the 'configuration'; there were various shapes which prevented the signalman from putting a tablet into the wrong instrument.

L. Crosier

Signalling between Plymstock and Yealmpton

As already stated in the description of Plymstock signal box, the line between there and Yealmpton was initially controlled by the Electric Train Staff system: the Train Staff stations were Plymstock and Yealmpton. However, unlike the Plymstock signal box, which was a LSWR affair, Yealmpton signal box was a standard G.W. Type 25 containing a frame of 23 levers. It was also second-hand, having first been used at Probus siding, between St Austell and Truro, in Cornwall.

The intermediate sidings at Billacombe, Brixton Road and Steer Point were all controlled by ground frames which could only be released by Annett's Key attached to the Electric Train Staffs; revolving discs were provided to indicate the catch points. In addition, the facing points at each location were all locked by facing point locks when the facing point levers were in the normal position, and these levers could only be reversed after the Annett's Key had been inserted. Further details appropriate to each location are as follows:-

Billacombe ground frame consisted of five levers. Facing point locks 1 and 5 were released by Annett's Key. Points 4 could not be reversed until points 2 were in the reverse position.

Brixton Road had two ground frames, East and West. Facing point lock 2 at the West ground frame and facing point locks 2 and 4 at the East ground frame were released by Annett's Key.

Steer Point also had two ground frames, again East and West. Facing point lock 1 at the East ground frame (consisting of two levers) and facing point lock 1 at the West ground frame were released by Annett's Key.
The West ground frame was the largest on the branch and consisted of seven levers. However, apart from facing point lock 1, only points 2 and independent disc 7 were actually used. This was because original proposals to construct a siding opposite the platform, which would have required the extra levers, failed to come to fruition. (Lever 3 was, nevertheless, also fitted with the Annett's Key for use had the siding been constructed.)

In May 1905 a new signal box was ordered from Reading Signal Department Works. This was subsequently constructed at Brixton Road Station, replacing the East and West ground frames, and contained a frame of 13 levers. Electric Train Staff instruments were also provided, which meant that the line would now be divided into two sections – Plymstock to Brixton Road and Brixton Road to Yealmpton.
Little is known about the reason for providing this box, but it was obviously done as cheaply as possible as the existing revolving discs were retained whereas it was normally standard practice in such circumstances to replace them with independent discs. One theory for the box, incidentally, was that a Mr Prowse, who owned a quarry near Yealmpton, could not do any blasting whilst a train was in the section between Plymstock and Yealmpton, and that dividing the line into two sections would be a means of easing the problem. Whatever, the box was to remain in use for less than 20 years, for between August 6th and 8th 1924 the signals at Brixton Road Station were removed, which suggests that it must have then been closed; once again, the Electric Train Staff section was Plymstock to Yealmpton.
When the decision was made to close the line to passenger traffic (for the first time) on July 7th 1930, plans were prepared at the Reading Signal Department drawing office to close Yealmpton signal box and to convert the mode of working from Electric Train Staff regulations to the Train Staff and 'one engine in steam' system. At the same time the revolving discs at each of the intermediate ground frames were to be recovered, as was independent disc 7 at Steer Point West ground frame.
These plans were subsequently approved by Mr Dannault (Divisional Superintendent) on May 22nd 1930, by Mr C. M. Jacobs (the Signal Engineer) on June 5th 1930, Mr A. H. Christison (the Divisional Locomotive Superintendent) on September 24th 1930, by Mr C. B. Collett (the Chief

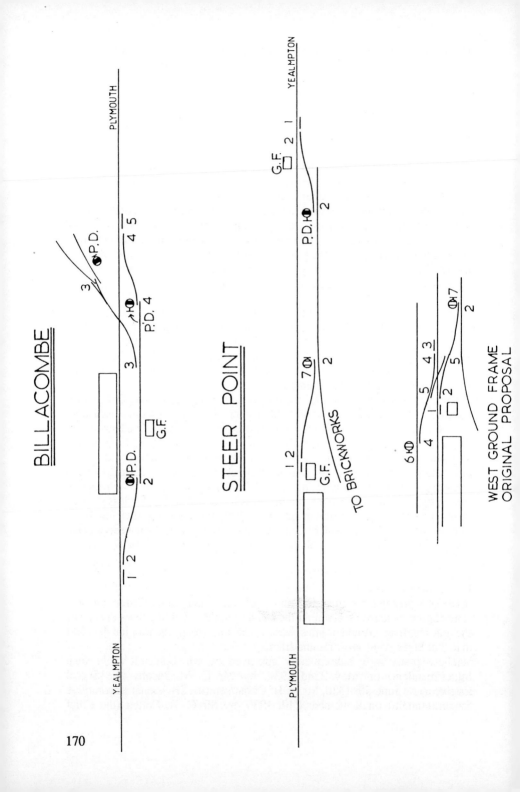

BILLACOMBE

STEER POINT

WEST GROUND FRAME
ORIGINAL PROPOSAL

TO BRICKWORKS

PLYMOUTH

YEALMPTON

170

Mechanical Engineer) on October 2nd 1930, by Mr H. Whitley (the Divisional Engineer) on November 11th 1930 and, finally, by Mr R. H. Nicholls (the Superintendent of the line) on November 30th 1930. The work was then carried out on January 23rd 1931.

Other changes quickly followed as on December 12th 1931 the Motor Trolley Maintenance system was brought into use between Plymstock and Yealmpton, while later, on June 27th 1933, the 'distant' signals for the Yealmpton branch at Plymstock Station were fixed at 'danger'. This then remained the situation until the line was re-opened for passenger services in 1941, when the mode of signalling was changed to the Elecric Train Token system. The section was still between Plymstock and Yealmpton, but an intermediate token instrument was provided at Brixton Road Station so as to allow a passenger train and a freight train to cross, provided that the latter kept to the loop line. In addition, a new two-lever ground frame was provided on the station platform at Yealmpton to control new 'down home' and 'up starting' signals.

The motor trolley used on the line rests upon its 'pitch' at Brixton Road Station.
C. Fennamore

Despite passenger services being withdrawn again in 1947, the Electric Train Token system remained until October 11th 1952, when it was replaced by Train Staff and 'one engine in steam' working. At the same time the loop line and the West ground frame at Brixton Road were recovered: ironically, a plan produced at the Reading Signal Department drawing office on January 1st 1926 refers to Brixton Road West ground frame as a temporary ground frame! The remainder of the ground frames, on the other hand, remained in use until the line finally closed on February 29th 1960.

Three photographs taken at Yealmpton Station during the final years of operation, showing the ground frame operated signals that replaced the originals in 1930. They depict the 'down home', looking eastwards *(above)*, the rear of the 'up starting', with the 'down home' in the distance, again looking eastwards *(below)* and the 'up starting', looking westwards, with Boldventure to its left *(opposite)*.

C. Fennamore

RATES OF PAY – TRAFFIC DEPARTMENT
YEALMPTON BRANCH
AUGUST 1914

MAXIMA of 2nd Class Station Masters

Brixton Road	29/-		Elburton Cross	31/-
Steer Point	33/-		Yealmpton	40/-

Signalmen

Yealmpton	Class: Local Cross Country and Branch Line Third	23/-

Signal Porter

Brixton Road	Second Class	21/-

Passenger Station Porters

Billacombe	Class 3	18/-	Brixton Road	Class 3	18/-
Elburton Cross	Class 3	18/-	Steer Point	Class 3	18/-
Yealmpton	Class 3	18/-			

THE YEALMPTON BRANCH – MEMORIES

(a) The Author's

In September 1933 my father, a serving officer in the Royal Navy, had purchased a house on the rural outskirts of Plymouth at Elburton. This move was in preparation for his retirement which was to follow in 1934/35. The house was called 'Gasgoyne' and stood in ample grounds in a quiet cul-de-sac off the Plymouth to Kingsbridge Road, just west of The Elburton Hotel where the local Western National service terminated from Plymouth.

It was during 1935, shortly after my father retired, that I was to acquaint myself with the little goods line that ran past the woods bordering the orchard at the bottom of our garden. Country walks taken with my father would often include a wait somewhere by the lineside for the pick-up freight to pass on its way to, or from, Yealmpton. I could not have guessed then how much, or how happily, this line was to re-enter my life in the later, wartime, years that were to follow, nor did I know the sad facts that had relegated it from a thriving passenger branch.

It was in the summer of 1943 that the Yealmpton branch was to enter my life again. The war had passed its dangerous phase, the bombing had almost stopped and our victorious armies were advancing steadily up the leg of Italy, who was about to capitulate. The tide of war, which had brought life anew to the line, had turned, but still prevented the unfortunate child of the day from straying very far from home. The beaches were out of bounds with their rusty barbed wire ribbons encircling the giant 'Dragons Teeth' anti-tank defences – pillboxes stood where once the swimmer laid in the sun – and the city parks were an assortment of P.O.W. camps, gun emplacements and 'Dig for Victory' allotment gardens.

At the outbreak of war my parents had moved into the city and, as a result, my school holidays were spent, up until 1943, mainly on North Road Station (near my home) or at Laira motive power depot. During that year my elder sister, some eleven years older than myself, was living with us, along with her two small children. She was a slight woman whose rather sheltered life with the middle classes of the 1920s had not been ideal training for the role of motherhood through the arduous rigors of the war-torn years in a front line city! These very years were taking their toll, and the strain of the Plymouth blitzes was beginning to show in mild hysteria of varying forms. One day my mother had suggested a trip to Yealmpton from Friary Station as "a change to take her out of herself" and to give her two small children a day out. This proved a success and, henceforth, was to become a weekly vigil during school term and, more often, during holidays.

Each trip would follow the same pattern, for once my sister had established a pattern of movement nothing would encourage her to try something else. At midday we would pack our lunch and tea for ourselves and her two children (then two and four years old) and load it all into a large bag with the other paraphernalia sufficient for a journey to the pole!

The pram that was to propel her offspring was rather the worse for wear as it had at one time been pushed too close to a Valor oil heater. Nevertheless, it was duly loaded with children and bags, and pushed with great haste through the streets towards Friary Station.

On arrival at Friary, my sister, without slowing the terrifying pace she had set through the town, would shoot through the well worn doorway towards the 'Left Luggage' office, carrying any poor unfortunate porter that may have got in her way partially impaled on the hood handles, which had long since been denuded of their rubber.

Once at the office, she would shout at the poor checking clerk "I want to leave this pram here" (as though he had already informed her of the contrary). He would then quickly issue a 1/3d. ticket, take the pram in order to rid himself of the peculiar woman and her 'tribe', before resettling into the comparative quiet of his office again to recover.

After she'd shouted at the booking clerk in the same way, we would tear out with our tickets onto the little bay platform to find the train wasn't even in. When the motor train did arrive and we were safely aboard with our gigantic pile of luggage spilling over onto the next pair of seats, we would wait patiently for it to depart. This seemed to take hours as the thin whiffs of steam drifted upwards from the leaky heating connections, and the driver and fireman grinned ruefully at their humourous cargo.

When we did get under way, however, certain rituals took place along the route. For example, we would all get up and look at the quarry where the woods once stood at the bottom of our orchard in the days gone by, and my sister would say to her charges "that's where we used to live". The whole complement of the carriage would look out, at what they were not quite certain!

At the commencement of Cofflete Creek, after leaving Brixton Road Station, we would all chorus out "there's the river", which, in fact, was grossly inaccurate as it was just a backwater off the River Yealm.

Following the course of the river to the next station, we would all chorus out "Steer Point – there's the brickworks"!

Later, as we were approaching journey's end, the train would burst out of the cutting and onto the embankment after Puslinch Bridge and this time we would shout out "there's the meadows," as though we were long lost travellers seeing home for the first time in many years! Little did the other passengers realise that it was only a week at the most since we had passed that way before to eat our tea in those same meadows, eyeing the cows whilst hundreds of horse flies tried to eat us.

On occasions our fellow passengers would be entertained in other ways, and one particular trip I shall never forget. My sister's watch had broken and so as not to miss the train home she took her very large, blue, square-faced alarm clock with her, tucked away secretly in the food bag. This brash object would tick loudly, so much so that when the train stopped at a station it could be heard plainly keeping time above the gentle hiss of steam and the creaking of springs. With this object accompanying us, we were eyed suspiciously as enemy agents trying to blow up this vital war link to the front line! (The repair, in wartime, of watches and clocks was not a speedy affair and during the wait my sister actually became attached to the giant alarm clock and it became a regular traveller!)

On this particular occasion the two children had been playing with the clock in the morning and the result, in the afternoon, was the complete disruption of an otherwise peaceful journey by a shrill and persistent ringing from way down under a pile of sandwiches. Of course my sister, being the calm person she was, leapt ten feet in the air, shot all the contents of the bag onto the seats opposite and finally ended up red-faced and holding the square blue monster in her hand. The time lapse, although quite small, seemed endless, but was sufficient for the thing to run down, whereupon it uttered a guttural clucking noise. The poor guard had thoroughly examined the train for faults, while the harassed driver was left wondering if the train was derailing itself!

Sometimes my mother would accompany us on the trip and would bring her sister, aunt Gladys, who was not the least bit like her. This wide variation in the characters of these two ladies would often add further humour to these outings. My mother was a very upright and straight-laced Victorian lady, haughty and strict, who would walk into Yealmpton from the station like some royal personage honouring the locals with her visit. My aunt Gladys, on the other hand, was a small, frail woman of humble outlook and with a clear Cornish accent. She would follow my mother, slightly behind her, and be carrying the bags which contained the tea-making kit, rugs and the stools – in that order of importance.

As we trotted on our way through Boldventure and on through Waltacre to The Clam, the youngest would be checked by me, who would, in turn, be kept in check by my sister and aunt. All of us would be kept in check by mother, as my aunt "Glad" would interject now and then with "Iss Floss, that buye'll be the death of 'ee." Finally, our walk would end by the little 'beach' next to the 'Wishing Stone' and we would sit and play and drink many cups of tea.

These then were some of my most vivid memories of our many wartime trips to Yealmpton until, alas, the railway finally closed to passengers for the last time.

Nostalgic Verse on the Yealmpton line:-

As I lay here fast decaying,
In pale autumn's waning sun
My rails gone, my buildings crumbled;
Weeds thriving where trains did run.

Reflect I on my days of use
When my life in fact began
That winter's day in ninety-eight
When the first proud train it ran.

Whistle blowing – wheels shrieking!
Gently rumbling o'er the ground;
Entered proudly, smoke ascending
the haven of my surround.

But alas in years to follow,
Very soon in fact to be
Great god car was being born to
Raise its mastery over me.

This and no permission granted
To run o'er some gentry's land,
So abruptly terminated
My progress to sea and sand.

So thus my rails did never reach
Beyond to Modbury fair
Thence 'cross the flowing Avon to
Kingsbridge, vainly waiting there.

So I was to be subjected
to an ever falling trade
For by the end of the 'twenties
Cars invaded every glade.

Further life is not warranted
The 'thirties came – my end is nigh,
Great Western decided closure
So thus I was about to die.

Through the 'thirties thus I struggled
Weekday goods were all I knew,
No excited childrens' voices –
No-one to enjoy my view.

But wait! – war clouds are to gather
The 'forties bring life anew
I am needed and re-opened
Cars vanish and are but few.

But this reprieve was very short
War in passing would restore,
Cars ever in their great profusion
So I am doomed as before.

The 'fifties came and with them brought
twice weekly goods, one apiece
And sadder days were to follow
For even these too must cease.

Then quietly and finally,
On one dismal winter's day
The last train left for Laira yard
And I – my last service paid.

The 'sixties came and but no more
Was I to remain in peace
Only two more years to pass
Whence I finally will cease.

And then it came that final train
And departing took with it
My rails and bridges, all for scrap
Leaving just a ballast pit.

Now o'er my track the bindweed strays
Station roofs sag in despair
My paint it flakes and woodwork rots
For the want of human care!

Now the 'seventies are all but here
Rural land is savaged fast
Sprawling mass of hallowed concrete
Takes the place of cool green grass.

Is this the plan for the future
Will all romance fade away,
Will future child ask in wonder
Dad, what was this steam railway?

Anthony R. Kingdom
September 1967

177

(b) Memories of some other people who knew the line well

Mr. B. Y. Williams of London:-

"My first journey over the Yealmpton branch was in August 1917, when an aunt rented a house at Newton Ferrers and I went to stay with her for a holiday; the approach was by train to Steer Point, thence by steamer down the river. Embarkation at Steer Point was from a small stone slipway; at low tide the steamer had to lie off and a rowing boat tender had to be used.

There was a brickworks at Steer Point: the Swilly housing estate was built with bricks from these works in, or about, 1926. They were conveyed by rail to Devonport goods where the railway borrowed a couple of A.E.C. 3^1/$_2$-ton flat lorries to deliver them to site."

"... I well remember the GWR buses standing in the station approach at Millbay. My first memories are of the high up type (AEC probably) painted in the old carriage colour of chocolate red: about 1920 this was changed to engine green, and later the buses took on the familiar chocolate and cream. In the later 1920s the long Maudsley and Guy buses were being used.

About 1929 the GWR bought the business of March at Kingsbridge, which included the GWR cartage agency at that point, the steamer service from Kingsbridge to Salcombe and the lorry service from Kingsbridge to Plymouth market. After purchase, the Plymouth lorry continued to run: it stood at the market in the afternoon to receive goods for delivery along its route to Kingsbridge.

The steamer service continued as a summer excursion business, although it was not generally known that the GWR owned it! The *Ilton Castle* was laid up and not used, later being sold for scrap. The *Kenwith Castle* ran for another two or three years, before being sold to Worths of Calstock in 1932: it was then later resold to the Millbrook Steamer Co. who renamed it *Whitsand Castle* and ran it as a ferry for some years."

Mr. G. St. C. Ellis of South Milton, Kingsbridge:-

"My earliest recollections of the Yealmpton line start with my schooldays (1915–1923), walking 2^1/$_4$ miles from Weston Farm, where I was born, to Yealmpton and leaving home at 7.30am. The Turnchapel train used to wait at Plymstock Station for us and we all used to feel very superior in our train, as the Turnchapel train only had wooden seats and a small engine. We often used to think as we passed it, that it would tip over as it stood there at a steep angle and looked most queer. I fear there was a good deal of skylarking amongst we youngsters on the train, so much so, that sometimes the conductor would make some get out at Brixton and walk home!

The GWR buses ran from Bigbury-on-Sea to Yealmpton, via Modbury; it was always very busy. The trains used to consist of three or four coach motors, hauling extra coaches on Thursdays (Plymouth's market day). Milk used to be sent in twelve gallon churns, these often spilling over from the luggage compartments into the passenger coaches, standing right down their centres. The first train to leave Yealmpton in the mornings was the 8.15am.

It was always a busy station at Yealmpton with passengers, goods and milk, parcels and rabbits being brought in from all the farms for many miles around.

During the summer months organised parties were brought to Yealmpton from Plymouth, sometimes by special train, to a Mr. Lane's tea field at Torre. Every Wednesday large numbers of children would come out, play games, have tea and, by the noise, seemingly enjoy themselves!"

Mr. W. C. Beard of Camborne, Cornwall:-

"Yealmpton Show day, known as 'Derby Day', was a difficult day operationally, as we would have thirty-odd horse boxes (Pacos) and (beetles) for the cattle, plus some Mex 'B's. Added to that there were two, or more, special trains to stable, and additional coaches left for strengthening the ordinary evening services back to Plymouth. To add to this we often had trouble with some fixed coupling sets of Southern stock which we could not divide when setting back into the goods yard for stabling.

There was a quarry about 500 to 600 yards out from Yealmpton Station towards Steer Point, quite near the line, and before they blasted permission had to be sought from the railway to do so; directions for this were on a special card in the signal box. Frost in winter would often present Staff failure and, until restored, pilot working would have to be employed. This was a difficult job to set up with six-odd miles of line."

"... One goods guard, who liked his 'scrumpy', had two fingers missing from his right hand and would often hold the remaining three up to the driver at Steer Point signalling 'Four off at this stop' ..."

"The upright boiler railcar (1927–28) was a nightmare to drivers and firemen working the branch. The enginemen were always 'in a state', sweating streams and seemingly unable to maintain sufficient steam. However, there was a driver and guard who delighted in playing 'Tag' around the boiler whenever they had a chance! ..."

"... when the *Kitty Belle* ceased to run from Steer Point to Newton Ferrers, the Hodge family set up a small bus service running in conjunction with the trains at Yealmpton, but they were bought out in later years by the GWR. Some GWR buses were themselves stabled at Yealmpton Station in a big galvanised garage by the Co-op stores in the yard. Ticket monies from them were paid in nightly to the booking office, but parcel monies were paid to the signalman on duty who dealt with all parcel traffic there ..."

"... I had heard that in the early days, when one of the local gentry, Lord Revelstoke or Lord Mildmay, made a periodical move to London, the whole village of Yealmpton would turn out to see them off. A special train for the whole family, all the staff, horses, luggage etc., etc., would be hired for the job ..."

"... at times we had the otter hounds from Brent come to Yealmpton by rail, they then worked back to the source of the River Yealm ..."

"... The Sunday School parties from St. Jude's church, and others in Plymouth, were catered for by Messrs. Lane at Waltacre, near the station, with swings etc. 'Pennycross Bill', an old Plymouth character, used to come with them with his tea can and Union Jack. He used to show the crowds of people his bank book at 1d. a time."

"Another character, 'Old Bill', used to come from Plymouth daily, picking watercress for some hotels. With his clay pipe and a couple of pints inside him, he would return to Plymouth after dinner with his mawn strapped to his back full of 'cress ..."

Mr. R. G. Perryman of Plymstock:-

"I remember when I joined the GWR in 1920, the Yealmpton branch to Plymouth was flourishing, with all the intermediate stations having a stationmaster; these were later replaced by senior porters. Yealmpton had a staff of five, including a stationmaster who later had charge of the stations from Yealmpton to Billacombe ..."

"... on market days store cattle were weighed on the station weighbridge before sale, later being trucked to their destinations. Prize cattle for county shows were frequently boarded here in special trucks and forwarded to the show ..."

Mr. S. J. Broad (a former signal porter at Yealmpton) of Thurlestone:-

"... the squire at Gnaton Hall always gave the station a pheasant when they had a shoot, a lovely gesture ..."

"... our wages were 18/- a week and, if passed for the morse code, that was an extra 2/- a week ..."

"... one lady told me she and her friends were late for the train; the engine driver saw them hurrying up the road, reversed the train to pick them up before departing proper ..."

"... We lived with granny Luke who kept a pork shop in the market and we paid her 10/- a week and on Thursday evenings, if off duty, we used to turn her mincing machine to help make pork sausages and hogs puddings ..."

"... Mr. Brown, the stationmaster, I found dead at the gates one morning..."

Mr. F. J. Cross of Yealmpton:-

"One old timer I remember was Bill Evans, a water-cress picker, who used the train a lot ... he was well known and a tale was told that a local landowner gave his gamekeeper the sack because he treated old Bill Evans roughly one day ..."

"... a Mr. Stevens used to drive a 'four in hand' from Modbury every day to meet the trains, for the people of Modbury would have no service through to Plymouth otherwise. There was also a bus service from Noss Mayo run by two men called Hodge. These two men also ran a boat from Noss to Steer Point ..."

180

" ... I think the journey to Millbay from Yealmpton used to take rather less than an hour, sometimes a train would be held outside Plymouth if an express was on the main line and due in ..."

"... Just before the 1914 war they did put on a few trains on Sundays and one clergyman preached against this abomination of the Sabbath! ..."

"... During the last war a lot of naval men were stationed at Lyneham, close to Yealmpton, and one Christmas morning at six o'clock a train was run to take them all to Plymouth to catch an express to London in order to get them home for Christmas dinner."

"... During the 1914 war a military guard used to travel with the train but I never heard of them catching anyone though! ..."

"... The first stationmaster I can remember was a Mr. Courtney; he used to call to see my grandfather and in doing so brought me a 1d. bar of chocolate from the station slot machine ..."

"... Before that I think it was a Mr. Brown, but the man that came after was Mr. Hoblin; his wife kept a shop in the village. He would have seen the closure to passenger traffic in 1930. A Mr. F. Bunney looked after the station after that, and during the period the line was re-opened in 1941–47 ..."

"... The last man here on the station who saw the complete closure was a Mr. A. Rowe ..."

Mrs. I. Rickard of St. Austell (daughter of Mr. F. Bunney, a former stationmaster):-

"During the blitz on Plymouth, so many people used to come out from the city to try and find refuge in our village ..."

"... The Western National buses came out every evening and parked in the station yard and the road to it, to avoid destruction in the city ..."

"... The station yard was used during the war as a searchlight battery and there was a balloon barrage site at Collaton Cross, nearby. The Yealmpton branch catered for the gas cylinders and supplies for these two sites. The gas cylinders used to go to Motherwell to be filled and, when they were returned, they used to stand in the siding right outside our window. We lived in the converted station buildings at this time and it was very dangerous at times ..."

"... Yealmpton Station was used as a cattle grading centre by the Ministry at this time ..."

"... The branch was put out of action no less than three times by bombs; the service was then carried out by buses ..."

Mr. H. Pitts of Plymouth (a former GWR bus driver stationed at Kingsbridge in the 1920s):-

"... The steam boats from Steer Point were operated by the Hodge brothers, Elliott and Ernest. These boats used to meet the trains from Plymouth and, when possible, in the reverse direction. With the closing of the line in 1930, the steam boats were no longer required and the GWR, faced with maintaining a bus service to the Yealm, offered Ernest Hodge a job as a driver. This bus connected at Yealmpton with the through service from Plymouth to Kingsbridge and Dartmouth ..."

"... Vehicles used in this area were a twenty-seater 'Thornycroft's' between Noss and Yealmpton and 'Maudsleys' on the main road routes ..."

"... For a little while after the closing of the line in 1930, a bus service operated from Brixton to Steer Point, but there was little call for it and it was soon withdrawn ..."

"At suitable tides the *Kitley Belle* started the trip to Steer Point from Noss Mayo, picking up passengers at Kiln Quay and the Yealm Hotel, Newton Ferrers – also calling at The Warren and Thorn. At low tide the trip started from the Pool.

The *Kitley Belle* was owned by my grandfather, Mr. George Hodge, and licenced by the Board of Trade to carry 78 passengers and ply within the Yealm. She never went outside the river, certainly not to Phoenix Wharf, Plymouth – and was regularly surveyed by the Board of Trade.

It may be of added interest that when the Yealmpton railway opened my grandfather, with a partner, started the ferry service to Steer Point in a small boat called the *Puffing Billy*. After a short time the partner gave up owing to ill health.

My grandfather then had the *Kitley Belle* built and ran a regular service of six trips a day – Sundays included in the summer – with the help of his three sons ... later adding the *Kitley Girl* and *Pioneer* to cope with the summer crowds."

F. W. J. Lawrance, OBE of Weston-super-Mare:-

"My first experience was a return trip from Millbay to Elburton Cross to attend a Sunday School outing on a Saturday (probably the third) in July 1923; I was then eight years old and had moved with my family to Devonport in April of that year. We travelled on the 1.08pm from Millbay, which was an ordinary passenger train with both first and third class accommodation – all other regular trains were 'rail motor cars – one class only'. For years I assumed that this exception to normal was provided for the convenience of certain customers – the 1.08 and its return journey made reasonable connections with the Cornish Riviera Expresses to and from Cornwall – but when I ventured to include this suggestion in a talk I once gave to the Bath Railway Society one of the senior members told me he thought it more likely that the arrangement was made to provide time for the regular rail motor engine to replenish its coal supply in the middle of its long working day. It might be interesting if someone locally could throw more light on this point.

That day we returned in the evening on the special 'tea party' train which evidently started at Yealmpton and was hauled by an Aberdare 2-6-0 goods tender engine, running tender first and presenting an odd picture with its very high cab, very low tender, and enormous cranks outside the frames rotating on its very small driving wheels. Stopping at most (if not all) stations, it took us right to Devonport (GWR) Station where it ran round its now empty train and gave me a most valuable and memorable practical lesson in railway operation and signalling.

Later that year (or maybe the next) we discovered the way to Newton Ferrers and Noss Mayo, going by train to Steer Point and then by the *ss Kitley Belle*. This, of course, meant a stop at Brixton Road which greatly fascinated me and soon became my favourite station on the branch. At that time its signal box was still open, apparently freshly painted and in full working order.

About a year later I found the box still standing, but – alas – out of use and disconnected; by remarkably good fortune I was able to walk over to it, climb the steps, and look at the abandoned lever frame inside. I wish I could tell you the exact date of this visit because, the next time I passed, the box had been completely demolished.

I never cease to wonder why the platform was on what looks like the passing loop. Perhaps the original intention was for it to be a regular crossing station – perhaps with two platforms; but throughout all the time that I knew it the trains in both directions had to negotiate the reverse curves at both ends.

For most of the time between 1923 and 1930 the trains providing the 'normal' passenger service were rail motor cars consisting of an 0–6–0 pannier tank engine with two, 70-feet long passenger coaches – one smoking and the other non-smoking. At one time the engines on this service were painted chocolate brown to match the coaches. I found it most interesting to note that on the Yealmpton line the engine invariably pushed its coaches outward and pulled them back to Plymouth; whereas on the Southern line to Turnchapel the engine pulled out and pushed home; further, on the Yealmpton (GWR) trains the fireman collected and delivered the Single line Staff or Tablet, whereas on the Southern trains the driver did these duties – even if he was riding in the leading coach of a 'pushed' train.

On one of our trips to Yealmpton I remember that a young lady in our party so enjoyed the journey between Steer Point and Yealmpton that she said "I'd like to go all the way to London in this train"!

My last trip on the branch was to Steer Point (and Newton and Noss) in August 1929; I think we travelled out in the usual motor train, but on our return journey the train was late and it consisted of the steam railmotor (ex-Chudleigh and Heathfield) towing a vintage trailer-coach; it was slow, uncomfortable and noisy, and it made one of our party quite ill. Towards the very end, in 1930, I saw the Yealmpton train two or three times consisting of just one railmotor trailing coach pulled by an ancient 'Bulldog' class tender 4–4–0 which, of course, had to return tender first – a weary, heart-breaking sight.

During the 'goods only' years I made one or two cycle trips and met the porter at Billacombe; he told me he had one train a day – "the same as any country station". And I learned that the normal procedure was for shunting to be done on the way out; wagons to go away were then left in the loop from which they would be collected by the train on its way back.

I was glad that passenger services were resumed during the war, using

Friary as the Plymouth terminus. I saw the trains once or twice; they never looked as clean and tidy as in pre-1930 days: and I noted that they followed the Southern practice in which the engine pulled the train out and (if fitted for auto operation) pushed it back."

Extract from 'Letters To The Editor', South Devon Times, 17th Feb., 1967.

Harbour View
Noss Mayo

You must realise that in those days the river trip and train were the only means of getting to Plymouth from the villages of Newton and Noss. Even school children who attended Plymouth schools did the trip daily.

During the '14–'18 war when the sons in the business were in the Services, my grandfather turned to his grandsons for help to keep the "Kitley Belle" running – and at times the young women of the family were pressed to assist.

At that time Membland Hall was taken by the Government as an officer training centre with an intake of 300 men at a time – in some cases the wives and families of the men living in the villages. So you can imagine how busy the trip to Plymouth became.

Of course the trip to Steer Point in the "Kitley Belle" ended with the closing of the railway and the boat was sold to a Plymouth firm who altered her structure and renamed her the "Tamar Belle" where she was used as a pleasure boat within the Breakwater for many years, taking people up the Tamar and, I think, to Cawsand.

N. G. Croft (Mrs.)

POST-CLOSURE DEVELOPMENTS

As stated elsewhere, the final closure to goods traffic had occurred on February 29th 1960, but by May 1962 fresh developments were already afoot with the commencement of work on a new spur line into the then Associated Portland Cement Works (opened in 1961) at Plymstock Station. Subsequently, it was reported in the *South Devon Times* for June 21st 1963 that new track had been laid into the factory site after the excavation and removal of 70,000 cubic yards of rock. The contractor was T. W. Ward Ltd of Sheffield, a firm better known at that time for its demolition contracts, and the work had cost the company £2 million.

The work, when fully completed, resulted in track running around the northern side of the factory and in the provision of special loading platforms. British Railways had produced purpose-built cement carriers, each with a capacity for 20 tons of bulk cement, and one of the regular destinations for this cargo was the storage and distribution centre at Chacewater, in Cornwall. Incoming freight to the factory consisted of quantities of paint and kiln bricks.

The renewal of the old LSWR bridge over The Embankment, which carried Yealmpton, Turnchapel and Cattewater trains. This work was carried out over a weekend in November 1962 and was done in order to facilitate the then new cement works traffic.

A.R.K.

During 1964/65 part of the site at Plymstock Station was also the subject of negotiation between British Railways and the South Western Gas Board. On this occasion it was for the construction of a depot to serve as an unloading

185

point for butane, a form of liquefied petroleum gas (LPG). Work on the site subsequently commenced in 1965 and was carried out simultaneously with the construction of a new gas production plant at Breakwater Works, on the site of the old Oreston quarries.

The production of commercial gas at Breakwater Works began in 1966, and shortly afterwards approximately 300 tons of LPG (butane) started arriving at the Plymstock depot every week in special rail containers, at a pressure of 20lbs/sq. in. This was needed so as to give the lean gas produced at the works an odour, for safety reasons, as well as to enrich it (increasing its calorific value by some 175 British Thermal Units), and, from the depot, was piped to a giant, 860-ton 'Horton Sphere' container through a four-inch main that passed under the adjoining roads. The final product then left the works by means of a high pressure grid system of pipes, one of which followed the trackbed of the disused Yealmpton branch for several hundred yards to the east before diverging across open countryside. Meanwhile, of course, accommodation had to be found for the South Western Gas Board traffic at Plymstock Station, and this resulted in the station site layout being remodelled so as to provide new sidings. In fact, this work was seen in progress on June 18th 1966, when a passenger train again found its way to the station – a 'special' run by 'The Plymouth Railway Circle', of which, unfortunately, no details are recorded.

The fomer Associated Portland Cement Company's 0–4–0 diesel shunter depicted at Plymstock Station site in November 1973. Curving away to the right of the photograph are the sidings leading into the works.

A.R.K.

Three studies of BR 0–6–0 diesel shunter No. 4158 working trains at Plymstock on Wednesday, December 12th 1973. *Top:* Arriving, at 11.45am, with 12 wagons of LPG – the second such consignment that day. *Centre:* Crossing the River Plym after leaving Plymstock Station site at 12.30pm with 'empties' from the earlier delivery, made at 8.15am. *Lower:* Shunting cement wagons in order to clear siding space.

A.R.K.

A photograph of South Western Gas Board's transfer plant at Plymstock Station site taken in late 1973.

A.R.K.

By now changes had also occurred elsewhere. For a start the over-bridge carrying Colesdown Hill over the line at Billacombe had been strengthened by girder trusses immediately following its closure, while later, in 1964, the underside of the bridge had been back-filled using spoil from the now-demolished embankment carrying the former Southern Railway line to Oreston, remaining thus at the time of writing. In addition, the Billacombe Station site, together with the trackbed between there and Haye Road bridge, had now passed into the ownership of English China Clays Limited, the contract of sale with British Railways having been completed on January 8th 1965. Furthermore, during the period of negotiation for the sale, planning permission had been granted for new company offices to be built on the site of the former goods yard, and also for the construction of a private road to the new work face just off Haye Road, using part of the old trackbed. The work had then commenced shortly afterwards and included, in its early stages, the dismantling and landscaping of the old Moorcroft Quarry at Billacombe Station as well as the renovating of the station building to serve as a test laboratory (before being allowed to fall into disuse again).

During the late 1960s British Railways disposed of even more of its land. On this occasion it resulted in Steer Point Station and the land eastwards, beyond the bridge over the River Yealm and up to and including Yealmpton Station site, reverting to its former owner, Kitley Estates. Meanwhile, the surviving end of the branch was now carrying some 500 tons of bulk cement daily as the special trains of 'Presflo' wagons shuttled to and from the cement works at Plymstock and the storage silos at Chacewater, Barnstaple and Exeter.

188

On November 23rd 1970 Yealmpton and Brixton Parish Councils held a meeting to decide on a proposition that the trackbed between their two villages should become a public footpath. However, the clerk of Kitley Estates, Capt John Bastard, stated that the land had been purchased from British Railways for the express purpose of keeping it private, adding that in spite of this vandals had already been at work damaging property and disturbing the pheasants. He also stated that the trackbed was becoming very overgrown and that the Estates were not prepared to spend large sums of money clearing it for such a purpose. Finally, he mentioned that the public were, however, permitted to use the section from Puslinch Bridge to Kitley Quay, although beyond that it was a dead end from Yealmpton due to the removal of Cylinder Bridge.

November 1971 saw the commencement of the clearing of Yealmpton Station site: it had now been sold by Kitley Estates to a firm of London property developers, Venture Estates. The land was to be cleared of all existing buildings and used for an executive housing estate consisting of 34 detached, luxury houses.

The demolition process was carried out by C. J. Howe of Greenham, near Taunton, throughout the winter of 1971/72, and work on the construction of the houses commenced in the following spring. (At this point it may be of interest to note that I, as chairman of the South West Group of the Great Western Society, negotiated with the contractors for several railway items for the Society's then new depot at Bodmin General Station, in Cornwall. Goods shed doors, platform slabs, fencing posts, timber and other building materials were freely given, and were then subsequently loaded onto a transporter and taken there by H. Stoneman's of Plymouth.)

A rain-swept day at Yealmpton in November 1971 only serves to accentuate the dismal sight of the now isolated station building – just before the arrival of C. J. Howe's bulldozer *(overleaf)*.

A.R.K.

190

November 1971 also saw the 3.85-acre site and buildings of Brixton Road Station sold to the Devon County Council by British Railways as part of a long-term county road improvement scheme.

On October 22nd 1973 the *Western Evening Herald* reported that the 'Plymouth Conservation Corps' and the 'Plymouth Polytechnic Environment Council' were hard at work clearing the trackbed between Puslinch Bridge and Kitley Caves. It was to become a nature trail, but the idea was contrary to the decision made in 1970 by Kitley Estates and the project had subsequently to be abandoned.

During 1976/77 a road widening scheme was in progress at Haye Road, which involved the infilling of the adjacent railway cutting and the bridge, the parapets of which were removed and used as part of the infill. The land comprising the infilled cutting to the east of the road was then purchased by a Mr Gunton, who later built a bungalow there – 'Ashleigh', No 38 Haye Road.

On November 30th 1977 a road widening scheme was also observed in Sherford Road, Elburton. Here again, this was achieved by the infilling of the adjacent railway cutting and by the removal of the parapets of the bridge, which were similarly used as part of the infill. Part of the land to the east, towards the former Brixton Road Station, was subsequently to be brought into use for the building of houses.

A view of the station building at Brixton Road in October 1978, shortly before being demolished.

A.R.K.

191

Another view of the station building at Brixton Road in October 1978, this time looking northwards and showing the adjoining road bridge.

A.R.K.

Less than a year later, on October 6th 1978, part of the site and buildings of Brixton Road Station were on the market. This, of course, was for the second time in only seven years, and on this occasion they were being offered for sale by tender. However, of the 3.85 acres originally purchased from British Railways, Devon County Council was retaining one acre, which included the bridge, for possible future road improvements.

The station site was subsequently purchased by a builder from Holbeton (a Mr Evans), who proceeded to demolish the original station building and use the limestone, and other materials, to build a seven-roomed house: this was eventually completed in late 1980, and much of the station's character was retained. (At the time of writing the house has recently been sold to a new owner for an undisclosed sum, although it had appeared for sale on previous occasions at a price of £250,000.)

February 29th 1980 was the 20th anniversary of the complete closure of the line, and to mark the occasion a special ceremony took place on the site of the former Yealmpton Station, by the entrance to Riverside Walk. This included a plaque, made of stainless steel and commemorating the railway, being unveiled by Mr William Dennis (chairman of Yealmpton Parish Council), Mr Michael Howarth (chairman of the 'Holbeton, Yealmpton and Brixton Society') and myself, whose name appears upon it.

At the time this plaque was the first of its kind to be erected in memory of a lost branchline, and even to this day the only other known to exist, at least in the area, is on a bridge abutment along the route of the former Turnchapel branch. This, in fact, appeared during 1994 and was donated by 'Intercity', no less!

192

Great excitement occurred in railway lobbies during 1984. First the *Western Evening Herald* carried a paragraph reporting that Mr Michael Bastard of Kitley Estates had applied to the South Hams District Council for planning permission to re-open a one-mile stretch of the Yealmpton railway between Kitley Caves and Kitley Quay, with the idea of running a narrow-gauge diesel train carrying up to 80 passengers. Then later, on August 20th and 22nd, came conflicting reports that a Mr John Moore, manager of Kitley Caves, was fighting local opposition to open a mile and a half of the line between Kitley Caves and the Yealm Estuary(!), running a two-carriage electric train.

Both of these proposals eventually led to a site meeting being called by the South Hams District Council, following protestations from the residents of mainly Yealmpton (still recoiling from the effects of the recently opened Shire Horse Centre), Brixton, Newton Ferrers and Noss Mayo, but thereafter nothing more came of them. Opposition, it seemed, had won the day and both Kitley Estates and Mr John Moore were over-ruled, mainly on the grounds of lack of space for parking and toilet facilities.

1984/85 saw the miners' strike against the Thatcher government, as a result of which there was a substantial increase in the amount of South Western Gas Board traffic at Plymstock Station in order that the Breakwater Works could step up the production of gas, in the short term, to cope with the extra demand.

In stark contrast, a serious decline in the use of the line surviving at Plymstock occurred during February 1987, when British Railways no longer desired to maintain the rail bridge over the Plym. This, together with a continuing rise in the cost of transporting bulk cement by rail, caused Blue Circle Industries (Associated Portland Cement Manufacturers prior to 1978) to soon close its three regional silos and switch all traffic to road haulage which, of course, meant that cement could then be delivered direct to customers' sites.

To make matters worse, so far as the future of the line was concerned, the gas production plant at Breakwater Works was, by then, nearing the end of its life due to the advent of North Sea gas, which was already flowing through an expanding national grid. Indeed, by 1990 the plant had been dismantled and, in consequence, Plymstock Station site had become virtually deserted.

Just beforehand, during 1988/89, Mr Gunton had sold the bungalow ('Ashleigh') built by him on the eastern side of Haye Road and constructed another at the rear, further to the east along the infilled cutting. This had then become No 40 Haye Road, and was named 'Parkside', while his previous property, No 38, had been renamed 'Inglenook' by its new owners.

On March 30th 1990 the 0–4–0 diesel shunter at Plymstock Station left, by road, for the Plym Valley Railway at Marsh Mills. It was being donated by Blue Circle Industries after having been redundant since 1987. Meanwhile,

Members of the Plym Valley Railway assisting a contractor with the removal
of the roof girders from Billacombe Station building.

A.R.K.

volunteers from this same group of railway preservationists were busy dismantling the Billacombe Station building. This had come about due to the generosity of Camas UK Limited (part of the English China Clays Group), and was a job that entailed taking the building apart brick by brick, labelling everything and then removing it to Marsh Mills. In all, this was to take almost two years, the work having commenced on April 2nd 1989 and not being completed until January 20th 1991.

During 1992 the sidings at the cement works were lifted and, apart from the pointwork, which was returned to British Railways at Laira for further use, was sold to the South Devon Railway at Buckfastleigh.

Early in 1994, almost without being noticed, the steel bridge over 'The Ride' was recovered by Plymouth City Council Works Dept. The precise date is unknown, but it is safe to say that due to the cessation of goods traffic it had become redundant. Its removal opened up the entry into the city's recycling depot at Chelson Meadow, which had been a refuse tip since the early 1960s.

With financial help forthcoming from the E.C., a new road junction was constructed under control of traffic lights. This, I consider, was a retrograde step, for it removed the possibility of a rail 'Park & Ride' scheme from Plymstock Station site to Plymouth (Friary), or North Road.

Later that year, at the end of September, track lifting at Plymstock Station was commenced by Weaver Plant of Bristol. All recoveries were removed by road, and the last rail was lifted at 3.50pm on Wednesday, October 12th 1994, as witnessed by the author: the last vestiges of the Yealmpton railway had failed to reach a centenary by just four years!

Footnotes

1. The latest news on the re-use of the branch at the time of writing was seen in the *Plymouth Extra* dated August 7th 1997. It read: 'Cycling or walking along the former railway line at Elburton could become a reality, even for commuters into the city centre. A path along the line through the Camas Quarry is being proposed by a substantial transport organisation, and is supported by Plymouth City Council. Planning application is now under consideration for the path, some two and a half miles long. If successful, the path would form a link along the West Country Way and provide a green corridor for people within the area, and would link up with the Plym Valley cycle route says Ben Hamilton – Baille of 'Sustrans', promoters of the national cycle network and the West Country Way'.

2. Another recent newspaper article of interest mentioned one of the uses of the railway in days gone by. It read: 'Devon County Council are considering a planning extension to 'Riverbank Cottage' in Newton Ferrers, a listed

The former sidings serving the cement and gas works on the old Plymstock Station site were lifted by Weaver Plant of Bristol, the last rail being lifted at 3.50pm on Wednesday, October 12th 1994.

A.R.K.

196

building with an interesting history. It was originally the village granary, the grain arriving by donkey before shipment by barge to Steer Point and thence by train to Plymouth'.

3. Finally, tracing the course of the old line around Elburton is becoming increasingly difficult due to building. However, from the rear of 'Parkside' (No 40 Haye Road) the course of the line runs through Nos 17, 19 and 21 Hazel Grove; from thence this road is constructed on the old trackbed up to the site of Elburton Cross Station. Here the site is distinguished by the railings and old station gates leading into Hazel Grove and Station Road, and which mark the periphery of the former halt.

A dwelling has been built upon the former station area and this, in turn, backs onto the site of the former Sherford Road bridge. Here stands No 26 Sherford Road, a large detached house, where a kissing gate to the south of its front garden boundary still marks the old station entrance. To the eastern side of the Sherford Road bridge site is 'Crosspark' (No 27 Sherford Road), and behind it, further to the east, is the 'Portway Close' housing estate. Eastwards from here no further building occupies the trackbed until Yealmpton Station site is reached, although new ownership and earthworks do occur along the way.

This road sign is still in situ, 38 years after the line's closure and 51 years after the last passengers!

A.R.K.

197

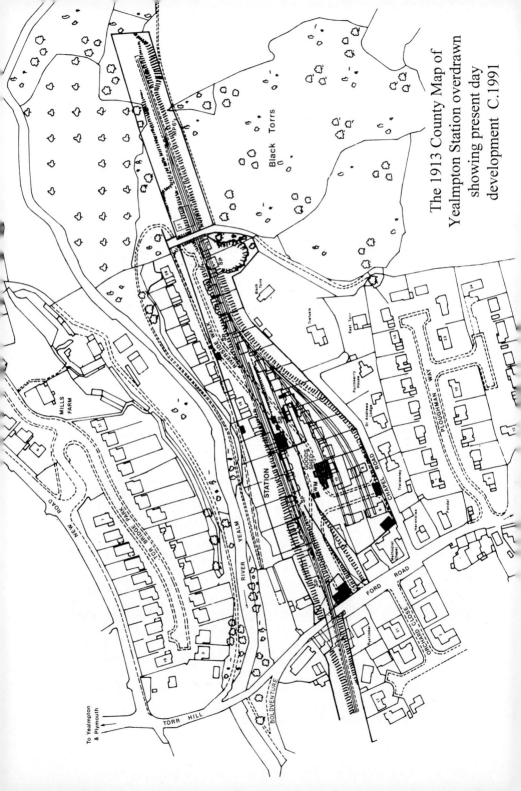

The 1913 County Map of Yealmpton Station overdrawn showing present day development C.1991

Black Torrs

Black Torrs

East Torr

Parkhearty House

Trelusts

St Andrews Lodge

PLOUGHMAN WAY

CHAPEL ROAD

Tresteway

Randal

Heronlea

Methodist Chapel

Myrtimbe

FORD ROAD

ORCHARD CLOSE

BOLDVENTURE

TORR HILL

STATION

GOODS SHED

RIVER YEALM

RIVER YEALM WAY

MILLS FARM

BRIDGE PARK

NEW ROAD

To Yealmpton & Plymouth

Further post-closure photographs taken by the author since the late 1980s:-

The new road junction at the entrance to 'The Ride'.

One of the few complete engineering stuctures still standing at the time of writing – the bridge over the road leading to Rock Gardens, just beyond the former Plymstock Station site.

Two views of Billacombe Station during the period that the building was being dismantled by members of the Plym Valley Railway, April 2nd 1989 to January 20th 1991.

Billacombe Station site as it is now, in 1998.

The site of the former over-bridge at Haye Road, Elburton, looking eastwards and showing No. 38 Haye Road built on an infilled cutting, with No. 40 Haye Road immediately behind it.

Two more photographs taken at Elburton where, due to housing development, the route of the fomer railway line is extremely difficult to locate. *Above:* Looking eastwards out of a bedroom window at No. 40 Haye Road and showing, on the left of the photograph, the hedgerow that previously marked the northern boundary of the line. *Below:* Looking westwards towards the same hedgerow and Nos. 17, 19 & 21 Hazel Grove. On the right of the photograph can be seen the rear of the pavilion in the playing fields and also, in the distance, the house on the far side of Haye Road.

Above: Looking westwards across the site of the former Sherford Road bridge and the adjacent Elburton Cross Station. Note the 'kissing gate' entrance to the latter still existing in the boundary wall.
Below: A close-up of the gate.

Brixton Road Station site, looking northwards and showing the desirable residence built of materials from the original station building by Mr. A. Evans, a local builder. The bridge carrying the A379 over the old cutting can just be seen in winter time, here with a white van conveniently marking its position.

The remains of the bridge that carried the line over the minor road in from the A379 at Chittleburn Cross.

A photograph of the underpass that forms part of a long-established footpath between Combe and Torr. Older members of the indigenous population claim that this tunnel was used as an air-raid shelter during World War II.

The 'kissing gate' near the eastern entrance to the tunnel depicted in the top photograph and adjacent to Holebay Cottage.

The railway bridge over the road leading to the site of the former Cofflete House is still intact and, nowadays, is used as part of the River Erme/Plym Trail. At the time that the photograph was taken the road was partially flooded as a result of water draining from the nearby fields following a spell of heavy rain.

Nature has almost completely reclaimed Steer Point Station site. However, if one searches carefully the old gates leading into the former goods yard can still be found *(above)*, and a few hundred yards to the east the accommodation over-bridge is still in situ *(below)*.

Cylinder Bridge. All that remains now are the cylindrical supports and the concrete abutments, themselves isolated by erosion of successive tides.

The terminus at Yealmpton has been erased and replaced by an executive housing estate, namely Riverside Walk. Its location, however, is marked by three items – the right-hand gatepost at the entrance, the lower part of an adjacent GWR lamp-post and the commemorative plaque erected by the 'Holbeton, Yealmpton and Brixton Society'. *Above:* The former entrance. *Below:* The lower courses of the brickwork of the eastern abutment of the bridge.

Another photograph taken at Yealmpton, showing a fine detached house straddling the site of the former embankment leading into the station.

The end of the line! The 'stopblocks' that were in the woods to the east of Yealmpton Station, just beyond the start of the proposed extension to Modbury.

A.R.K.

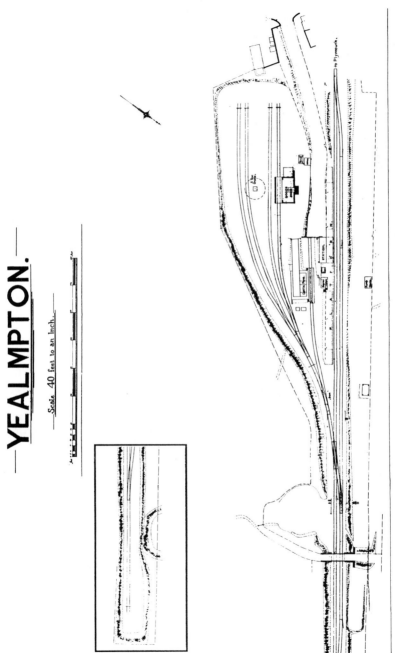

YEALMPTON.

Scale 40 feet to an Inch.

A reduced copy of a GWR Engineers' Drawing Office plan of Yealmpton Station plotted and completed on August 29th 1905.

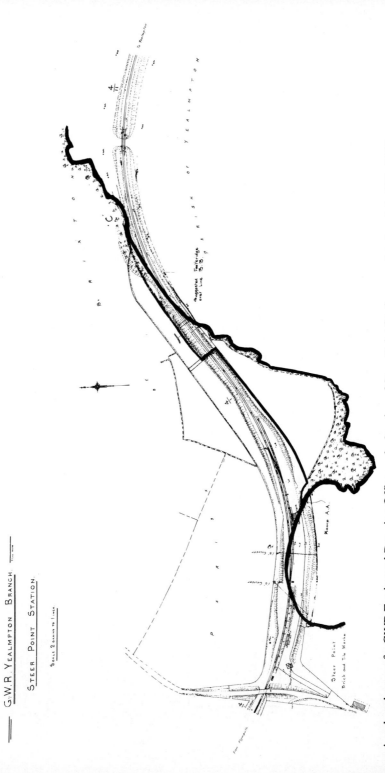

═══ G.W.R YEALMPTON BRANCH ═══

STEER POINT STATION.

Scale 2 Chains to 1 Inch

A reduced copy of a GWR Engineers' Drawing Office scale drawing of Steer Point Station completed on July 20th 1899.
Below: A reduced copy of a GWR Engineers' Drawing Office scale working drawing of Elburton Cross Station completed on October 26th 1905.

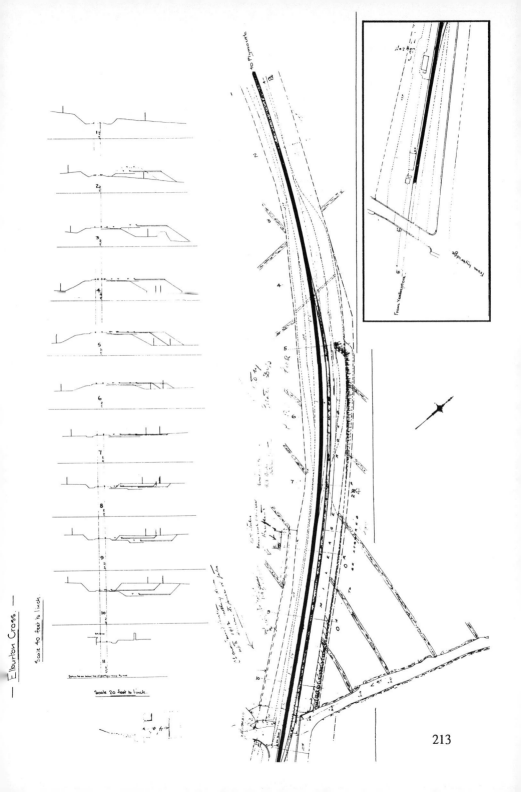

Elburton Cross.

Scale to feet to 1 inch.

Scale 20 feet to 1 inch.

213

APPENDIX II: SOME IMPORTANT DATES

1883	–	The Plymouth & Dartmoor Railway Company's first proposal for a line from Plymstock to Modbury, via Yealmpton.
1887	–	The Plymouth & Dartmoor Railway Company's second proposal for a line from Plymstock to Modbury, via Yealmpton.
1898 (January 15th)	–	Lady Morley officially opens the Yealmpton line.
1898 (January 17th)	–	Public passenger and freight services commence on the Yealmpton line.
1906 (May 30th)	–	First sod cut for the proposed line from Newton Ferrers to Yealmpton.
1906 (July)	–	Work commences on constructing the proposed line from Newton Ferrers to Yealmpton, but the project is later abandoned.
1909	–	The Wembury (Plymouth) Commercial Dock and Railway Company Limited (formed in 1908 by a group of Plymouth businessmen) propose building a line from Wembury to Plymstock in order to serve a commercial dock scheme planned at the former location.
1930 (July 7th)	–	Passenger services cease on the Yealmpton line.
1941 (July 21st)	–	A passenger service for workmen ('Workmen's Specials') commences on the Yealmpton line.
1941 (November 3rd)	–	Passenger services recommence on the Yealmpton line.
1947 (October 6th)	–	Passenger services cease on the Yealmpton line for the second time.
1960 (February 29th)	–	The Yealmpton line is closed to all traffic.
1962 (November)	–	Track lifting commences between Yealmpton and Plymstock stations.
1963 (June 12th)	–	Track lifting completed – only some 11 chains leading into Plymstock Station are left.
1971 (November)	–	Yealmpton Station site demolition commences.
1972	–	Venture Estates of London start the construction of houses on the site of Yealmpton Station.
1980 (February 29th)	–	Plaque erected at the entrance to Riverside Walk, Yealmpton, commemorating the Yealmpton line.
1994 (October)	–	The last rails are lifted on the former Plymstock Station site, together with the surviving 11 chains of track of the Yealmpton line.

APPENDIX III: PASSENGER STEAMERS ON THE RIVER YEALM, LINKING NEWTON FERRERS AND NOSS MAYO WITH STEER POINT RAILWAY STATION

Until the Great Western Railway opened its Yealmpton branch in January 1898, the people of Newton Ferrers and Noss Mayo had no form of public transport to Plymouth other than the weekly carrier's cart and the occasional summertime excursion steamer from Plymouth promenade pier. Soon after the opening of the railway, however, a Mr Hartnell began to provide a limited ferry service between Noss Creek and Steer Point with a paraffin (or naptha)-engined launch.

This was followed, about a year later, by James Ford (the architect and property developer responsible for building the Yealm Hotel and laying out plots for villas in Newton Creek) inaugurating another ferry service from Steer Point to the Yealm Hotel – where a landing pier was built – using a small steam launch with the engaging name of *Yam Yam* ('Yealm', pronounced 'Yam'). No doubt operated with a waterman's licence for 12 passengers, the *Yam Yam* looked like a typical river day-launch, or Admiralty steam pinnace, of the period. She measured about 40 feet in length, had a well deck forward, a small after cabin and a slim, upright funnel amidships. She also flew a triangular name pennant from a large jackstaff astern, was fitted with canvas dodgers around her deckrails and provided with awnings over her fore and aft well decks. However, it would appear that the *Yam Yam* was operated mainly for prospective buyers of villas in the creek as any service offered to the locals seems to have been by way of a favour.

At around the turn of the century George Hodge of Noss Mayo, seeing the need for an all-the-year-round public steamer service to Steer Point, purchased a vessel called *Lady of the Lake*, which he subsequently renamed *Puffing Billy* and operated, initially, with a partner (thought to have been Mr Hartnell, the pioneer of the ferry) for the purposes of meeting each of the weekday trains. This was a composite (iron frames, wooden planking) steamer that had been built at Waterman Bros. yard at Cremyll in 1890 (with engines by Willoughby Bros. Ltd. of Millbay) to the order of John Parson of Millbrook, for use on his Millbrook to Devonport steamer service. Later, in 1892, it had been sold for £650 to the Saltash, Three Towns & District Steamboat Co. Ltd., when that company absorbed Parson's steamer company.

In 1905 (when James Ford stopped running the *Yam Yam*) George Hodge took delivery of a new steamer, the well-remembered *Kitley Belle* which derived its name from the fact that the navigable channel of the Yealm was also known as the Kitley River because the highest commercial quay was at Kitley. Built by Isaac Darton of Mount Batten, the *Kitley Belle* was a pretty little wooden steamer measuring 54 feet in length and 12 feet in width, and whose appearance was further enhanced by an attractive all-white livery and a scarlet, black-topped funnel. She was open-decked fore and aft, had a passenger cabin which shared the same deckhouse as the engine room – a typical Plymouth district arrangement for small ferry steamers – and top deck

One of George Hodge's sons casts off the *Kitley Belle* in Noss Creek. The Dolphin Inn, the then comparatively new school and Holy Cross Church can be seen in line above the stern, c1912.

L. Foster, courtesy of H. Pitts

The Kitley Belle moored off the southern side of Noss Creek, with the Swan Inn and St. Peter's Church above it, to the right of the photograph. Date unknown.

Alan Kittridge collection

seating on the deckhouse roof. She was steered from the customary unsheltered position in the bows, where passenger space was partly encumbered by the need to carry a long gangplank. Nevertheless, she had still been granted a Board of Trade licence for 78 passengers within the River Yealm.

The *Puffing Billy* , meanwhile, was rebuilt at around this time, possibly by Isaac Darton, and later re-entered service under the new name of *Kitley Girl*. She was needed to help during the summertime, when paddle steamers from Plymouth called and some of their often 200 or more passengers wanted to be ferried to Steer Point for return by train.

The *Kitley Girl* in a differing role, that of committee boat for the Yealm Regatta at some time during the 1920s.

Devon Library Services

A possible threat to the ferry services emerged in 1906, when work commenced on the Devon & South Hams Light Railway. This project, however, was soon abandoned and so, instead, the ferries continued to prosper with a regular service of six trips being made each day, Sundays included in the summertime. By now George Hodge also had the assistance of three of his sons – George jnr., Ernest and Elliot – as well as a nephew, Lionel Baker. Hodge snr. skippered the *Kitley Belle* with George jnr. as deckhand (later to be the relief skipper and, eventually, skipper of the *Kitley Belle*) and Ernest as engineer/stoker, while Elliot was a boatbuilder, his workshop being adjacent to Pope's Quay. In addition to building small boats and repairing local crabbing boats, Elliot maintained and repaired his father's steamers and also served as a relief crewman at times. Lionel Baker, meanwhile, served as a relief engineer on either steamer. As Mr Edgar Foster of Newton Ferrers recalls: "All the staffing was done by members of the family. Mind you, they were a large family!"

During World War I, when his sons were away in the Services, George Hodge had to turn to his grandsons for help in order to keep the ferry running, and at times the young women of the family were also required. The government had taken over Membland Hall (situated a mile from Bridgend, but since demolished) as an officer training centre with an intake of 300 men for each course; and the wives and families of some of the trainees came to stay in Newton and Noss. The requisitioning of Membland Hall increased the need for direct contact with Plymouth, and made the ferry busier than ever.

After the war, George Hodge snr. retired and the business was carried on by his sons, with George jnr. as the senior partner. The service started from Pope's Quay (or from The Pool at low water) about an hour before the train was due and called at Kiln Quay in Newton Ferrers, Wide Slip near Ferry

A view of Noss Creek taken from the top of St. Peter's Church and looking towards the River Yealm estuary, showing the *Kitley Belle* turning to negotiate Kiln Quay with passengers from Steer Point, c1920.

Author's collection

Road, the Yealm Hotel pier and, if hailed, at The Warren on the opposite shore of The Pool and also at Thorn Quay, about half way up on the Wembury side of the river, before reaching Steer Point. When the tide was out the run started from the mouth of the creek, off Wide Slip and the Yealm Hotel pier.

When it was full tide at Steer Point the steamer could land at the slipway just inside Cofflete Creek, which was connected to the railway station by a track. On other tides a small beach just around the corner on the river was used as a landing point, but when the tide was out the steamer had to lie off and a rowing-boat tender was used. Mr. Bernard Williams of London, recalls from his boyhood days, that: "The service was not confined to daylight hours – I remember one dark night when my cousin's husband was arriving on the

218

The *Kitley Belle* heading for Steer Point following its departure from Pope's Quay, Noss Mayo. Date unknown.

Alan Kittridge collection

last train and I was kept up to see him: we stood down on the foreshore and, following arrangements made beforehand, he signalled to us with a torch to show he was on board".

Train passengers, who included a number of children from Newton and Noss attending schools in Plymouth, had a mile-long walk between Steer Point Station and the steamer slip. Moreover, that was not the only trial, for at low spring tides the steamers could get to within only about 550 yards of Steer Point. As a result the passengers had to be put into a rowing boat which had been towed astern, and then rowed by the ferry crew as near to the slip as possible. However, this might still be some 50 yards short, and resulted in ladies (and others unsuitably shod for traversing the mud) being carried pick-a-back by the ferryman. This duty, it seems, usually fell to George jnr.

It was common for the ferries to tow a boat astern so that passengers could be embarked or disembarked at points en route irrespective of the tide. This towing, however, was taken a considerable stage further when the Hodges acquired two mercantile ship's lifeboats, one wooden-hulled, one steel. When the queue awaiting the ferry exceeded the number for which she was licensed, the remaining passengers would be embarked in one of these lifeboats and towed astern! If this procedure didn't actually break safety regulations, it certainly broke the spirit of the law and leads one to believe that it was only due to the river's remote location that the Hodges survived undetected!

Although the ferries did not operate a regular parcel service, there was the luggage of summer visitors and other train passengers to be handled, for which a small charge was made. A handcart was kept at Steer Point for moving trunks and cases between station and steamer. At Newton and Noss all luggage was manhandled, usually by George jnr., who seems to have been the official strongman! Coaling ship was another strenuous chore. Most services could get this done before embarking passengers, but it was different on the Yealm. Coal for the steamers arrived by rail at Steer Point Station, from whence it was carted the mile to the waterside and tipped into a rock crevice which the steamers could reach when the tide was in.

By the early 1920s passenger traffic on the Yealmpton railway was at its peak, and the service of the 'Kitley' ferry steamers made Steer Point the busiest of the intermediate stations, for all trains were met by ferry. As the years rolled on, however, motor bus services started becoming established and this, together with a growth in private car ownership, led to a steady decline in passenger traffic on the Yealmpton line. Needless to say, there were also less people wishing to use the ferries, but up until the coal strike of 1926 there was little other apparent change. But then, during the coal strike, all steamer excursions from Plymouth ceased, and when coal imports eventually became available the cost proved prohibitive for the Hodges' steamers. As a result, the *Kitley Girl* was laid up, never to be used again, while the *Kitley Belle* was fitted with a paraffin engine and had her funnel, along with part of her deckhouse, removed. At around this same time also, the more economic motorboat *Pioneer* was purchased from St. Mawes, in Cornwall, and took over the greater part of the work. She looked like a converted yacht and was fitted with a semi-diesel Gardner engine (to start the

The *Pioneer*, seen here at Steer Point in the late 1920s with passengers from the nearby railway station.

Alan Kittridge collection

engine, glass bulbs were heated by blowtorch to pre-heat the cylinders). A Kelvin engine was fitted later. Photographs indicate that she might have received some of the *Kitley Belle's* discarded deckhouse, probably fitted by Elliot Hodge.

In 1929, a year before the passenger trains first ceased on the railway, the Hodge brothers brought the ferry service to an end. This may have been because the GWR, which had started advertising joint rail and motorboat excursions to Steer Point and Noss Creek in 1926, withdrew the 'through' tickets following the amalgamation of National and GWR Buses as the Western National: alternatively, it may have been because by now it had become clear that the steamer route (with its one mile walk at Steer Point) could be bettered by a motor bus to Yealmpton, and the Hodges wished to forestall such competition. Whatever the reason, the ferries never ran again and, instead, Ernest and Elliot Hodge ran their own bus service between Newton Ferrers and Yealmpton to meet the trains until Ernest Hodge took a job with the Western National in 1930, while George Hodge, who did not drive, moved to Saltash to run a market-gardening business.

As for the three ferry boats, the *Kitley Girl* (seen laid up at Bridgend, in Newton Creek by Bernard Williams in April 1930) was subsequently broken up in situ; the *Pioneer* was reportedly used occasionally in the early 1930s for carrying passengers on a waterman's licence (up to 12 passengers) until being left to rot away on the foreshore at Noss; and the *Kitley Belle* was sold, in 1929, to William Worth of the Tamar Transport Company. At that time she was in a bad condition and appeared to have been laid up for one season, at least, but she was subsequently rebuilt at Rogers Yard at Cremyll, fitted with an Atlantic diesel engine and renamed the *Tamar Belle*. The Tamar Transport Company then used her on Tamar excursions and on some of the last Tamar Valley market day services to North Corner, for Devonport Market, before offering her for sale to the Oreston & Turnchapel Steamboat Co. Ltd., in 1932, along with the business of the Tamar Transport Company. However, the Plym steamer company rejected the offer, and the *Tamar Belle* eventually passed to the Millbrook Steamboat & Trading Co. Ltd. in 1942, when that company had just taken over the running of the Cremyll Ferry from the Mount Edgcumbe Estate. After that, in 1959, she was sold for scrap to George Pill of Falmouth. Mr Pill, however, put her into service on the River Fal and she survived three more years before being sold for scrap in Looe, where her hull was hulked in the mud of the West Looe River.

Today, little evidence remains to indicate that the ferries ever existed. However, by following the road along which George Hodge once trundled the handcart, one can find the steamer slipway at the beach, and at Newton Ferrers the Yealm Hotel pier is still in situ, albeit somewhat shorter than in the days of the ferries. Kiln Quay, on the other hand, has now become a private garden, whilst Pope's Quay at Noss, after being allowed to fall into decay, has been rebuilt. Finally, one of the *Kitley Belle's* lifebuoys can still be found on display in The Ship Inn at Noss.

BIBLIOGRAPHY

A Regional History of the Railways of Great Britain (Vol. 1), D. St John Thomas & C. R. Clinker (Phoenix House Ltd, 1960)

Branch Lines Around Plymouth, V. Mitchell and K. Smith (Middleton Press, 1997)

Great Western Railway Journal (No. 9), (Wild Swan Publications, Winter 1994)

Historical Survey of Great Western Engine Sheds 1837–1947, E. Lyons C. Eng., M.I. Struc. E. (O.P.C., 1972)

History of the Great Western Railway (Vol. 2), E.T. Macdermot & C. R. Clinker (Ian Allan Ltd, 1964)

History of the Great Western Railway (Vol. 3), O. S. Nock (Ian Allan Ltd, 1967)

History of the Western National, R. C. Anderson & G. G. A. Frankis (David & Charles, 1979)

Passenger Steamers of the River Tamar, A. Kittridge (Twelveheads Press, 1984)

Passengers No More, G. Daniels & L. A. Dench (Ian Allan Ltd, 1973)

Plymouth Extra (7 August 1997)

Plymouth Steam 1954–1963, I. H. Lane (Ian Allan Ltd, 1984)

Railway Magazine (1898, 1906, 1941 & 1948)

The Great Western in Devon, K. Beck & J. Copsey (Wild Swan Publications Ltd, 1990)

The Lee Moor Tramway, R. M. S. Hall (Oakwood Press, 1963)

The Plymouth & Dartmoor Railway, H. G. Kendall (Oakwood Press, 1968)

The Plymouth to Turnchapel Railway (and The Cattewater Goods Line), Anthony R. Kingdom (ARK Publications (Railways), 1996)

The Wembury Docks and Railway Proposal of 1909, P. W. Broughton (Wembury Local History Society, 1995)

Track Layout Diagrams of the GWR/BR (WR) Sec. 12, R. A. Cooke

Western Evening Herald (Various copies)

Western Morning News (Various copies)

THE AUTHOR

There can be few people more well known in local railway 'circles' than Tony Kingdom. Born in Plymouth in 1931, the son of the late Engr. Comdr. Charles M. S. Kingdom, himself a steam engineer with the Royal Navy from 1906 until 1934, Tony became interested in steam at a very early age and still vividly recalls 'interviews' with the driver and fireman at the start and, often again, at the completion of a train journey during the 1930's. Similarly, he also has vivid memories of trainspotting at Plymouth Laira, North Road and Mutley during the war-time years and seeing many locomotives and rolling stock 'foreign' to the area.

With the demise of the steam era in the early 1960's, Tony turned his attentions towards the field of preservation, and the many activities that followed included being Chairman of the South-West Group of the Great Western Society from 1968 until 1972 and a founder member of the Dart Valley Railway Association.

Pressure of work and the responsibilities of a young family ultimately weaned Tony away from preservation work during the early 1970's, but the vacuum was to be immediately filled by him becoming an author of Railway books. This, in turn, subsequently led to the successful publication of no less than seven titles between 1974 and 1982, while in 1990 the lack of a publisher did nothing to prevent the appearance of his eighth book: using the name ARK Publications, he published it himself!

Tony, now retired after a long career in the Post Office Engineering Dept. (now British Telecom), in which he graduated to the position of Engineering Training Manager, Westward District, currently lives in Newton Ferrers with his wife Marjorie. He has two grown-up children, Roger and Nicola, and three young grandchildren, and enjoys gardening, is a keen photographer and, during the summer months, looks forward to boating and caravanning with his wife. In addition, he likes to spend any spare time researching the history and experiences of the Second World War and, looking to the future, hopes to produce further works on Westcountry Railways as well as seeing some more of his out-of-print titles republished.

Other books by A. R. Kingdom:

The Yealmpton Branch	OPC	1974
The Railways of Devon	Bradford Barton	1974
The Great Western at the Turn of the Century	OPC	1976
The Ashburton Branch	OPC	1977
The Princetown Branch	OPC	1979
The Newton Abbot Blitz	OPC	1979
The Turnchapel Branch	OPC	1982
The Plymouth Tavistock and Launceston Railway	ARK Publications	1990

The Bombing of Newton Abbot Station (RAILWAY ARKIVES SERIES No. 1)	ARK Publications (Railways)	1991
The Yelverton to Princetown Railway	Forest Publishing (In Assoc. with ARK Publications)	1991
The Totnes to Ashburton Railway (and The Totnes Quay Line)	ARK Publications (Railways)	1995
The Plymouth to Turnchapel Railway (and The Cattewater Goods Line)	ARK Publications (Railways)	1996

The Author, photographed here with his wife Marjorie.